IE

W9-DCF-873

MANITOBA

HISTORICAL AND

Scientific Society,

WINNIPEG.

PUBLICATION No. 1.

"The causes of the Rising in the Red River Settlement, 1869-70."

ALEX. McARTHUR. ESQ.

Cover of the first *Transaction* of the Manitoba Historical Society

A Thousand
MILES OF PRAIRIE

THE MANITOBA HISTORICAL SOCIETY AND THE HISTORY OF WESTERN CANADA

EDITED *by* JIM BLANCHARD

UNIVERSITY *of*
MANITOBA PRESS

© Jim Blanchard 2002

University of Manitoba Press
Winnipeg, Manitoba R3T 2N2 Canada
www.umanitoba.ca/uofmpress
Printed in Canada on acid-free paper by Friesens.

Cover Design: Doowah Design
Text Design: Sharon Caseburg
Cover: *Upper Fort Garry* (1907) by Frederick Challener

National Library of Canada Cataloguing in Publication Data
Main entry under title:

A thousand miles of prairie : the Manitoba Historical Society and the
history of Western Canada / Jim Blanchard, editor.

   Contains selections from early members of the Manitoba Historical
Society.
   ISBN 0-88755-665-5

   1. Manitoba--History--1870-1918--Sources. 2.
Manitoba--History--Sources. 3. Northwest, Canadian--History--Sources.
I. Blanchard, J. (Jim) II. Manitoba Historical Society.
FC3373.T46 2002   971.27'02   C2002-911344-X
F1063.T46 2002

The University of Manitoba Press gratefully acknowledges the financial support for its publication program provided by the Government of Canada
through the Book Publishing Industry Development Program (BPIDP); the
Canada Council for the Arts; the Manitoba Arts Council; and the Manitoba
Department of Culture, Heritage and Tourism.

To my mother, Mabel Blanchard

Contents

Preface

———— ·•· ————

THE IDEA FOR THIS BOOK WAS BORN DURING THE planning for the Manitoba Historical Society's 125th anniversary in 2004, and the royalties will be used to help fund anniversary events. This collection is intended to celebrate one of the society's important achievements—the *Transactions*—and to draw attention to these authors, all interesting individuals who played important roles in building our province.

I wish to acknowledge the enormous amount of hard work put into this project by David Carr, Patricia Sanders, and Sharon Caseburg at University of Manitoba Press. The staff of the Manitoba Legislative Library and the Provincial Archives of Manitoba, and of that group I would mention especially Chris Kotecki, have given much invaluable help.

The *Transactions* printed here were published over a period of more than forty years, and different printers and individuals were involved in preparing them for their original publication. Because of that, these pieces display a variety of spellings, punctuation, and grammar. In particular, names are often spelled in different ways, and no accents are used in the originals in French names or words. Sometimes even within one *Transaction*, the usage is inconsistent. Thus, for instance, spellings of the "North West Company," the Hudson's Bay Company," or "pemmican" vary widely. I have chosen to reprint these pieces as they originally appeared—inconsistencies, phrasing, and all—in order to preserve more fully the flavour of the times these papers represent.

In some cases, I have also omitted parts of the original *Transaction*, usually sections that are digressions from the main topic. These deletions are indicated by ellipses. Finally, my editorial notes are contained inside square brackets.

A THOUSAND MILES OF PRAIRIE

Introduction

—•—

ON THE EVENING OF FEBRUARY 28, 1889, PRESIDENT Charles N. Bell delivered his inaugural address to the members of the Historical and Scientific Society of Manitoba, assembled in the council chamber of Winnipeg City Hall.[1] He began by reminding the members of the ambitious objects of their ten-year-old society, which included "to rescue from oblivion the memory of the early missionaries, fur traders and settlers" of the Northwest; to establish a library of books, pamphlets, and maps, and a "museum of minerals and archaeological curiosities"; and to promote the study of science and history by lectures and publications.

The Historical Society had experienced the same boom and bust roller-coaster ride as Winnipeg and Manitoba had during the previous decade. The great real-estate boom of 1881 and 1882 had brought thousands of new people to Winnipeg, all hoping to make their fortune. The new historical society was swept along on the same wave of optimism, swelling to almost 500 members and renting a suite of rooms

---

1. Although the legal name is unchanged, the society is now commonly known as the Manitoba Historical Society. A history of the society is given in Gerald Friesen's "The Manitoba Historical Society: A Centennial History," in his *River Road* (Winnipeg: University of Manitoba Press, 1996), 91-106.

Charles Napier Bell, c. 1917

to house its library, museum, and meeting space. Then, in 1882, the boom collapsed, along with the optimism that had driven it. By 1887, the society had only about seventy members and was forced to move into space in the new City Hall, where they stayed for almost twenty years.

In spite of these setbacks, Charles Bell could still speak with pride of the society's accomplishments. These included a library with a circulation of 6400 books a year and a museum with a wide variety of objects. The museum and library have long since been absorbed by other public institutions; what remain today as a testament to the early society's endeavours are its publications.

By the time of Charles Bell's inaugural speech, the society had already sponsored and published thirty-three lectures. These lectures and talks, called *Transactions* when published, numbered seventy-two by 1909, when the first active period of the society came to an end. The early papers were later designated the First Series *Transactions*, to be followed by the Second Series from 1926 to 1936, and the final Third Series from 1944 to 1980. This sampling of the *Transactions* is intended to give modern readers a taste of the interests and pursuits of these early Manitobans, and to help "save from oblivion" some of their writings.

The early *Transactions* are fascinating to read today. They offer a unique insight into the world view of the dominant groups during modern Manitoba's formative years. Their words give us a clear sense of their intellectual curiosity and vitality, their confidence in the future of the Northwest, and their own colourful personalities. Although they were printed verbatim in the newspapers of the day and usually also issued as pamphlets that were widely circulated, the early *Transactions* are largely unknown today, available to researchers in only a handful of libraries.

The *Transactions* of the First Series reflect a remarkable range of interests. Twenty-three were scientific papers, investigations of the geology, water resources, climate, and the animals and birds of the Northwest. These studies were similar to myriad others written at the time, dealing with the natural world in newly opened colonial areas. Others are edited reprints of journals, letters, and other original source documents useful for the study of western history. The early *Transactions* even include a long talk given by the Arctic explorer John Rae, delivered when he visited Winnipeg in 1882. The prolific Dr. George Bryce was responsible for twenty of the early *Transactions*, covering western history, archaeology, geology, and edited source materials.

The project of the *Transactions*, and the topics and tone their writers chose, reflect not only the Manitoba Historical Society at the time, but also the larger Victorian world. In this earlier age, the liberal bourgeoisie devoted itself to the glorification of progress and the spreading of useful knowledge. The Historical Society, with its museum and library, was, in its members' view, as essential a part of the new city they were building as were its churches, schools and public parks. Objectives similar to those outlined by Charles Bell in 1889 could have been found in the minute books of hundreds of other nineteenth-century institutions all over the European world. The most prestigious of these organizations were the beautifully housed and richly endowed Athenaeums and private subscription libraries in cities such as Boston and London. The great societies and museums, like the Royal Geographical Society in Britain, and the National Geographic Society and Smithsonian Institution in the United States, pursued ambitious and well-funded research programs. On a more modest scale, most towns had Mechanics Institutes, devoted to the education and betterment of working men and, later on, public libraries, idealistically called the "people's university."[2]

All these institutions flourished in a world where universities and technical colleges were still small in number and scope, and not yet

---

2. See J. Blanchard, "Anatomy of Failure: Ontario Mechanics' Institutes 1835-1895," *Canadian Library Journal* 38, no. 6 (1981): 393-400; J. Blanchard, "A Bibliography of Mechanics' Institutes," in Peter McNally, ed., *Readings in Canadian Library History* (Ottawa: Canadian Library Association, 1986), 3-18. See Carol Budnick, "Books to the People in Winnipeg," *Canadian Library Journal* 38, no. 61(1981): 417-422, for a discussion of attempts by working-class Winnipeggers to set up their own library.

dominant in the enterprise of doing and publishing research. For the most part, they all used the same core methods to educate and improve: the lending library of high-quality books, the informative public lecture, the museum of educational objects. They hoped to morally uplift young people, the poor, the working man. Andrew Carnegie, the boy from humble origins who had educated and improved himself at Col. James Anderson's Mechanics' and Apprentices' Library in Pittsburgh, stood as their paragon, their good example. To the businessmen and lawyers and teachers—the membership was almost solely middle class—who founded the Historical and Scientific Society of Manitoba, such institutions were familiar from their homes in Ontario and other parts of eastern Canada or Great Britain.

The society's *Transactions* also had much in common with the work being done in these other institutions. The *Transactions*, like much of nineteenth-century writing on history, was largely the work of lay historians—people not primarily employed in teaching and researching historical topics. Professional academic historians did not make their appearance in the field of Canadian history until G.M. Wrong was appointed to the chair of Canadian history at the University of Toronto in 1894. Some would mark the beginning of academic Canadian history in Manitoba in 1909, when the young Chester Martin first arrived to teach at the University of Manitoba. Until that point, organizations like the Historical Society filled the gap in the research and dissemination of western Canadian history. As W.L. Morton later wrote, "the society performed much of the work that today would be called a research institute. It provided the means and encouragement . . . to pursue historical and scientific studies and attempt original work."[3]

In Winnipeg, the Historical Society had a further objective: that of promoting immigration to and development of the Northwest. The very

---

3. W.L. Morton, "President's Address on the Occasion of the Seventy-Fifth Anniversary of the Society," *Transactions of the Historical and Scientific Society of Manitoba*, Series III, No. 9, 1954, p. 3.

George Bryce, as seen by a Winnipeg cartoonist in 1909,
surrounded by his historical and scientific work

first lecture the group sponsored in 1879 was a talk by John Macoun,
just returned from his extensive survey trip out on the prairie. When he
pronounced the west "destined to be one of the most important parts of
the globe," it was music to their ears. Many of the scientific papers heard
in the years to come were practical assessments of resources that might
be profitably exploited. Even the humble prairie chicken of Ernest
Thompson Seton's paper had potential, and he offered to help any society member who might want to raise them domestically.

As we read the words of these early writers, we are transported
back to those gas-lit rooms of nineteenth-century Winnipeg, where
the audience came looking for enlightenment and stimulation, and to
escape the bleak winter night. Just outside the windows, dwarfing the
clapboard and brick city, lay the great prairie, stretching away unbroken to the Rockies, silent and waiting. The lecturers and their listeners sought to bring this great, lone land under their control by
cataloguing it, listing its inhabitants, digging out its history, and

ordering it according to their view of the world. Perhaps the most remarkable aspect of the *Transactions* is what they reveal of the enormous self-confidence of these men—the early society was overwhelmingly male—their absolute certainty that they were the vanguard who would bring the benefits of progress to the land, by, as George Bryce wrote, "throwing open the fertile land of the Northwest to the world—a land too good to be kept as the preserve of bears and foxes."

Bryce, one of the founders of the society and the most prolific contributor to the *Transactions*, saw the west as offering rich possibilities for all kinds of scholarship. In this wonderful passage written in 1904, Bryce expresses the enthusiasm he and other new arrivals felt for the history of their new home and the liberation they experienced at leaving behind the confines of Ontario society:

> This comes to us as a part of the large inheritance which we who have migrated to Manitoba receive. No longer cribbed, cabined, and confined, we have in this our "greater Canada" a far wider range of study than in the fringe along the Canadian lakes. Think of a thousand miles of prairie! The enthusiastic Scotsman was wont to despise our level Ontario, because it had no Grampians, but the mountains of Scotland all piled together would reach but to the foot hills of our Rockies. The Ontario geologist can only study the rocks in garden plots, while the Nor'wester revels in the age of reptiles in his hundreds of miles of Cretaceous rocks, with the largest coal and iron area on the continent. As with our topography so with history. The career of the Hudson's Bay Company, which is in fact the history of Rupert's Land, began 120 years before the history of Ontario, and there were forts of the two rival Fur Companies on the Saskatchewan and throughout the country, before the first U. E.*[United Empire]* Loyalist felled a forest tree in Upper Canada.[4]

---

4. George Bryce, "Among the Mound Builders Remains," *Transactions of the Historical and Scientific Society of Manitoba*, No. 18, 1884-85, p. 1.

Many of the society's speakers in the early period played important roles in the public life of the Northwest: Dr. Schultz, Gilbert McMicken, and Sigtryggur Jonasson are examples. Other prominent men, whose papers have not been reprinted here, included the American consul in Winnipeg from 1870 to 1893, James Wickes Taylor, an enthusiastic supporter of the society, who contributed a paper on Lord Selkirk. W.J. McLean was another of these men, a forty-year veteran of the Hudson's Bay Company by the time he spoke to the society about a trip he had taken through the Great Slave Lake region. He was nicknamed "Big Bear" because he and his family had been the prisoners of that Cree chief during his long retreat after the failure of the 1885 rebellion.

Common themes emerge as we read the *Transactions*. Many contain descriptions of the trip that brought the writer or his or her subject to the Northwest, this strange new land, so different from their homes. The extreme isolation of the Red River Settlement in the days before railroads eased the journey from the outside world meant that the trip took on an epic quality, remembered for the rest of the travellers' lives. Schultz, McMicken, and Jonasson all describe such journeys, as do authors whose works could not be included here.

In the early *Transactions* we hear, overwhelmingly, the voice of Protestant Ontario, whose sons, like Gilbert McMicken and John Christian Schultz, had wrested control of Manitoba away from their rivals in the decades after Confederation. George Bryce and, to a lesser extent, some of the other authors of the *Transactions* helped to give the political triumph of the Ontario immigrants its intellectual underpinnings. Non-Anglo Canadian groups were not usually given much prominence in the history of the Northwest. Although Charles Bell called on the members to research the ethnology of local Aboriginal people, the resulting papers were sometimes marred by inaccurate information and outright prejudice. The French and Métis roles were also downplayed. A notable early exception was the paper by Father Lewis Drummond on "The French Element in the Canadian West," presented in 1887. Father Drummond, a Jesuit who taught at St. Boniface College, was of Irish and French-Canadian parentage, a background that allowed him to feel at home in both camps.

Main Street, north from Portage Avenue, c. 1910

Some have also found in Bryce's writing the beginning of a distinct western view of Canadian history, one that, among other things, portrayed the Red River Settlement as a sort of utopia in the wilderness.[5] In this view, the Selkirk settlers are portrayed as the true founders of Manitoba, and they became, as one modern historian has suggested, adopted ancestors who gave legitimacy to the dominance of Ontario immigrants in Manitoba's life.[6] In papers like his tribute to Alexander Isbister, Bryce attempted to build a bridge between the older world of Red River and the new Manitoba being constructed by the newcomers from Ontario.

Bryce's version of western history did not go unchallenged. When,

---

5. See Doug Owram, *Promise of Eden: The Canadian Expansionist Movement and the Idea of the West, 1856 - 1900* (Toronto: University of Toronto Press, 1992). The final chapter, "The West as Past," pp. 192-216, discusses the so-called "Red River myth" and the work of the Historical and Scientific Society in the larger context of Canadian history at the time.

6. Lyle Dick, "Historical Writing on 'Seven Oaks': The Assertion of Anglo-Canadian Cultural Dominance in the West," in Robert Coutts and Richard Stewart, eds., *The Forks and the Battle of Seven Oaks in Manitoba History* (Winnipeg: Manitoba Historical Society, 1994), 69.

in 1890, he spoke on "Two Provisional Governments of Manitoba," he challenged the authenticity of the version of Riel's Bill of Rights, which was being used at the time to argue for separate schools in Manitoba. He was questioned by Father Cloutier, who was in the audience, and later, in writing, by Archbishop Taché. The archbishop asked if the society endorsed Bryce's conclusions about separate schools, a delicate topic at the time. The secretary of the society was quick to assure him that the society took no responsibility for "statements made in papers published under its auspices."[7]

After 1900 there is evidence of more interest in the stories of the non-Anglo Canadian inhabitants of Manitoba, no doubt because their increasing numbers made them difficult to ignore. In 1902 the society published, in translation, an account of the life of Marie Anne Lajimonière by Abbé Georges Dugas, an historian whose work focussed on the French contribution in the Northwest. Sigtryggur Jonasson's paper on the Icelanders was delivered in 1900, and Michael Sherbinin, a member of the society, spoke on Ukrainian history in 1906, at a time when the Ukrainians and the Icelanders were the victims of a great deal of prejudice at the hands of the English-speaking majority in Manitoba.

While the primary focus of this selection of the *Transactions* is the period from 1879 to 1909, the first active period of the society, the final three papers collected here date from the 1920s and 1930s. Yet these papers as well relate to that important period. The account of Winnipeg's fur-trade forts by Charles Bell, a topic he envisaged as early as 1889, is a workmanlike piece of historical research that remains a useful source. The papers by Archbishop Matheson and John Dafoe, delivered in the 1930s, are, like many of the earlier *Transactions* reprinted here, reminiscences of prominent men about events in which they participated.

Over the years, the method of delivering and publishing the *Transactions* changed very little. They were presented as public lectures in the

---

7. Minutes of the Executive Council, April 1890, Public Archives of Manitoba, Manitoba Historical Society Papers.

meeting rooms of the society and then in the council chamber at Winnipeg City Hall. When the society lost its space at City Hall, it used other locations, such as the YMCA or the lecture halls of the University of Manitoba building in what is now Memorial Park on Broadway.

In the early years, the *Manitoba Free Press* published the lectures verbatim and most, but not all, were then issued in the form of a pamphlet. The cost of the pamphlets was normally shared by the society and the author,[8] the bill for 300 copies of an 1887 pamphlet being $21.00. The publication of some papers was delayed because of lack of money. Of the thirty-eight papers from the 1926 to 1936 period, only a few were printed, and those much later in the 1940s and 1950s. In 1933 the society's annual report expressed the hope that they would be published "when times improve," but added, "times have not improved nor is there much sign of improvement."

The pamphlets could be ordered from the society's secretary or purchased in Winnipeg bookstores. No profit was made on this venture: the cost of printing for the 1885-86 season was $45.00 and the income from sales was $10.00. The pamphlets probably had more value as exchange items, traded for the publications of other societies, which were added to the library.

As an organized and sponsored approach to researching the natural and human history of Manitoba, the *Transactions* have no equal. They stand as an impressive achievement and legacy of the early society members. The work of the Manitoba Historical Society continues today, but these early lectures and papers, presented with the distinctive language and viewpoint of the time, give us an authentic glimpse of the visions of people who help to lay the groundwork for modern western Canada.

---

8. Minutes of the Executive Council, January 1885, Public Archives of Manitoba, Manitoba Historical Society Papers.

GEORGE BRYCE

(1844-1931)

GEORGE BRYCE WAS THE PERFECT CLERGYMAN, PROFESSOR, and historian for the young City of Winnipeg and Province of Manitoba. Like the city he lived in, he was self-confident and noisy, and he possessed enough energy to produce a volume of writing noteworthy for its size, if not always for its quality.

Bryce was born on a farm near Mount Pleasant, Ontario, in 1844, a year after his parents had immigrated to Canada from Scotland. He received what was, for the times, a good education, at the high school in nearby Brantford, the University of Toronto, and Knox College, where his success as a student was marked with medals and scholarships. He was an athlete, playing on the college football team. He had served as a militia volunteer during the Fenian troubles of 1866 and was present at the disastrous Canadian defeat at Ridgeway.

As a young Presbyterian minister, Bryce was part of the influx of Ontario immigrants who came to Manitoba after the collapse of Riel's Provisional Government in 1870. He was selected in 1871 by the General Assembly of the Presbyterian Church to come west to Red River to organize a Presbyterian college and a new church. He set up Manitoba College in the same year and taught there until 1909. In 1872 he founded Knox Church, the first Presbyterian church in Winnipeg. He was also one of the founders of the University of Manitoba, and taught science on the university faculty and served on the University Council until his retirement in 1904. Bryce was one of the founders and a president of the Manitoba Historical and Scientific Society. He was a prolific author, who wrote nine books and forty or fifty pamphlets as well as numerous sermons and speeches. He delivered thirty papers before the Historical and Scientific Society of Manitoba alone, on topics as diverse as geology, archaeology, and Red River history. In 1902 his scholarly work was given national recognition when he was elected to the Royal Society of Canada. In 1910 he served as the Royal Society's president and he was also a member of many other learned societies.

In his later years, after the death of his wife, he grew frail and moved back to Ontario to live with his brother. He died, largely forgotten, in 1931.

The *Transaction* by Bryce chosen for this collection is a memorial written soon after the death of Alexander Kennedy Isbister, a famous son of the Northwest who lived most of his life in London. Dr. Bryce began his talk with a description of a visit he paid to A.K. Isbister in London in 1881. Isbister took him to lunch at the Middle Temple, where, as a barrister, he was a member. Bryce said Isbister was a good host: "Mr. Isbister, with great gusto, entered into the traditions of the place, and was a most pleasant cicerone." There is no doubt that George Bryce was impressed with his introduction to one of the most exclusive preserves in the Empire. But Bryce writes that despite a successful career in the great metropolis of the British world, Isbister and his mother, who lived with him, missed their home in the Northwest and longed to return.

For Bryce, Isbister serves as an important figure in that, as a native of the Northwest who succeeded in the sophisticated world of London, he provides a link between the raw, wild west of the fur-trade times and the new era of progress being ushered in by Ontario immigrants like Bryce. He is extremely complimentary about Isbister's career and is careful to play down the fact of his mixed blood, saying he had a "trace" of Indian blood. Alexander Isbister was in reality one-quarter Cree, but this fact would not have fitted conveniently into Dr. Bryce's historiography, where Aboriginal and Métis people were made to represent the old, outmoded ways of the past.

One of the first of a long list of westerners who left their home to make good in some faraway place, Isbister did not forget where he came from and made generous donations of money and of his library to the University of Manitoba. Many of his books were sadly lost in a fire in the 1890s but the Isbister Scholarships are still awarded today by the university.

In Memoriam.
The Late A.K. Isbister

———◆———

. . . THE WINTER BEFORE LAST ONE SUNDAY MORNING BY appointment we met Mr. Isbister in London to go to service in the Temple Church. Mr. Isbister was a barrister and so had a right to all the privileges connected with the legal profession including admission to this church. Turning in at Temple Bar, . . . entering by the passage we came to the ground and enclosure of the middle temple of which Mr. Isbister was a member. There lay stretching through courts and gateways eastward the buildings of the inner temple. Tradition says there was once an outer temple though nothing trustworthy remains of it. These temples are now the abodes of the legal fraternity, whose predecessors were the Knight Templars, a society of military clerics. The master of the temple is the well known Dr. Vaughan, the clergyman who officiates in the Temple Church, who has as a privilege freedom from the supervision of the Bishop of London. We entered the church which is one of the few remaining round churches of England. . . . Coming out to Fleet street we crossed it and through a few passages came to Bolt Court. For many years, Mr. Isbister, in connection with the educational work he had in hand, occupied offices—the very rooms, indeed, where the great Dr. Johnson had lived. Indeed it was in Bolt Court that the burly English man-of-letters died. Homeward bound, we left the part of London whose every foot was instinct with memories of dramatists, poets and literateurs, and we were glad to have had so kindly a guide. This was our first acquaintance, though but preliminary to other opportunities of knowing and appreciating the man more fully.

EARLIER LIFE

Alexander Kennedy Isbister was born in 1822 at Cumberland House, on the Saskatchewan. On both sides he was Orkney descent, as his name indicates. He had also a trace of Indian blood in his veins. He was thus thoroughly identified with the earlier population of the country, and always retained that strong love for the land of his birth so characteristic of the natives of the Northwest. It is somewhat remarkable the part taken by people from the Orkney Islands in the earlier history of the country. They did a large part of the severe pioneer work which made the Hudson's Bay Company strong. . . . Young Isbister was the son of an officer in the Hudson's Bay Company, whose family, on the father being killed in the company's service at Norway House, settled in the parish of St. Andrews about the year 1833—alongside the rapids of the Red River. On the maternal side Alexander Isbister was a Kennedy. His mother is an elder sister of Capt. Kennedy, of St. Andrews, well known as one of Lady Franklin's captains, who delivered two most entertaining lectures on his "Arctic Explorations" before this society. Old Mrs. Isbister lived with her son till his death. She is now an old lady of 83. In the winter of 1881 she was still hale and hearty, and had a passionate longing to see the Red River of her early life. It is with sorrow her friends will learn that she is not now in such good health. The Kennedy's were formerly proprietors of some of the islands between the Orkney's and the mainland, notably the Island of Stroma. At the time of the Pretender, when so many estates changed hands in Scotland, one brother favored King George and the other Prince Charlie. The fortunes of war were in favor of the other line, and the Kennedys, of whom we are speaking, as the subject of our sketch, in relating the ins and outs of the matter with great glee confessed, were left "out in the cold." Mr. Isbister, by the Kennedy side, is related as a third cousin or so to the Hon. A.G.B. Bannatyne, and was a nephew by marriage of Chief Factor Christie.

Alexander Kennedy Isbister

BOYISH DAYS

Settled on the Red River at the age of eleven, the subject of our sketch showed an early inclination for study, and soon was sent to the nucleus of what has now become St. John's College, in this city, then known as the "McCallum School". Spending a few years here the young student, at about the age of sixteen, entered the service of the Hudson's Bay Company as an articled clerk. His lot was cast in the far-off Mackenzie district, and here he gained his acquaintance with the fur trade and the company's affairs, so useful to him in his after career. With strong desire to obtain a professional education the young clerk, having served his three years time in the company's offices left the service and returned to Red River. Having spent a year in "the settlement" as Assiniboia was called up to only a few years ago, he left his native land for England in 1842, and though ardently attached to it never had the privilege of seeing it again.

AT THE UNIVERSITY

The well-developed fur trader now entered upon scenes of a different kind from the remote Mackenzie river. He was a successful student, and took both his M.A. and L.L.B. degrees. In appearance he was stalwart, standing about 6 feet 3 inches, and was a fine looking man. He was a man of excellent address, of very great conversational power, and enthusiastically devoted to any cause he espoused. After a successful student career he entered upon the study of law, and in due time became an English barrister. His mind was upon his native country, and at that time the questions arising in England were peculiarly interesting to the young and the ardent. It was a few years after the passing of the Reform Bill, and it was in the air to examine into the affairs of

OLD MONOPOLIES.

For the Young man of high hopes and a broad sense of justice not to be a Liberal and a Reformer is unnatural. It is as men get older and find that the world is not so easily set to rights as they had supposed that they become conservative. One can quite imagine the ardency with which one, who retained even to the last buoyancy and hopefulness as to the triumph of true and just principles, entered on the work of bringing his fellow-countrymen to enjoy all the rights of British subjects. Mr. Isbister related to the writer his experience in dealing with some of the affairs of a society called the "New England Society," which was supposed to have outgrown its usefulness, indicating a thoroughgoing and practical turn of mind.

RED RIVER OPENED UP

With great perseverance in England and on the Red River the case was worked up by which Representative Institutions were to replace the Hudson's Bay Company Regime. The Hudson's Bay Company's rule, it must be said, was patriarchal, on the whole kindly, but could not have stood the strain of a larger population, or a people less docile than the English half-breeds of Red River. Mr. Isbister ardently undertook the task of liberalizing the government of Red River, and throwing open the fertile land of the Northwest to the world—a land too good to be kept as the preserve for bears and foxes. Petition after petition from the people of Red River was sent to the British Government by the hands of Mr. Isbister, and he became known as the champion of popular rights for the people of the settlement. He had acquired a quantity of Hudson's Bay company stock and so was enabled to speak from a more influential standpoint. The excitement culminated in the appointment of a committee by the Imperial Parliament, the results of which are embodied in the Blue Book of 1857. In a general sketch such as this, it is unnecessary to enter into a statement of the details of the struggle. The Hudson's Bay Company wisely discerned the signs of the times, made excellent terms with the Government, and has now in a wholehearted and earnest way thrown in its lot with the country, and become one of the strongest forces in its development. Mr. Isbister informed the writer that he had long ago made up his quarrels with the Hudson's Bay company. He looked back with no regrets on the part he had taken, but he recognized in the Hudson's Bay Company an honourable and useful corporation. As a retired official of the Company he had the feeling of attachment that is so strong a feature of all its employees.

AS AN EDUCATIONIST

Mr. Isbister had, however, a strong leaning to the cause of education. It was not strange, that one of his ardent and sympathetic mind should be fond of teaching. It is surely one of the most honourable and useful of professions. For many years in Bolt Court he labored in connection with an education institution. In 1851 he became a Fellow of an organization since grown to large dimensions, "The College of Preceptors." Its object was to serve as a high class examining board to give certificates of acquaintance with certain departments of knowledge. In 1881 this board issued 11,000 certificates. Mr. Isbister was also Dean of this College of Preceptors. He was the author of several textbooks on education subjects, and up to the end of life had the responsibility of editing an educational magazine of some importance.

HIS BOUNTY

The generous nature of Mr. Isbister did not confine itself to sympathy for the people struggling for their rights, nor to the efforts of the young to gain an education. He gave about the time of the transfer of this Province 100 pounds sterling in American bonds, of which the interest has been used in the shape of prizes to the Public Schools of this Province and in 1881 he gave a handsome subscription to Manitoba College. It is known that for years he has been considering the propriety of establishing in his native land some useful educational institution. At one time this was thought of as a 'Normal School' and the University Act bears traces of an intention to provide for this on the part of the framers of the Act. Since that, the University of Manitoba has shown itself to have the "potency" for future good. Mr. Isbister was greatly delighted with the unsectarian character of the University, so thoroughly uniting all ideas in the country. He had a great desire to see the Province. He has now left a monument more enduring than brass in the splendid gift of upwards of $60,000 to the Manitoba University, and his large library which the writer had an opportunity of examining.

KIND MEMORIES

As a society striving to commemorate the deeds of generosity and worth of those belonging to our territory it becomes us while mingling our tears with the friends of our departed brother to yet rejoice in the honor done to us by achievements of our late Honorary member.

His efforts for the cause of civil liberty: his lifelong devotion to education and every benevolent and humanizing agency: and his overflowing of generosity to this Province and the University of Manitoba make his name one that surely we shall not willingly let die.

Transaction No. 8, read July 26, 1883.

A sketch of Ernest Thompson Seton, c. 1901

ERNEST THOMPSON SETON
(1860-1940)

ERNEST THOMPSON WAS BORN IN ENGLAND IN 1860 AND died in New Mexico in 1946. He took the name Seton because his family claimed to be descended from George Seton, the Jacobite Earl of Winton, who was exiled from England in 1715 because of his support for the Stuart cause. Ernest's father, Joseph Thompson, moved his family to Canada after the failure of his shipping business in 1866. He tried farming but the upper-crust Thompsons were not suited to Canadian frontier life, nor to the back-breaking work of clearing the land. The family moved to Toronto in 1870 and Joseph Thompson earned his living thereafter as an accountant.

Ernest Thompson wanted to be a naturalist from a very early age but his father sent him to the Ontario School of Art and the Royal Academy in London, where he was recognized as an artist with great promise. He combined the two interests to become one of the greatest artist/naturalists of his time.

In 1881 he returned to Toronto and the next year made the journey to Manitoba to join his brother Arthur on a homestead near Carberry. Their father and the rest of the family soon followed and Seton travelled extensively in the western part of Manitoba in search of the best locations for homesteads. But his real passion, as always, was sketching and writing about the natural life of the districts through which he passed.

It was during this period in Manitoba that he wrote the *Transaction* included in this collection—one of his first pieces as a naturalist. On May 8, 1884, the society's Minute Book recorded that Mr. Seton, a corresponding member living at Carberry, had sent in "an interesting and valuable paper on Prairie Chickens," and that J.B. McKilligan would read it at the next meeting.

He wrote other papers for the Historical and Scientific Society, some of which have been reprinted by the Manitoba Naturalists Society.[1] One of these, entitled "A List of the Mammals of Manitoba," consists of his field notes from his travels in the province. In his introduction he mentions that the identification of specimens was done by C. Hart Merriam, who was the secretary of the American Ornithological Union in New York. Merriam had become Seton's mentor, helping him to find work as a nature artist in New York. Seton had spent the winter of 1883 in New York, attempting to establish himself as a nature illustrator. His success there and the contacts he formed made him finally decide to give up homesteading and leave Manitoba for good.

In his later years he became an international figure because of his illustrations and writings, and because of the Woodcraft movement he founded to teach boys about outdoor life. In this charming piece about prairie chickens, we are given a glimpse of the great naturalist at the beginning of his writing career, a young homesteader observing and noting his impressions in that sympathetic and clear style that would make him beloved of readers all over the world.

---

1. Ernest Thompson Seton, *Ernest Thompson Seton in Manitoba, 1882 - 1892*, (Winnipeg: Premium Ventures in co-operation with Manitoba Naturalists Society, 1980).

The Prairie Chicken or
Sharp-Tailed Grouse

——•——

FOR BREVITY IT MAY BE DESCRIBED AS A GROUSE, resembling the other members of the family in its general anatomy and appearance, but differing in that its neck is without any specially developed feather-tufts, and its tail feathers are very short and stiff, except, however, the central pair, which are softer and so long that they project an inch beyond the others and end the tail in a point.

It is a matter of doubt whether these two long feathers are true tail feathers or merely developed coverts. The fact that their insertion is slightly above that of the true quills would seem to indicate that they are coverts, but in color and shape they grade perfectly into the adjoining quill feathers, which fact, I think, establishes their claim to be considered as true rectrices. It is from this peculiarity of the tail that the bird gets the name of "sharptailed" or "pintailed" grouse, though, throughout this country, it is best known as the prairie chicken.

In Manitoba at least this bird in its distribution is co-extensive with the prairies. I have found it abundant in the Big Plain, Turtle Mountain, Souris and Shell river districts, but cannot say how far west it extends. In the east it has been found as far as the north shore of Lake Superior. It is supposed that at one time it ranged much further to the south than at present, but that it is retreating before the pinnated grouse (tetrao cupida) which has already entered Manitoba by the Red River Valley. I have seen a number of specimens taken within twenty miles of Winnipeg. It is desirable that a record be kept of any new facts regarding this encroachment. . . .

When the snow disappears and warmer weather sets in the chickens meet every morning in companies of from four, six to 20, on some selected hillock or knoll to indulge in what is called "the dance." They commence at dawn. The birds may be seen standing in ordinary attitudes until suddenly one lowers his head, spreads out his wings horizontally, but slightly dipped, and his tail perpendicularly, distends his air sacs and erects his feathers, then taking the very shortest steps, but stamping his feet so fast and hard that the sound is like that of a kettle drum, he careers about, beating the air with his wings and vibrating the tail so that it rattles loudly, uttering a sort of cribbing crow, which seems to come from the air sacs. When one commences all join in rattling, stamping, drumming, dancing, louder and louder, faster and faster, till as they madly whirl about they are fairly leaping over each other in their excitement. This continues for a minute or two, then they gradually relax, but only for a short time, when they are again started by some one leading off. The whole performance reminds one so strongly of a "Cree dance" as to suggest that the dance of the birds was the prototype of the Indian exercise, the drumming noise, stamping hi-hi's of the Indian corresponding to the wing drumming, tail rattling, stamping and crowing of the chickens. The space usually beaten by the dancing is from fifty to one hundred feet square, and is called in the Western States by the name of their "scratching ground." The dance is indulged in at any time of the morning from dawn till noon, but generally till the sun is up, and is carried on throughout the month of May.

It will be seen that this corresponds somewhat to the manoeuvres of the Old World Ruff, a bird that is well known to be polygamous and for this and other reasons I expect that it may yet be proven that the grouse do not pair. . . .

[Seton now describes his efforts to raise some prairie chickens.]

Having determined to raise some of the grouse in the barnyard, I set two common hens with prairie chicken eggs. The eggs were subjected to some very rough usage, all of them having made a long journey, either with a man on horseback or in a buggy over the prairie.

The amount of shaking they bore would have endangered the vitality of any barn fowl egg. Besides this, through the negligence of the hen, they were several times left cold for some hours. Notwithstanding these disadvantages, after about twenty days the whole of the eggs came out. I put them with one large hen and enclosed for them a piece of prairie, in its natural state, so as to have their surroundings as natural as possible. They were bright little chicks, clad in golden down, with black spots above. When they squatted in the grass their color was a perfect concealment. Their only note was the triple whistle call, in a higher key, however, than that of the old ones. At first their wings all appeared with rows of large blood quills. As soon as they could run they showed a desire to drink, and on water being set before them they drank much and often. This was rather surprising, as in a state of nature they are hatched in the driest places and far from water.

2nd Day.—They are very active, catching flies, etc., they care little for any kind of food but that of living insects, but will now and then eat a little hard-boiled egg, or if oatmeal be wetted and splashed about the grass they will peck off a good deal of it.

3rd Day.—Three are dead; one was drowned and two were killed by the hen trampling on them. The hen was a Brahma and weighed about six pounds. I would recommend that a Game or Bantam hen be used in future, as the mother prairie chicken weighs barely two pounds at this time. This left me now twenty-two chicks.

4th day.—The chicks are now developing their scapulars.

7th day.—They can now fly a little, as the wing quills are very large and strong. I have reason to believe that when wild, that their development is even more rapid.

8th day.—They are now fledging on the neck, the wings are completely feathered; otherwise they are clad in down. At this time, when in a state of nature, should the old bird be surprised, she goes off with a loud whirr, but immediately a dozen little "whirrs" are heard as she flies, and is followed by what appears to the unpractical eye, like a flock of sparrows, but in reality by her brood, which are already strong on the wing.

9th day.—All fly well, and their voices are changing from the high-pitched "peep" to the deeper "chuck" of the old ones.

13th day.—They now number but fifteen, the loss being caused by the clumsiness of the foster mother and the strict confinement. Yet if they be let out, they would be lost in the long grass, and could not be gathered together again by the hen, as they do not understand her "chuckle." They are now well grown and feathered on the back. They still adhere to insect food, rarely eating anything of a vegetable nature except that they are fond of wild strawberries. An ant's nest that would quite fill an ordinary bucket they pick clean in a day.

14th day.—A cold day, though this is the 13th of July. Fearing for the safety of the chickens I took them into the house. They sat under the stove on the tin. Here they chanced also to receive the direct rays of the sun as it shone through the window. Suddenly one of them jumped up and commenced to dance in the same manner as the old ones did on the hill, immediately the whole brood joined, their little feet stamping together on the tin under the stove, sounded like so many kettle drums, while their miniature crowing and strutting combined to form a most ludicrous spectacle.

17th day.—They number 13. They are now more than ever fond of the dance. They show the bare skin patches over the eye and on the neck, but these are neither colored nor inflated. Their heads are beginning to fledge and their tails to grow. Their wings are now much longer in proportion to those of adult birds.

About this time I was traversing some scrub land by night when suddenly I heard at my feet a well-known whirr. I clutched in the darkness and caught a young prairie chicken in each hand. . . .

18th day.—The wild chickens apparently of the same age as my penned in birds, can fly a mile or more, indeed they seem as strong on the wing as the adults.

20th day.—The chicks number 12. A small one which died weighed only one ounce. I would here contrast its wing development with that of an adult. An adult prairie chicken weighs two pounds, each of its wings is eleven inches long and five inches across, which gives a total wing surface of 110 square inches or 3 1/2 square inches to each ounce of weight. The young one weighs an ounce, each of its wings is four inches long by two inches across, which gives a total wing surface of

16 square inches to its one ounce of weight. Therefore the young chick has in proportion nearly five times as much wing support as the mature bird, although, of course, the latter is more than compensated by the vastly greater proportion of muscular power.

22nd day.—They now have the adult voice and are all feathered except on the throat, neck and breasts, where they still retain the yellow down. They will now eat a little grain and are fond of curds, eggs and soaked bread, but insects continue to be their favorite food. Burrowing beetles, however, they will not eat.

28th day.—To-day I emptied a lot of ashes into the pen, whereupon they indulged in the most extravagant expressions of delight, and for a long time continued to dust themselves most vigorously.

31st day.—Tried them with a dead hawk. All chuckled and squatted except two, the latter spreading their wings and tail and raising their feathers, crowing loudly and defiantly. I imagine the wild mother will often battle for her young successfully against harriers and other inferior birds of prey.

It is not necessary to follow further in detail the growth and development of the young grouse, as sufficient has been stated to illustrate the rapidity of their growth and to guide all who desire to raise them. . . .

. . . Like most wild birds they have a foreknowledge of storms and when some firewood searcher returning from the woods reports that the chickens are going into the bush, that is leaving the open timber for the denser fir coverts, the settler makes ready for a severe storm.

The prairie chicken like most of the grouse family spend the night in winter in a snow drift. Out on the plains the wind pounds the snow into drifts of ice like hardness, but in the bush it continues soft, this softness affording another security to the chickens by causing the wolves and foxes to quit the bush in the winter, though they live there by preference the rest of the year. In the evening the chickens fly down either headlong into a drift or run a little and then dive. Each makes his own hole. They generally go down six inches or so and along about a foot. By morning their breath has formed a solid wall in front of them so that they invariably go out at one end. In Ontario observers are less likely to have the non-conducting powers of snow impressed upon them as in Manitoba, so I may illustrate this. For days together the thermometer may range at twenty degrees below zero (F) with six inches of snow resting on a quarter of an inch of ice, completely keeping the water beneath at a temperature of thirty-two degrees above zero. Without the snow the same ice increased in a day to a thickness of two inches. Likewise, under ten inches of snow the ground continued unfrozen, after the thermometer had for one month ranged from zero to forty degrees below. Thus we can easily see that under six inches of snow and one inch of feathers, the chickens do not suffer even at fifty degrees below. . . .

So long as the prairie chicken are abundant in their wild state it is unlikely that farmers will try to domesticate them, but with the anticipated influx of immigration it is just possible they will not be so abundant in a few years. I think that the experiment is worth trying, however, and if any member of the Historical Society is inclined to take the trouble, I will endeavor to find the necessary stock to start with. . . .

Transaction No. 14, read May 22, 1884.

GILBERT McMICKEN
(1813-1891)

GILBERT MCMICKEN WAS IN MANY WAYS TYPICAL OF THE young men who immigrated to Upper Canada from Scotland in the first half of the nineteenth century. In one respect, however, he was unique: he was Canada's first secret policeman.

The *Transaction* printed here, delivered when he was seventy-five years old, offers a fascinating glimpse into the professional life of a secret agent, a man who "made himself useful," in many ways and many different situations, to the new Dominion and its first prime minister, Sir John A. Macdonald.

Born in Wigtonshire, Scotland, in 1813, McMicken immigrated to the Niagara district in 1832. He was involved in many business enterprises, none very lucrative: he was a forwarder and commission agent, and a banker, and he operated the horse-drawn Erie and Ontario Railroad. Like many businessmen in Ontario at the time, he also speculated in real estate, but it was as a politician and political appointee that he enjoyed his greatest success. He served as a customs collector, Warden of Lincoln and Welland counties, and mayor of Clifton. As a Conservative he represented Welland County in the Legislative Assembly of Canada from 1857 to 1861. During this time McMicken became acquainted with John A. Macdonald and began a relationship that lasted for two decades. It was Macdonald who asked him to work as a secret agent and he seems to have been a "natural." Macdonald described him as a "shrewd, cool, and determined man who won't easily lose his head, and who will fearlessly perform his duty."[1] He made McMicken a magistrate with powers to set up the

Western Frontier Constabulary, a special force assigned to watch the Ontario-United States border during the American Civil War.

McMicken and his undercover detectives attempted to control the "substitute brokers" who paid or shanghaied young Canadians to go south and fight in place of conscripted Americans in the Union Army. His agents gathered intelligence in American cities such as Chicago, Detroit, and Buffalo. After the American war ended, McMicken continued as an agent of the government and, among other things, spied on the Fenians.

The Fenians were an American branch of the Irish Republican movement. In their oath they swore to "labor with my earnest zeal for the liberation of Ireland from the yoke of England, and for the establishment of a free and independent government on the Irish soil,…" The Fenians planned to conquer British North America and use it as a bargaining chip to bring pressure on the British, and in 1866, Fenian bands had crossed the border into New Brunswick, Quebec, and Ontario. The Fenian leader O'Neill showed considerable skill in defeating the inexperienced Canadian militia at the Battle of Ridgeway in the Niagara Peninsula. He and his followers, however, soon retreated across the border, not wishing to face approaching British regular troops.

In 1868, when Sir John A. Macdonald set up the Dominion Police force, and put Gilbert McMicken in charge, one of its main duties was to keep an eye on the Fenians. The force also provided security for Members of Parliament (the murder of Darcy McGee was fresh in everyone's mind) and important foreign visitors. McMicken played a role in the Red River troubles of 1870 when he met Manitoba representatives Scott and Ritchot at Ogdensburg, New York, and escorted them safely to their meeting in Ottawa with the prime minister.

In the summer of 1871, Gilbert McMicken was sent to Manitoba by Macdonald, ostensibly to open the Dominion Lands Office and the First Government Savings Bank. But he had other work to do as

---

1. Carl Betke, "Gilbert McMicken," *Dictionary of Canadian Biography* (Toronto: University of Toronto Press, 1965-).

well, watching the Fenians believed to be preparing an invasion of Manitoba. The Fenians were under the leadership of W.B. O'Donoghue *[whom McMicken calls "O'Donnahue"]*, a former member of Riel's Provisional Government, and the same John O'Neill *["O'Neil" in McMicken's account]* who had fought at the Battle of Ridgeway. McMicken was also to keep an eye on Lieutenant-Governor Archibald, who was unpopular with the Ontario faction in Red River and judged too sympathetic to the Métis and original settlers of the Red River Colony.[2] He was specifically ordered by Macdonald to gather what evidence he could about Riel's involvement with the Fenian raid.[3] Much has been written about whether Riel supported the Fenian invasion, but no evidence has been found that he planned to do so.[4]

McMicken, however, portrays Riel as a traitor, "haranguing" his followers and offering to help Lieutenant-Governor Archibald only after the Fenians were arrested by the American army.

McMicken's colourful language—the Fenians are "green ribbon decorated rapscallions" and a stage driver is a "vile lame lump of

---

2. Betke, "Gilbert McMicken," p. 678.

3. Ruth Swan and Edward A. Jerome, "Unequal Justice: The Metis in O'Donoghue's Raid of 1871," *Manitoba History* 39 (Spring/Summer 2000): 24-38.

4. Perhaps the definitive discussion of this issue can be found in J.M. Bumsted's *Louis Riel vs. Canada* (Winnipeg: Great Plains Publications, 2001). Dr. Bumsted concludes that Riel and the Métis remained loyal to the Canadian government, in spite of their frustration with Macdonald over land allocation and continued inaction on an amnesty for Riel and his colleagues in the Provisional Government. McMicken's version, stated in this *Transaction*, that Riel only pledged his loyalty to Lieutenant-Governor Archibald when he was sure the Fenians were defeated, was false, but it was the line taken by the press in Ontario and by the *Manitoba Liberal*, the newspaper of the Ontario group in Manitoba. Other research on the issue includes A.H. de Tremaudan, "Louis Riel and the Fenian Raid of 1871," *Canadian Historical Review* 4 (1923): 132-144, and John Pritchett, "The Origin of the So-Called Fenian Raid on Manitoba in 1871," *Canadian Historical Review* 10 (1929).

humanity"—and the strong-arm methods he unabashedly describes—attempting, unsuccessfully, to bully Bishop Taché, and threatening the unfortunate Mr. Goldie with a gun—make for entertaining reading and reveal a ruthless character.

McMicken's attitude toward Riel and the Métis was uncompromising: they could not be trusted and were bound to join the Fenians. He ends his talk with a final sneering story about Joseph Royal and a squad of Métis raised by him to defend the province. He says they appeared only after the danger was over, demanding rum. When that was gone, "Mr. Royal demanded and obtained for himself and each member of the squad, six dollars per diem. To this extent did so many of the Metis profit by the threatened insurrection and the raid."

McMicken, who came to Manitoba at the age of 58, never returned to live in Ontario. He found a new career in the west: as Dominion Land Commissioner, member and Speaker of the Manitoba Legislature, and Assistant Receiver General for the province. Two of his sons also settled in Winnipeg. One of them, Alexander McMicken, was mayor of Winnipeg in 1883, a provincial magistrate, and one of the founders of the Historical and Scientific Society. Gilbert McMicken passed away in 1891 in Winnipeg.[5]

---

5. An account of McMicken's career is found in Cheryl Macdonald, "Gilbert McMicken, Spymaster: Canada's Secret Police," *The Beaver* (June/July 1991): 44-49.

Gilbert McMicken in his robes as Speaker of the Legislative Assembly, c. 1880

The Abortive
Fenian Raid on Manitoba
Account by One Who Knew Its Secret History

TOWARDS THE END OF SEPTEMBER, 1871, WHILST
holding a commission under the Great Seal of Canada as Commissioner of Dominion Police, and acting as secretary to the Intercolonial
Railway Commissioners, I was appointed Agent of the Dominion Lands
for Manitoba, in connection with other important offices and duties.

Owing to the disturbed state of public feeling in the Province I was
hurried from Ottawa, and again, whilst stopping a day or two over at
Windsor, arranging my family affairs, was still further hurried by a
telegram from the Premier of the Government urging my departure,
owing to information he had received relative to the threatened Fenian
movement on Manitoba, in connection with the apprehended uprising of the half-breeds, subsequent to my departure from the capital.

My two days stay in Windsor involved no loss of time, for anticipa-
tory of just such a possibility, I had instructed my agents in the United
States to meet me in Chicago prepared to communicate the fullest
information respecting Fenian matters up to the latest moment. To
keep tryst in this behalf, and in fullest compliance with the wishes of
the Government, I on the following morning took my departure from
Windsor en route for Fort Garry. Accompanying me were my astute
and courageous son George, and Frank Ritchie equally trustworthy;
both most useful and reliable members of my Secret Service Police.
Merely stopping over in Chicago between train connections, so as to

lose no time, and meeting my agents promptly as expected and arranged, I received the exact information I needed in respect to the condition of Fenian matters and especially as to the projected movement upon Fort Garry. The body was at this time very much disorganized and General O'Neil found it impossible to galvanize into it a spark of enthusiasm by which O'Donnahoe might be encouraged by an offer of either men or means to any available extent. The fact was amongst themselves, there was no fund, to provide either sustenance or transportation.

The "sinews of war" had all been dissipated at Eccles Hill the preceding year.

O'Donnahoe had not wherewith to pay his own fare from Chicago to St. Paul.

Under such circumstances it was not to be wondered at that only forty-one (41) volunteers were found foolhardy enough to form a forlorn hope and by means of contributions from sympathizers started in the wake of O'Donnahoe—to conquer Manitoba. This was the meagre result of the most pathetic appeals, the earnest urgings and the specious statements made as to the absence of all opposing force—the overwhelming numbers of the Metis whose hospitable homes would at once yield quarters and hospitality while the rich plunder to be obtained from the Hudson's Bay Company's stores at Pembina and Fort Garry would serve to enrich them all at an unbounded extent.

O'Neil had managed to forward from their hidden depository in Michigan at Port Huron two hundred and fifty (250) breech loaders that had been converted from Springfield rifles at the Fenian armoury in Trenton, New Jersey.

It may not be out of place here to mention that, in all, 5,040 in number of Springfield rifles had been so converted at this armoury at an expense of $13.50 each whilst the Colts Arms Manufacturing Company had tendered to effect the conversion for $6.50 per rifle. You will see this operation caused a draft on the Fenian treasury of $68,040. This aside, however, I proceeded by first outgoing train for St. Paul. . . .

Arrived in St. Paul on Tuesday— . . . . I could not proceed on my way before Thursday morning I utilized my detention as best I could in endeavouring to ascertain some points of information, but, except the acquisition of a knowledge of the route and its exigencies, discomforts and topography, I had little success.

In St. Paul I met with the Honorable Alfred Boyd, a member of the Manitoba Cabinet, and as a matter of course congratulated myself on the immediate prospect of some useful information in regard to the state of affairs in the Province. In reply to my inquiry … he said the half-breeds intended pretty serious doings, and queried further said he thought they would make a fuss ere many days. It appeared uncommonly strange to me that a member of the government should not refer more seriously to such a grave subject and being under such apprehensions, and still more so did it appear to me when he told me he was going to do some shooting on the way home, as he had his own conveyance, and he might be some weeks on the way.

All the elucidation I could extract out of this, to me, very strange manner of a Cabinet Minister, was a remark by a gentleman who knew him well, and who said … : "Oh, he's queer."

On Thursday morning we started by train on the Breckenridge Railway, then in course of construction, and came to "Morris," at that time the terminal point. We arrived at an advanced hour in the afternoon and put up at the temporary station building for the night. It was Hobson's choice in this respect, the station building comprising at that day the whole town of Morris. Under the circumstances the meals were satisfactory and the quarters, on the plan of "forty for a garret," acceptably good.

Here I fell in with my companions for the trip booked, like myself, from St. Paul to Fort Garry in their totality. Mr. Wylie, a gentleman, representing the firm of James Turner and Co., of Hamilton, and who in that capacity had been over the route several times previously, with him was Mr. James Turner, jr., son of the senior of the firm a fine young lad; in years somewhat short of his majority. Mr. Richard Fuller, also from Hamilton, with whom and myself an acquaintanceship had sprung up some 16 or 17 years before. Besides these, there were Colin Strang a younger brother of Robert and Andrew Strang, well known citizens of Fort Garry then as they are now of Winnipeg; and a Mr.

Klotz from Berlin, County of Waterloo, Ontario. These with myself, my son and Ritchie, made a party of eight. After supper, at about 9 o'clock, the arrival of the stage vehicle from Fort Garry was announced, and with it the Rev. Bishop Tache.

Mr. Wylie, who knew His Lordship, at my instance, introduced me to his reverence, whom I found at once exceeding affable and quite willing to converse freely on the topic which at that moment interested me most, and engrossed my thoughts. ... [R]etiring somewhat apart from the other guests in the apartment, [I] asked what he could tell me about matters at Fort Garry.

. . . He apprehended troublous time. . . . [T]he Metis were intensely agitated over the unfulfilled promises of the Government and the harsh and insulting conduct of the more recently arrived Canadians from Ontario. Alluding to the Ontario volunteers who remained behind of the first expedition as intending settlers, he said they were so hostile and abusive as to invoke severe retaliation, and he feared ere many days scenes of a deplorable character. His Lordship of his own accord told me that on the previous evening he had met, where he stopped for the night at Macaulayville, O'Donnahoe and had a long interview with him; tried to persuade him not to proceed. O'Donnahoe said he was going in with some friends as settlers, as he had a right to do under the recent order-in-council, and to take up homesteads. I asked the Bishop if he saw the friends of O'Donnohoe referred to, and how many of them there were; also if Gen. O'Neil was with him. In reply he said there was a stranger with O'Donnohue who might be O'Neil, and as to the number of men he could not tell how many, but as they walked along they seemed a very considerable number, and this in connection with the state of affairs at home gave him great anxiety and uneasiness.

I counselled and entreated his Lordship to return to Fort Garry with me, as doubtless his presence and influence would be all-powerful to allay the excitement and maintain peace. He said he was on mission to Quebec according to appointment and the carrying out of this duty was paramount to all other present considerations. I spoke very candidly and plainly; said he would, if trouble ensued, as he apprehended, be looked upon as leaving the country under a full knowledge of the intended raid and insurrection, and had purposely left the country so as to give countenance and passive aid as well as encouragement to the movement; and he might take my word for it that it would not be many days ere the *Globe* of Toronto would express this view of the matter, and he could infer this as readily as myself. It was now between 11 and 12 o'clock, and on shaking hands at parting for the night, I besought the Bishop to ponder the situation and the free words I had spoken to him: a mutual "Good Night" was expressed and we parted, he to his couch and I to the work of preparing a duplicate despatch in cipher to the government at Ottawa. One to be sent by telegraph from the station, the other to be sent by His Lordship from St. Paul on his arrival there. This occupied me, letter-writing included, until between 3 and 4 a.m. As our coach was to start at 6 o'clock, and it required an hour previous to have breakfast, etc., I had no time for repose. Between 4 and 5 I went to the Bishop's bedside and again urged and besought him by every consideration in behalf of preserving the peace and preventing bloodshed to give up his trip to Quebec and return with me, that I would assume all his expenses, etc. He said he was deeply sorry, but his trip to Quebec was paramount with him and he must proceed thither at all hazards. He kindly consented to hand my duplicate despatch to the telegraph office in St. Paul on his arrival, which he did. We shook hands and parted.

It may be mentioned now that on our next meeting, which was on the 16th January, 1872, immediately after the Bishop's return, he reminded me laughingly of what I had predicted would appear in the *Globe*, saying "You see it was just so, but it did not make it any more the truth for all that."

I was fully impressed by this interview with a conviction that, however insignificant the Fenian force might be, there was great and immediate danger of a general rising of the French Half-breeds, and was burning with impatience to reach Fort Garry.

The morning was clear and cold; with one or two passengers added to our list, we started at 6 o'clock sharp, sped along fairly well over a good prairie road; saw many flocks of wild geese here and there on the ground; reached the first stopping place for exchange of horses about half past 8, this time on the edge of one of the small lakes with which Minnesota abounds. . . .

. . . At Macaulayville, which we reached about sunset, we found comfortable, clean and tidy accommodation, the hostess, an Eastern Townships woman, cleanly, good-looking, intelligent, and possessing a loving and loyal Canadian heart. Mr. Wylie had, in the course of his several journeys over this route, become well acquainted with this good lady and her husband, and stealing an opportunity whilst she with her assistants were busied in preparing a good supper for us, learned from her "ready discourse" a good deal respecting the bishop's stay . . . and his interview with O'Donnohoe, communicating this to me. Immediately after enjoying a hearty acceptable supper he made me acquainted with our good hostess. . . .

. . . Her intense Canadian loyalty had led her to play the eavesdropper while O'Donnohoe was closeted with Bishop Taché and repeated much of the conversation that was carried on between them. Interrupting her from time to time with trying questions and searching scrutiny I was convinced, apart from her exuberance of intense Canadian sentiment leading her to hasty conclusions, that what she told me was the truth pure and simple. What the Bishop had told me she fully corroborated. In addition, however, she informed me that a man of the name of Bodkin had raised in the village a company of men for the Fenian service; that they had that day been sworn in by Bodkin as their captain and were to start for the taking of Fort Garry on the morrow; that the men had paraded around the village that day with badges of green ribbon on their breasts. . . .

Frank Ritchie . . . had learned by some means that the hospital-sergeant with the U.S. force at Fort Abercrombie, which was immediately across the Red River, had just returned from St. Paul and had slipped a word or two as if he knew something of the Fenians, and had fallen in with them. Ritchie and the sergeant had been intimate in Ottawa while the latter was a member of the Prince Consorts Own Rifles stationed there for a time. It was now about midnight, but we crossed the river by an extra dollar to the ferryman, and, to Ritchie's message sent into the sergeant, he promptly responded. He told me he knew Major Watson, who was in command of the Fenians; that he came upon them on his way in at Old Crossing where they were encamped for the night. He ridiculed the movement to Watson and laughed at their meagre force. Watson said it would be all right at Fort Garry, that O'Donnahoe and the whole native population would be ready to greet their arrival, and their ranks would be filled up at Pembina. The sergeant said he saw but two wagons with the party. They had some arms, some barrels of pork, etc.; that their numbers were, so far as he could judge, not above forty if even so many; that they were a rough, hard looking set. All this information, coupled with what Bishop Tache had conveyed to me, very naturally caused me some anxiety, and induced serious cogitation. I consumed the rest of the night in writing dispatches, some for the mail and some in cipher to be sent by wire. At 6 a.m. Saturday I aroused Wylie and asked him to interview the stage agent at once and induce him to give us the coach as an express the rest of the way, telling him he must accomplish this at all hazards or at any cost, yet to economize as much as possible.

The result was, after no little difficulty in the negotiation, that by paying him five hundred dollars the coach would go to Fort Garry with us without stopping anywhere over at night. A new way bill was made out, all names being excluded except Wylie, who figured on it as eight. The reason of this was to prevent my name appearing, as O'Neil being ahead of us it was well known to him.

Owing to this change and the preparations it entailed, we did not get away from Macaulayville until late in the forenoon, hence I had the opportunity of an interview with Mr. Bodkin and of seeing a number of green ribbon decorated rapscallions.

Except breaking a thorough brace, which caused a little detention, and a detestable colation of rubabboo, at a changing station, nothing noteworthy occurred until we arrived at Georgetown. It may be remarked here that the whole country through which we passed presented no sign of life or settlement; the desolation caused by the Sioux Massacre still reigned supreme.

Daylight was just gone as we reached Georgetown. The prairie all around seemed to be lighted up with a lurid conflagration at once to us, strangers to prairie life, as grandly imposing and dread inspiring.

We had hardly freed ourselves from the coach when Mr. Wyllie was accosted by Mr. Pearson, father of Harry and Alfred Pearson, since well known as good citizens of our good city. He addressed Wylie in a very excited manner and asked him if Mr. McMicken was one of the passengers, Wylie hesitated and answered evasively, owing to the injunction of secrecy respecting my name, as it might bring danger to the whole party. Mr. Pearson said: Wylie this is no child's matter, I ask you on the square if Mr. McMicken is with you; it means for him life or death, and my anxiety is to save him from danger which lies in his way. Wylie replied "he is on the square too, and I'll introduce you shortly."

During this episode the order of the stage agent had been presented to the driver, who had only an hour or there abouts before arrived over a stage of about 20 miles. Such a hurricane of blasphemous swearing as issued from that profane driver's lips I never heard before, and could not imagine so vile a lame lump of humanity to exist anywhere out of the "inferno". Yet even in this there was hid a germ of virtue, a trait of humane feeling, for it was in consideration of his team (which he idolized) that he was excited into the indulgence of such revolting profanity, polluting the very atmosphere around him.

However, when exhausted and some what solaced with tobacco from Fuller and rum from Ritchie, Lame Jack concluded to feed his horses, while we fed, and get ready to go back and retrace with us the 20 miles over which he had come so recently.

At our introduction Mr. Pearson abruptly said: "You must on no account go on any further, but return the way you came. You will be robbed and killed to a certainty." Whilst at Grand Forks in the morning waiting the stage to start he heard a Mr. Goldie state in the presence of 13 or 14 persons that his friend, Mr. McMicken, the Receiver-General of Manitoba, was on his way in by the stage which was to leave St. Paul on the Thursday and he had a million of dollars with him, and if there was any truth in what they said about the trouble in Fort Garry he felt awfully sorry for him.

Goldie was in the stage which preceded me in the start from Morris by two days, and had O'Neil and O'Donnahoe with a Mr. and Mrs. Lathom as fellow passengers, and to them, not knowing them, he repeated this same statement. Mr. Pearson further said in coming down he met on the way two wagons laden with barrels and arms convoyed by a lot as villainous cut-throat looking ragamuffins as any one ever saw together; then addressing me said, "You won't attempt to go on; no, no, you must go back. You can do nothing to save yourself in this wild lone country—to proceed would be self-murder."

I said I would think the matter over and after supper would confer with him further. . . .

It need not be told how heartily I thanked Mr. Pearson, or how deeply I appreciated his warm-hearted friendship for me as a brother of the "mystic tie"*[i.e. a Mason]*.

I said to him: I must proceed; kindly answer me one or two questions and I shall be fully prepared for emergencies. At what hour did you leave Grand Forks? At what hour did you meet the Fenians? At what hour did you arrive here? At what rate were the Fenians travelling?

His replies gave me a basis for the calculation that the party had by that time reached Grand Forks, and to assure him said: Now you can see I shall pass over these 62 miles scatheless, and when there will be governed by circumstances as I find them.

The prairie fires were raging in every direction far and near. Others present who knew nothing of Fenian dangers urged these as an insuperable obstacle to our getting on to-night. They said that it would be impossible to pass through them, and the team would not be kept under control, etc., etc. Lame Jack was now, however as fully determined to proceed as he at first had so strenuously objected. So we started. The team of four horses was superb. I do not think I ever saw four such handsome, well conditioned, spirited horses hitched together, not even amongst those of the four-in-hand club in London; and notwithstanding their lately finished trip of twenty miles, were proudly champing the bit and fretting for the start. We had covered a distance of some three or four miles; all the party exuberant in spirits and enjoyment, when suddenly our driver held up and asked us hurriedly to leave the coach as he had to turn about and try, after escaping the fire, to find a way of picking us up after it had passed; out we all sprang quicker than it is written. As the stage left us I admired the sight as it receded from our view. The white canvas covering the proud stepping of the horses as seen in the light of the burning prairie afforded as weird a scene as did the witches in Macbeth over the caldron on the Scottish heath. The fire came roaring and leaping down towards us with, to us as it seemed, race-horse speed. The flames varying in height from 6 to 12 feet, immediate cremation seemed our inevitable fate. Furnishing each of the party with a few matches, a supply of which I always carry on my person, and some pieces of newspaper, I ordered them to spread out along the trail and, at distances of two or three yards apart, to fire the grass to leeward. This was done; none too soon, for young Mr. Turner got a slight scorching. As the grass burned we followed the flames on to the seared and blackened sward. The flames from windward were stopped by the trail and the absence of anything to feed upon, and we were safe. The stage, having taken a turn far off beyond our vision, got in rear of the flames, and our friend Swearing Jack soon picked us up. From this to Grand Forks, although constantly on the alert and keenly observant at each stopping for change of horses, no incident worthy of note occurred except it be that, *nolens volens*, at Frog Point (I think it was) we were summarily made to exchange from our roomy 4-horse coach to a 2-horse jerky. Cramming and ramming was the order and some discomfort resulted, and our progress was proportionately slow. Sunday morning dawned upon us, promising a beautiful day. We drove up to Stewart's door at Grand Forks about 10 o'clock in the forenoon, hungry and tired. After a hurried and rather imperfect ablution Mr. Stewart soon had set before us wherewith to refresh and satisfy our appetites. In the meantime, however, I had seen Mr. Trail, the officer in charge of the Hudson's Bay Company's post there, and from him had Mr. Pearson's statement fully corroborated. He told me the marching Fenians got in there late in the evening and left about four hours previous to my arrival. The Fenians and probable half breed troubles at Fort Garry were freely talked of. . . .

. . . So the vehicle was got ready, I left all my cash but a few dollars and my papers to the safe-keeping of Mr. Trail and my baggage with Mr. Stewart. . . . Here I may note that, had the Fenians got hold of me, they would have been woefully disappointed in their financial expectations, for, having purchased three safes for the Government use in Detroit—one of them burglar-proof—I had Mr. Hamilton G. McMicken set the quadruple combination of the lock and placed all the funds in my charge excepting $5,000 in it, leaving it with the other two to be forwarded by ordinary conveyance. The delay occasioned some apprehension at Ottawa, for I was wired by Sir Francis Hicks (the telegraph line was now working), asking if they had arrived. Fortunately just that day, the 2nd of December, they were brought in by sleigh from Pembina, intact. . . .

Night set in upon us and we hoped to slip past the Fenians, encamped somewhere along the route. We kept a strict watch. Fuller and Ritchie sat with the driver outside. They were to use as a watchword "Is that dog all right?" . . . About midnight as we were drawing near a changing station, "Is that dog all right?" in clear tones struck our ears. Stillness and expectancy of undefined apprehension ruled us all. Soon we heard Ritchie saying "A fine cool night for travelling boys"; the response, "You bet," we heard, and straining our eyes through the openings in the canvas-covered jerky, we saw the wagons and some of the men. The coach soon turned off the main trail, going in to the changing station. . . . Our horses were fresh and we started out at a rattling pace. Very shortly after reaching the main trail; again we passed the Fenians. Three were ahead of the wagons as an advance guard, and five were behind them. Nothing was said, as I had ordered, and we shot ahead in silence and with such speed as we could. At the next stage house we picked up a driver who knew nothing of the road, having only came in from Pembina over it the previous day. He, we found, was an Irishman Americanized; a full blown Fenian. Ritchie and Fuller pretended to be Americans and in full sympathy with his views. He told them he had been sworn in about two weeks ago, that they would see fun at Garry although he did not know how it would be now, as the leaders had made a big blunder. The raid was planned to take place in November when the route by the lakes could not be passed over, and now the raid was ordered for Wednesday. All were to gather at Pembina then, so as to start on the march for Garry Thursday morning. "It was a d—d mistake," he said, for now the Canucks could send up their soldiers by the lakes and rivers. Still he said, "You'll see fun anyhow."

We neared Pembina as the day was breaking and were astonished to find a man on horseback close to, and following, our coach. Dubious of the road we pulled up, and I inquired of the man on the horse which was the way into the village. He said he was a stranger and did not know; was following us as he supposed the stage would take the right road. Before this, however, at some unperceived bend in the road, we lost sight of the telegraph poles (the poles were planted, but no wire strung yet). We halted for consultation. Rumor said that at that time there were 1,500 men encamped up on the boundary of St. Joe, and Wyllie was afraid the driver was heading for this encampment. I struck a light, saw what time it was, and scanned a pocket compass. The course of the Red river was known, and so a little calculation and reflection assured me that keeping the course we were pursuing we would strike the Red river before very long. This was correct; in about 20 minutes the poles were hailed with joy and a heap of nervousness abated. Before entering Pembina, knowing that we would overtake the previous coach there and find Mr. Goldie at the inn, I instructed Mr. Wylie . . . to find out before I got out of the coach what room Goldie occupied. He did so, and I at once sprung out with face blackened and begrimed with the black-burned dust from the prairie, rushed into Mr. Goldie's room. I found him just up and buttoning his suspenders. Having a Colt's navy revolver in my hand I addressed him in language interlarded with what might have been taken as lessons learned from Lame Jack and referring to the extreme danger he had thrown around me, forbade him on penalty of instant death to show any recognition of me before any one, by word or look, and not to go out of range of my observation. He trembled and promised, I promising to explain fully when we met at Fort Garry. Poor man, his cup and saucer rattled together as he attempted to take a cup of coffee, but he was mum and undemonstrative. Here the stage people wanted to put us all together into one coach, I would not assent and insisted on my rights as having hired mine as an express. I managed to have the "regular," with Mr. Goldie and Mr. and Mrs. Latham start first, followed immediately by my vehicle. While waiting in Robertson's O'Donnahoe sat at one end of the stove, and I at the other—thanks, however, to my precautions and our stage arriving 2 days ahead of time, no suspicions were aroused as to my being there; few were astir, as it was only 6 a.m. We were now in the crisis of our danger, and excitedly apprehensive and watchful, for a couple of men on horseback armed with repeaters could have made us an easy prey.

Coming in view of the post which conspicuously pointed out what was then assumed as the boundary line, we felt as if nearing home, as coming under the aegis of never failing British protection, forgetting, or casting aside all fears as we passed the welcome post, our pocket pistols were drawn and the remaining drops of inspiring old John Barleycorn were quaffed to the toast of "The Queen", and cheer after cheer testified to our loyalty and returning confidence and courage. Changing horses at the Marais, at Klines (here a dinner characteristic of the route and needing starvation sauce, a little going a long way) next in St. John Baptist, then at D'Lorme's we arrived, the two conveyances always within hail on the south bank of the Assiniboine. About Sunset Fort Garry was reached safely on Monday the 2nd day of October 1871. The river was very low the crossing narrow, the ramshackle old scow in use lay on the north side, and the halfbreeds in charge made haste at great leisure, and more time than was at all necessary was consumed in bringing us over; down what is now Main Street, then an open prairie road, we were driven with a dash up to the door of the Davis hotel. Nothing inviting, everything forbidding— dirt, discomfort and whiskey abundant. What few houses there were, mean and insignificant in appearance, and as if dropped down here and there at random, without order and at haphazard.

A room could not at once be allotted to me although I proposed that my son and myself could room together. Davis was the autocrat of the whiskey ranch and we must wait his will to eat and sleep. It may be readily inferred that having come in from St. Paul's in 4 1/2 days, and with less than four hours sleep, I stood greatly in need of the latter, and of the former, seeing the kind of food we had on the way "it goes without saying". Supper announced, I entered a room with a table running lengthwise in the middle of it—every seat filled with occupants some with coats on, others without. Several who thought it no breach of law or etiquette to eat with unwashed hands. I managed to hustle into a seat and satisfied my stomach pro tem with a fried gold eye, a boiled potato, in his jacket fortunately, and a cup of tea. I was not allowed to enjoy even this undisturbed, for Capt. Villiers, the chief of Provincial police, in gold lace and spangles, introduced himself to me and said the Lieut.-Governor had heard of my arrival and was anxious to see me; that it was now dark and he would wait to see me up at Government House. He needed not to wait long; we walked up and I entered the vice regal hall, begrimed with the black dust from the burnt prairies, which the Red River water could effect little in the way of cleansing power. Shirt and collar in keeping with the color of the epidermis—having been donned at Grand Forks 36 hours before—I felt my outward appearance had little to recommend me to a favourable reception, but the Lt.-Governor, Mr. Archibald, received me with demonstrations of gladness. I apologized for my appearance and on not having letters of introduction, as I had left all but as I appeared before him at Grand Forks. He said I needed no introductory papers for he had heard from headquarters and otherwise of me and was indeed very glad to see me.

We entered at once into conversation upon the state of affairs. I told him exactly how matters stood with the Fenians and assured him the report of a large gathering at St. Joe was a baseless rumor; that O'Donnohue and O'Neil could not possibly muster over 70 men at Pembina, and probably not half that number. He had nothing to fear from outside forces; all would depend on how it stood with the Metis and others within the Province. He said there was every reason to apprehend a rising; that he was doing what he could to operate on them through Fathers Dugas and Ritchot, but they insisted as a condition that he would give them a satisfactory assurance that the promise of a full amnesty would be fulfilled at once. Without this they could exercise no influence upon their people; that Riel had their hearts and he would not yield unless the amnesty was granted forthwith. After some discussion upon the state of affairs, Mr. Archibald having told me of the unpleasant state of feeling between the Canadians, as they were called, and the Halfbreeds; that it was bitterly hostile on both sides, and towards himself personally as Lieutenant-Governor, the former as a whole were malignantly antagonistic. His Honor then said, Mr. McMicken, you have had large experience in circumstances of this kind, and I have had none. What would you advise me to do? Without hesitation I advised the issue of a proclamation calling the whole body of the people to arms, and this without a moment's delay. Assuring him if he could get 400 or 500 men under arms he could make himself master of the situation, but all depended upon the celerity with which it could be done, for his force must be enrolled before the Metis took the field. This is Monday night, I said, and the raid was planned to be made by crossing the line on Wednesday afternoon or Thursday morning. Mr. Archibald said "there are about 70 men in the fort (volunteers) under arms now, and I do not know how far the feeling obtains amongst them that is so vindictively shown towards me by the Canadians in the village and settlements, and I fear the proclamation may not receive a hearty response."

Dread nothing on this score, I said; I know no one here personally, but I do know well and thoroughly the genius and bent of mind of the Ontario people, in fact their human nature, and call upon them without distinction of party or prejudice, to rally round the nation's flag and to stand by their Queen. You will find not a laggard among them, not even the most hostile in feeling against yourself.

The proclamation was decided upon, was forthwith drawn up, and Mr. Cunningham, who was the government printer, and publisher of the Manitoba newspaper, was called from downstairs where he had been waiting to learn the upshot of the interview between the Lt.-Governor and myself; and to him was handed the draft of the proclamation with instructions to have it printed before morning—it was now midnight and Capt. Villiers would see to its distribution and posting. This celebrated document was printed in wonderful display of type:—

(The Royal Arms)

PROCLAMATION

PROVINCE OF MANITOBA

Victoria by the grace of God, of the United Kingdom of Great Britain and Ireland, Queen, defender of the faith, etc.

Sd. Adams George Archibald

To our loving subjects, the inhabitants of the Province of Manitoba, Greeting:

Whereas, intelligence has just been received from trustworthy sources that a band of lawless men calling themselves

FENIANS

have assembled on the frontier of the United States at or near Pembina and that they intend to make a raid into this province, from a country with which we are at peace, and to commit acts of depredation, pillage and robbery, and other outrages upon the persons and property of our loving subjects the inhabitants of this province. While not unprepared to meet the emergency with our regular forces, we do hereby warn all our said loving subjects to put themselves in readiness at once to assist in repelling this outrage upon their hearths and homes. We enjoin them immediately to assemble in their respective parishes and

ENROL THEMSELVES

For this purpose we call upon all our said loving subjects, irrespective of race or religion, or of past differences, to

RALLY ROUND THE FLAG

Of our common country. We enjoin them to select the best men of each locality to be officers, whom we shall duly authorize and commission, and we enjoin the officers so selected to put themselves in immediate communication with the Lieutenant-Governor of our said Province. We shall take care that persons possessing military skill and experience shall be detailed to teach the necessary drill and discipline. All officers and men when called into service shall receive the pay and allowances given to the regular militia. The country need feel no alarm. We are quite able to repel these outlaws if they were numerous. The handful of them who threaten us can give no serious difficulty to brave men who have their homes and families to defend.

RALLY THEN AT ONCE!

We rely upon the prompt reply of all our people of every origin, to this our call.

In testimony thereof, we have caused these our letters, to be made patent, and the great seal of Manitoba to be hereunto affixed.

Witness our trusty and well-beloved the Honorable Adams George Archibald, Lieutenant Governor of our province of Manitoba, member of our Privy Council for Canada, etc., etc., at our Government House in Fort Garry, this 3rd day of October in the year of our Lord one thousand eight hundred and seventy-one, and in the thirty-fifth year of our reign.

By Command,
Thos. Howard
Provincial Secretary.

On the following evening a public meeting was held at the Police station, then standing about where the St. Julien restaurant now is. It

General John O'Neill, Fenian leader, 1870

was addressed by the Revs. Black, McLean and Young in fervid expressions of loyalty and patriotism.

The enthusiasm of the audience was unbounded. The wonderfully large assemblage astonished me, for it was difficult to imagine where they all gathered from. But still more was I astonished when, ere 48 hours had elapsed from the issuing of the proclamation, over 1,000 men had enrolled themselves. Where were they domiciled? It was to me a mystery; but the enrollment was a great and gratifying fact.

The Hudson's Bay officials to a man enrolled themselves, and formed a goodly company in number and physique, under the command of Capt. D.A. Smith, now Sir D.A. The most virulent of those antagonistic to the Lieut.-Governor were amongst the first to offer their services. A strong company of unswerving Loyalists were placed under command of Mr. Stewart Mulvey, late an ensign in the first expedition of volunteers from Ontario. I think they numbered nearly 100 strong.

Mr. Cunningham organized a company as a "Home Guard" with Mr.—now Mr. Justice—Bain as his lieutenant.

The difficulty now was to arm the number who had enrolled themselves, for besides the arms in the hands of the 79 regular volunteers the total number at the command of the Lt.-Governor was only 650. Rather unwisely, Mr. Cunningham the bold captain of the home guard, obtained arms for his command. This soon became known and the Kildonan men represented by Mr. Harrower and Mr. Sutherland, then, and still known as "Scotchman" protested most strongly against the distinction, and insisted upon having arms served our to them, the scarcity of supply could not be made known to them and they were unreasonable. Mr. Sutherland, whose courage and loyalty appeared far above boiling point, said they must have arms or know the reason why. "Bombardinian had received a blow and Cornontrotonthologus must die" *[a reference to an eighteenth-century burlesque]*. Harrower said "Mr. McMicken, I admit you have the best of the argument but 'the Kildonan men must have arms for all that.'"

That morning I sent Ritchie off by the stage to Pembina to watch matters there and report. I endeavoured to obtain two saddle horses for myself and son to go to the Hudson's Bay Co.'s post near Pembina, but failed, and was obliged to remain at the Fort. Many perplexing difficulties cropped up, to annoy the Governor. Fathers Ritchot and Dugas had daily interviews with him but they invariably ended by their refusing to urge Riel to enroll with his people unless the amnesty was assured to them. During the night of Tuesday or Wednesday one of the cannon was spiked. The circumstance at the time was suspicious and rather alarming, but it had no ill effect.

On Monday morning Major Irvine who was in command of the volunteers assembled a force of 200 men and in the evening dull, dark and drizzling, started out with all the panoply and pomp of glorious war, crossed the Assiniboine with some confusion and delay, baptizing the chief of the commisariat, Major Peebles, in the river. This valorous force with the temerity begotten of the occasion marched without holding to St. Norbert. Here Pere Ritchot was indebted to the good feeling and watchfulness of Capt. Mulvey for his escape from danger he little suspected. Three or four scouts, factors in the Hudson's Bay Co. started out for the Company's fort at Pembina. Except an intimate acquaintance made with the prairie by Mr. Factor Christie having been catapulted over his horse's head nothing special occurred on the way.

Capt. Villiers, of the police, was directed to establish videttes between Fort Garry and Pembina for the purpose of maintaining communication and obtaining information. The least said of this service the better; it was not only nil—it was worse.

In the meantime, however, the banditti under O'Neil and O'Donnahoe to the number of 15 or 20 crossed the boundary and stormed the Hudson's Bay fort, opposed as vigorously as he could by the officer in charge, Mr. Watt, who had but one arm. They commenced rifling the stores, and when about preparing to establish themselves there Col. Wheaton, of the United States regular troops, dispersed and captured a number of them. This, thanks to the prompt and high-minded Wheaton, ended the raid—how O'Neil and O'Donnahoe and those with them were dealt with by the United States civil authorities is a matter of historical record and does not come within the object of this paper.

Meanwhile great excitement prevailed in the then hamlet, the germ of Winnipeg and Fort Garry. Apprehensions were entertained that Col. Irvine and his small force would be gobbled up by Riel and his followers. Rumors obtained that the villagers were to be attacked by a large force of Metis from St. Boniface. The home guard were active; several were incarcerated on suspicion. In Mr. Cunningham's eyes an Irish name, especially if the person who bore it was a Roman Catholic, was a strong ground for suspicion and a justifiable cause of arrest.

On Sunday forenoon, the Raid being a thing of the past, Mr. Archibald felt very anxious on the score of the arrests made by Cunningham's home guards, and requested me to give it my attention. I proceeded to the police station in the cells of which the prisoners were held, and on the way introduced myself to Mr. Bannatyne, who was a J.P. for the province. He accompanied me and informed me that one of those held in custody was a nephew of his. Mr. Ashdown, also a

J.P., joined us as we entered the office of the police clerk, Mr. Barton, who was then the officer in charge of the station. I asked him to show me a list of his prisoners, this he readily complied with.

There were six in number. Taking them in order consecutively, I inquired who ordered this man's imprisonment? He answered, Mr. Cunningham. By what authority did you receive him or retain him in custody? By Mr. Cunningham's order. A written order? No. Have you no written order or warrant of commitment? No. And so through the list. Turning to Messrs. Bannatyne and Ashdown, I asked them if the laws of Manitoba authorized such despotic authority, under such circumstance. No, no, they both said, "certainly not."

I immediately directed Mr. Baron, under my authority as an officer of the Dominion specially charged with matters within the criminal jurisdiction of the General government, and the sanction of His Honor the Lieutenant-Governor of the Province, to set the prisoners at liberty. This he instantly did, greatly to the relief and satisfaction of them and their friends.

One more episode, and I shall draw to a conclusion:

On that Sunday Riel, at the church door at St. Norbert, harangued the people. He told them their friend O'Donnahoe had failed, and it became them to offer their services to the Governor. Quite a large number of them turned out on horseback and came up to St. Boniface on the south bank of the river. Senator Girard, then a member of the Provincial government, came over and with much precision induced Mr. Archibald to cross over and formally accept the proffered services of Riel and his followers. This be it noted, when all occasion for his services had passed away, so that the move on Riel's part was a hollow mockery.

Humane feelings and a desire to conciliate prompted the Governor into yielding, contrary to his convictions and better judgement on this occasion.

The memorable handshaking took place, a scene over which prudence or other virtue draws a veil.

Yet one more episode and I have done. On the Tuesday following, a squad of Metis, numbering some thirty or more, headed by Mr. Joseph Royal, mounted on horseback, accoutred in their own fashion and with much braggadocio binding themselves to give a good account of the enemies of the Province wherever found. The only enemy, however, they were likely to encounter besides the majority of themselves (for of the lot it might be doubted if in the bosom of any of them excepting Pascal Breland and one or two others, a heart had a beat of loyalty within it) lay in the large quantity of 50 overproof rum which Royal insisted should be served out to them and would not stir without it.

They had a glorious time of it, a time of free frolic and feasting never in all their lives before enjoyed, and certainly never since. But their good fortune did not end here. On their victorious return from their valorous campaign on the exhaustion of their commissariat and the rum, Mr. Royal demanded and obtained for himself and each member of the squad, six dollars per diem. To this extent did so many of the Metis profit by the threatened insurrection and the raid.

The raid is ended. It is my turn to end; I have done.

Transaction No. 32, read May 11, 1888.

Unveiling the Seven Oaks Monument, June 19, 1891

GEORGE BRYCE & CHARLES BELL

ON JUNE 19, 1891, THE HISTORICAL AND SCIENTIFIC Society of Manitoba unveiled a monument commemorating the seventy-fifth anniversary of the Battle of Seven Oaks. The cairn, paid for by the Countess of Selkirk, was one of several such monuments erected in the early 1890s, manifestations of different French and English points of view about the history of the province. These included the stone erected on Riel's grave and the large La Vérendrye monument in St. Boniface.

A photo of the unveiling survives. Standing on and around a rough wooden platform hastily built next to the stone monument, dignitaries pose with grave expressions for the photographer. At the far left of the platform is Samuel P. Matheson. He is, not yet, in 1891, archbishop of Rupert's Land, but a professor at St. John's College and dean of St. John's Cathedral, and a representative of the old Red River settlement through his family and birth. The president of the society, John McBeth, was there, also a member of an old Red River family. Representatives of the new order of Ontario-born English-Canadians, who had assumed the dominant role in local society and politics in the years since 1870, were also on the platform in the persons of Dr. George Bryce, Charles N. Bell, and John C. Schultz. In an open landau parked beside the platform and hidden by parasols are two or three women, likely Agnes Schultz and Marion Bryce, each of whom, like their husbands, had played an important role in the development of the new province of Manitoba and the new city of Winnipeg since 1870.

This group is not formally posed, looking instead as though the photographer had caught them as they were preparing to leave the platform after the ceremony. But they are serious and formal, as though they considered that what has just transpired has deep significance.

The bare facts of the Seven Oaks incident are that on June 19, 1816, Cuthbert Grant, the Métis community leader, and a party of Métis connected with the North West Company had been riding across what was called La Grenouilliere, or Frog Plain, just west of present-day Point Douglas. They came within sight of Fort Douglas, the headquarters of Robert Semple, the governor recently appointed by Lord Selkirk. Semple, with a group of settlers and Hudson's Bay Company employees, rivals of the North West Company people, came out to parlay with the Métis. What exactly happened next has been and undoubtedly will continue to be the subject of debate. What is certain is that shots were fired and Semple and twenty-one of his party, and one of the North West Company men, were killed. Some, including Semple, had initially only been wounded in the battle, but were then finished off, and some of the bodies of Semple's party were mutilated by one of the Métis and his sons, adding to the heat generated by the incident at the time and in the years since.

The battle at Seven Oaks, with its tragic loss of life, was a milestone in the long struggle for dominance of the fur trade between the Hudson's Bay Company and the Montreal-based companies that, by 1816, had coalesced in the North West Company. But the fight also became an event of symbolic importance, one that "epitomized" larger historical themes.[1] For the Métis, it was "la Grenouillere," an epic battle immortalized in verse on the very night of the conflict by the Métis poet, Pierre Falcon. For English Canadian historians, such as Dr. Bryce, it was a brutal massacre of civilized White settlers by wild and savage Bois Brûlés, a bloody reminder of what the forces of

---

1. Jennifer Brown, "Commentary," in Robert Coutts and Richard Stuart, eds., *The Forks and the Battle of Seven Oaks in Manitoba History* (Winnipeg: Manitoba Historical Society, 1994), p. 90.

progress were up against. The Seven Oaks cairn, erected by an historical society dominated by English-speaking Manitobans, was intended to commemorate Dr. Bryce's Seven Oaks. Dr. Schultz, in his remarks, for example, said the monument would serve to remind people how far the country has come since those dark days.

In addition to the speeches made that day in 1891, the *Transaction* includes the text of two different descriptions of the events at Seven Oaks: one taken from Bryce's book *Manitoba: Its Infancy, Growth and Present Condition*, and one written by Bell in his *The Selkirk Settlement and Settlers*. Both men quoted extensively from eyewitnesses, although the two accounts differ slightly because of their authors' viewpoints. In this, as in all his writing, Bryce is interested in establishing that the Métis were less than civilized, being "lithe, cunning, turbulent, but adventurous and lively." His account leads the reader in the direction of a cold-blooded massacre designed to drive out the Selkirk Settlers, who were threatening the North West Company's fur trade and who were the representatives of civilization and progress. Bell takes a more neutral stance, commenting that it is "difficult to get at the exact truth" of what happened when Semple went out to meet the Métis. His answer to this problem is to present "a version of the affair emanating from each side," leaving readers to draw their own conclusions.

This *Transaction* is important not only because of the story it tells, but also because it gives a fascinating early example of the orchestrated manipulation of public history to promote a particular view of an historical event.

Seven Oaks

In 1811 the Earl of Selkirk, a Scottish nobleman of great energy and breadth of view, secured a large tract of country from the Hudson's Bay Company, of which he was a prominent stockholder, to found a settlement on the Red River, in the heart of North America. The fur traders from Montreal, organized under the name of the "Northwest Fur Company" (See Mackenzie's *Voyages* 1801, and Vol. I. Masson's *Les Bourgeois de la Compagnie du Nord-Oest*), had at the time establishments all through the country, from Lake Superior to the Pacific Ocean. The "Nor'westers," as they were popularly known, had the prestige of a generation of successful trade, and were led by Canadianized Highlanders of great energy and daring. Lord Selkirk's first settlers arrived, by way of Hudson Bay, at the Red River in 1812, and took up holdings on the Red River, near the site of the present City of Winnipeg. Several parties arrived in the years succeeding by the same route, until the Selkirk settlement in 1814 numbered about two hundred souls. In that year a "jauntily-dressed" officer of the Nor'-west Company, named Duncan Cameron, succeeded in inducing about one hundred and fifty of the settlers to desert the Red River and take up their abode in the western part of Upper Canada. (See Ross's *Red River Settlement*, 1856, and Bryce's *Manitoba*.) Governor Macdonell had erected buildings within what are now the limits of the City of Winnipeg; but the Nor'-westers resisted his authority, and even took the Governor prisoner; and their chiefs, one of whom was Cuthbert Grant, on June 25th, 1815, issued the mandate: "All settlers to retire immediately from the River, and no appearance of a colony to remain." In that year, however, another party of Highland colonists arrived from Britain, making the number up again to about one hundred and fifty. The deserted homesteads were again occupied. The colonists' buildings were erected in a more substantial form, a barricade was built around them, and reprisals were even made upon the Nor'-wester establishment, Fort Gibraltar, which stood at the junction of the Red and Assiniboine Rivers. (See Bryce's *Five Forts of Winnipeg*, 1886.) An officer, Robert Semple, had been sent out by Lord Selkirk as Governor, and he took up his abode in Fort Douglas (1816). The Nor'-westers now determined to make a great effort, and the events which led to the battle of "Seven Oaks," in which the Governor and his attendants were killed, are given in the following extracts from *Manitoba: its Infancy, Growth and Present Condition* by Dr. Bryce, a life member of this Society.

THE BOIS-BRULES.

[From George Bryce's book Manitoba.*]*

A lithe, cunning, turbulent, but adventurous and lively race were the Bois-Brules of those early times. They were chiefly the descendants of the French voyageurs of the North-west Company, who had taken Indian wives and settled down on the shore of some lake or river in the fur country. Some of the Scotch partners, too, from Montreal, had become enamoured of the country, and had cast in their lot with this half-blood race, who now, in 1812, the time of the arrival of the Selkirk settlers, had begun to speak of themselves as the "New Nation." Grant, Mackay, McLeod, McGillivray, and many other Highland names, are found among these hunters and trappers of the western solitudes.

By what name they should call themselves seemed to have been a subject of considerable interest among these mixed bloods of the prairies. The name then and now most in favor among them is that of the French word "Metis," of which the word half-breed is a fair translation, and which is now used in Acts of the Canadian Parliament as the legal title of this race.

At the time of which we write, the Metis, or Bois-Brules, were almost entirely connected with the North-west Company. The Hudson's Bay Company had up till this time been exclusively an English company. They had traded with the Indians entirely; and hardly a trace, at least in the interior of their territories, could be found of the admixture of European and Indian blood.

Since that date there has been a great change. The Hudson's Bay Company employed, subsequently to 1812, a large number of Orkney men in their service. These, after the manner of the early French voyageurs, intermarried with the Indian women, and founded a race of Scotch half-breeds, also known as English, i.e., English speaking half-breeds. In the year 1869, in which the Hudson's Bay territory was transferred to Canada, these Orkney half-breeds equalled in number those of French extraction, and altogether both summed up at that time 10,000 souls. The English half-breeds are far less volatile and more industrious than their French fellow-countrymen.

It is only with those of French origin that we are at present concerned, as the Orkney men had not, to any extent, begun to come to the Red River country previous to the union of the North-west and Hudson's Bay Companies in 1821.

How strange the sight of a race sprung up at this early date in the interior of the continent, combining the characteristics of the French and the Indian. Chateaubriand, who traveled in America, has indeed pointed out a fact, noticed by many other observers, that of all the Europeans, the French are most in sympathy with the Indians, and this arises from their liveliness, their dashing bravery, their love of the chase, and even of the savage life; though the English have far surpassed the French in management of the Indian tribes. There can be no doubt that the French half-breeds are of greater stature, are more restive under restraint, more inclined to the wandering life of the Indian, and more given to the hunt and to the use of arms, than those of Orkney descent.

The Bois-Brules, as the French half-breeds were commonly called, were admirably adapted for the purposes of the Nor'-westers, and indeed had a passionate attachment to the Company. The Company, recognizing the power it gave them with the Indians to have as agents those having Indian blood in their veins, encouraged the idea of an autonomy—a nationality among them. One of themselves had risen to be a ruling spirit among them, and though his name would not have betrayed his origin, Cuthbert Grant had all the ascendancy of a chief over this singular people. On him was afterwards conferred the title, of rather vague meaning, of "Warden of the Plains;" and he was evidently one of those men, found in all ages and countries, born to rule; and who, in spirit of governments and in the absence of government, under monarchy, republic, or absolutism, give the cue, direction, and force to the ideas of the community or mass. Happily, he seems to have been humane.

Cuthbert Grant was known far and wide among the hunters and trappers of the North-west; and regions, hundreds of miles apart, on account of the sparse population, were brought into close connection. He had been educated in Montreal, had risen to be one of the most enterprising and energetic agents of the Company, and had been placed in charge of many of their expeditions.

THE NOR'-WESTER ATTITUDE.

The Nor'-Westers were, from the first, averse to the establishment of Lord Selkirk's Colony. On the 22nd of May, 1811, at the very time the scheme was originating, one of the leading partners of the North-West Company, then in England, stated to Mr. Miles Macdonell, that he was "determined to give all the opposition in his power whatever might be the consequences;" that "such a settlement struck at the root of the North-West Company, which it was intended to ruin." If other people did not clearly see their own interest, he did; that the settlement "must at all times lie at the mercy of the Indians," who would not be bound by treaties and that "one North-West Company's interpreter would be able at any time to set the Indians against the settlers to destroy them."

It is stated by different writers, that no sooner had the settlers arrived than efforts were made to stir up the Indians against the colonists; and failing in this, the agents of the North-West Company had induced the Metis to disguise themselves as Indians, and, on the way to Pembina, rob one man of the gun his father had carried at Culloden, a woman of her marriage-ring, and others of various ornaments and valuable articles.

No specially hostile acts were observed during the years 1812 and 1813.

We come now to the celebrated proclamation of Governor Miles Macdonell, which undoubtedly had something to do with hastening the collision. The following is a copy of the document itself;—

PROCLAMATION.

Whereas the Governor and Company of the Hudson's Bay have ceded to the right Honorable Thomas, Earl of Selkirk, his heirs and successors for ever all that tract of land or territory bounded by a line running as follows, viz:—

Beginning on the western shore of Lake Winnipeg, at a point in 52 and 30' north latitude, and thence running due west, to the Lake Winipiquarish, otherwise called little Winnipic; then in a southerly direction through the said lake, so as to strike its western shore in latitude 52; then due west to the place where the parallel of 52 north latitude intersects the western branch of the Red River, otherwise called the Assiniboin River; then due south from that point of intersection to the height of land which separates the waters running into Hudson's Bay from those of the Mississippi and Missouri rivers; then in an easterly direction along the height of land to the source of the River Winnipic (running by such last-named river, the principal branch of the waters which unite the Lake Serginagus), thence along the main stream of the waters, and the middle of the several lakes into which they flow, to the mouth of the Winnipic River, and thence in a northerly direction through the middle of Lake Winnipic to the place of beginning; which territory is called Assiniboine, and of which I, the undersigned, have been duly appointed Governor.

And whereas the welfare of the families at present forming settlements on the Red River in the said territory, with those on their way to it, passing the winter at York or Churchill Forts in Hudson's Bay, as also those who are expected to arrive next autumn, renders it a necessary and indispensable part of my duty to provide for their support, in the yet uncultivated state of the country, the ordinary resources derived from the buffalo, and other wild animals hunted within the territory, are not deemed more than adequate for the requisite supply; wherefore, it is hereby ordered, that no persons trading in furs or provisions within the territory, for the Honorable, the Hudson's Bay Company, the North-West Company, or any individual or unconnected traders or persons whatever, shall take out any provisions, either of flesh, grain, or vegetables, procured or raised within the said territory, by water or land carriage, for one twelve month from the date hereof; save and except what may be judged necessary for the trading parties at this present time within the territory, to carry them to their respective destinations, and who may on due application to me, obtain license for the same.

The provisions procured and raised as above, shall be taken for the use of the colony; and that no losses may accrue to the parties concerned, they will be paid for by British bills at the customary rates.

And be it hereby further made known, that, whosoever shall be detected in attempting to convey out, or attempting to carry out, any provisions prohibited as above, either by land and water, shall be taken in custody and prosecuted as the laws in such cases direct; and the provisions so taken as well as any goods or chattels of what nature soever, which may be taken along with them, and also the craft, cattle and carriages, instrumental in conveying away the same, to any part but the settlement on Red River, shall be forfeited. Given under my hand, at Fort Daer, Pembina, the 8th of January, 1814.

By order of the Governor.

(Signed) MILES MACDONELL, Governor.

JOHN SPENCER, Secretary.

Here, then, is the loudly denounced and oft-spoken of proclamation. Were the question asked, "Did the Governor act wisely?" subsequent events afford an answer in the negative. No doubt Governor Macdonell, armed with the opinion of the legal gentlemen we have already quoted, regarded himself as fully authorized. No doubt there was need for preventing the starving multitude of settlers being driven away every winter to Pembina. No doubt it was the difficulty, under December and January weather, of their getting sufficient food from the buffalo that urged the Governor to take the strong step he did at Pembina, of obviating the recurrence of the suffering he was then witnessing. Further, it was well known that instructions had been given the Nor'-Wester agents, in their western posts (as shown by the evidence of Pritchard, at that time one of their employes), to buy up all the provisions possible and prevent the settlers getting them.

All these things can be urged and have great weight; but the fact that the idea of law was yet new, that the feeling of the Nor'-Westers was hostile to a certain extent, and that they had the turbulent Bois-Brules thoroughly under their control and ready to carry out any plans of attack, should have caused great caution on the part of the Governor, so newly created in his chair of authority. Further, all laws of non-intercourse, embargo, and the like, are regarded as arbitrary.

Expedience would have dictated a more conciliatory a less drastic policy; especially when he was not possessed of a force sufficient to carry out his commands.

But if the question be transferred to the region of abstract right, the case is different.

The legal opinions given certainly justify the Governor in the steps taken. He proposed, what is usually considered the right of government, to take possession of supplies if life is at stake, and not only so, but to recompense in full for the amount taken. But it was a claim of supremacy; it meant the diminution of Nor'-wester influence over the Bois-Brules and Indians, and must be resisted at all hazards.

The council of Nor'-westers that met at Fort William in the summer of 1814, was presided over by the Hon. William McGillivray, the principal partner of the North-west company. Mr. Pritchard gives evidence that he received direct information from Mackenzie, one of the North-west agents, that the following plan had been devised to accomplish the ruin of the settlement:

> The intention of the North-west Company was to seduce and inveigle away as many of the colonists and settlers at Red River as they could induce to join them; and after they should thus have diminished their means of defence, to raise the Indians of Lac Rouge, Fond du Lac; and other places, to act and destroy the settlement; and that it was also their intention to bring the Governor, Miles Macdonell, down to Montreal as a prisoner, by way of degrading the authority under which the colony was established in the eyes of the natives of that country.

Who shall say after that that the spirit of the Nor'-Westers since the days of Peter Pond had been in any way ameliorated?

Had they a grievance, the courts of England, where they had much influence, were open to them. But no! Indians and Bois-Brules must be stirred up, like the letting out of water, to end no one could tell where; and the words of Simon McGillivray, a Nor'-Wester partner, in writing from London in 1812: "Lord Selkirk must be driven to abandon the project, for his success would strike at the very existence of our trade," are seen carried out into action. The smoking homesteads of 1815, and the mournful band of three-score persons taking the route down Red River, across Lake Winnipeg, and seeking Hudson Bay, as if the broad continent had no room for ever so small a band of peaceful and industrious settlers, tell their own tale.

Cuthbert Grant again appears upon the scene, and along with him figure also the leading chiefs of the Nor'-Westers. The return of the settlers to their homes in 1815 had filled the minds of their enemies with rage. The contempt of the wild hunters of the plains for the peaceful tillers of the soil can hardly be conceived. They despised them for their manual labor; they named them, by way of reproach, "the workers in gardens;" and their term "pork-eaters," formerly applied to the voyageurs east of Fort William, was now used in derision to the Scotch settlers. During the whole winter the fiery cross of the Nor'-Westers had been flying; and they looked forward to a grand gathering in the spring at "The Forks," to give a final blow to the infant colony.

We have seen how the refugees returned to their devastated homes. Fortunately the crops sown by them had not all been destroyed; and under Colin Robertson, and with their new friends from Scotland, they settled down to endure in the following year the fear and uncertainty of continued threatenings, at last to have the crisis reached in atrocious acts of bloodshed, and to be again driven from their unfortunate settlement.

The expeditions were both to come from the east and west. Fort Qu'Appelle, some 350 miles west of Red River, was the rendezvous of the force expected from the west. The Bois-Brules wherever found during the whole winter throughout the territories, at the most distant posts, exhibited signs of unmistakeable hostility. A party of these warlike Metis were reported as coming from the far-off Fort des-Prairies, on the Saskatchewan; while from the east, a leading partner, McLeod, was journeying all the way from Fort William, with a strong band to assist in the complete extinction of the colony.

Of the western levies Grant was, as has been already said, the controlling spirit. He was the leader of the "New Nation."

On the 13th March, 1816, he writes from the River Qu'-Appelle the following letter to one of the partners, showing the intentions for the spring:

My Dear Sir,—I received your generous and kind letter last fall, by the last canoe. I should certainly be an ungrateful being, should I not return you my sincerest thanks. Although a very bad hand at writing letters, I trust to your generosity, I am yet safe and sound, thank God, for I believe it is more than Colin Robertson or any of his suit dare to offer the least insult to any of the Bois-Brules, although Robertson made use of some expressions which I hope he shall swallow in the spring. He shall see that it is neither fifteen, thirty, nor fifty of his best horsemen, that can make the Bois-Brules bow to him. Our people of Fort des Prairies and English River are all to be here in the spring; it is hoped we shall come off with flying colours, and never to see any of them again in the colonizing way in Red River, in fact, the traders shall pack off with themselves, also for having disobeyed our orders last spring, according to our arrangements. We are all to remain at the Forks to pass the summer, for fear they should play us the same trick as last summer, of coming back; but they shall receive a warm reception, I am loath to enter into any particulars as I am well assured that you will receive more satisfactory information (than I have had) from your other correspondents; therefore, I shall not pretend to give you any; at the same time begging you will excuse my short letter, I shall conclude wishing you health and happiness.

I shall ever remain,
Your most obedient, humble servant,
Cuthbert Grant.
J D Cameron, Esq.

After the settlers returned in 1815, Colin Robertson had organized the colony on his own authority, there having been no opportunity of communication with Lord Selkirk; and during the same year a new governor there came, Robert Semple, seemingly of Pennsylvanian origin, who had gone in early life to England. He was an author of some note, an officer of experience, and moreover a man of amiable and generous disposition. Too good a man he was for the lawless region to which he was sent. He was appointed by the Hudson's Bay Company as their governor, and with all the powers conferred by their charter.

As soon as spring was open the movement was begun. Governor Semple had dismantled the Nor'-Wester Fort, on account of the alarming rumours heard by him, but more especially because of definite information obtained from the letters intercepted by Colin Robertson during the winter. We shall allow an eye-witness of the event to tell his own tale as given on oath in Montreal, in 1818.

It is the account of a gentleman in the Canadian Voyegeurs—the corps that had so distinguished itself in the war against the United States in 1812-15. At the close of the war he entered the service of the Hudson's Bay Company as a trader. He gives a very clear account of the expedition from Fort Qu'Appelle against the colony.

STORY OF PIERRE CHRYSOLOGUE PAMBRUN.

I had been for some time under the orders of Mr. Semple, and on the 12th of April, 1816, I left Fort Douglas under his directions, to go to the Hudson's Bay Company's house on River Qu'Appelle. I set out with as much provisions as would last us six days, when we would get to Brandon House, about 120 miles west of Red River. To this place, according to my instructions, I was to go first, and from thence, if prudent, to the Hudson's Bay fort at Qu'Appelle. On the 1st of May I left Qu'Appelle with five boat-loads of pemican and furs. As we were going down the river on the 5th of May, near the Grand Rapids, I made the shore in a boat, and a party of armed Bois-Brules immediately came and surrounded me, and forced me to give up the boats and furs, and the pemican. The pemican was landed and the boats taken across the river. I was kept a prisoner five days. Cuthbert Grant, Peter Pangman, Thomas McKay were of the party who made me a prisoner. I was taken back to River Qu'Appelle, to the Northwest Company's post. I was kept there for five days. Mr. Alexander Macdonnell was in command at this station, and I asked him why I had been made a prisoner, or by whose orders I had been arrested ? He said it was by his own. There were about forty or fifty Bois-Brules at this fort. Cuthbert Grant frequently said they were going to destroy the settlement, and I was told Mr. Macdonnell said the business of the year before was a trifle to what this should be. Cuthbert Grant frequently talked with Bois-Brules about going, and they sang war-songs as if they were going to battle.

On the 12th I left Qu'Appelle. We drifted down to the place where I had before been stopped, and the pemican, which had been landed from our boats, was re-embarked by the North-west people. When we got to the forks of the River Qu'Appelle we encamped. The people who were taken with me had been liberated some time before, and had gone away. I had been left a prisoner. The next morning after we had encamped, that is, the people in the two boats which went with Mr. Macdonnell, a number of Indians who were in camp at some distance were sent for, and they came and went into Mr. Macdonnell's tent, who made a speech to them; a party went also on horseback from Fort Qu'Appelle armed, but I was in one of the boats with Mr. Macdonnell. In going down the river they talked freely of breaking up the settlement and taking Fort Douglas; and the people frequently told me that Mr. Macdonnell had said the business of the year before had been nothing to what this would be. Mr. Macdonnell's speech to the Indians was to this effect:

'My Friends and Relations,—I address you bashfully, for I have not a pipe of tobacco to give you. All our goods have been taken by the English, but we are now upon a party to drive them away. Those people have been spoiling fair lands which belong to you and the Bois-Brules, and to which they have no right. They have been driving away the buffalo. You will soon be poor and miserable if the English stay; but we will drive them away if the Indians do not, for the North-west Company and the Bois-Brules are one. If you (addressing the chief) and some of your young men will join, I shall be glad.' Mr. Macdonnell spoke in French, and Pangman and Primeau interpreted.

The chief said that he knew nothing about it, and should not go himself; if some of the young men went, it was nothing to him.

Mr. Macdonnell then said: 'Well, it is no matter, we are determined to drive them away, and if they make any resistance, your land shall be drenched with their blood.'

The next morning the Indians went away, and the party drifted down the Assiniboine River to the Grand Rapids. From there, about thirty started, among whom was Mr. Macdonnell, Cuthbert Grant, and a number of Bois Brules. I was left behind and still a prisoner, but in the evening a spare horse was brought by two of them for me, and I accompanied them on horseback to the North-west fort near Brandon House. When I approached, I saw a crowd assembled about the gate. I suppose there were from forty to fifty persons assembled. Their arms were down by the gate, and as I entered it a number of them presented their guns at me, making use of insulting language. I complained to Mr. Macdonnell of this treatment, and asked him if it was by his orders, and he said he would speak to them about it, but I do not think he ever did. I saw at this fort, tobacco, carpenter's tools, a quantity of furs, and other things, which had been brought over from Brandon House—our fort near by.

About the 24th or 25th of May the party was separated into smaller divisions, and chiefs appointed. The property was embarked, and the whole set off to go to Portage la Prairie; a part went by water, but the Bois-Brules generally went by land on horseback. Having arrived at Portage la Prairie, the whole of the pemican and packs were landed and formed into a sort of breastwork or fortification, having two small brass swivels there, which the year before had been taken from the stores of the settlement.

On the morning of the 17th of June, being at Portage la Prairie still, which is about sixty miles from the settlement, the Bois-Brules mounted their horses and set off for it; they were armed with guns, pistols, lances, and bows and arrows. Cuthbert Grant was with them, and a number of his race. I remained behind, so did Mr. Alexander Macdonnell and others; about thirty or forty men stayed to help guard the pemican. The object of this expedition was to take Fort Douglas and break up the settlement. If the settlers took to the fort for protection, then the whole were to be starved out. The fort was to be watched strictly at all times, and if any of them went out to fish or to get water, they were to be shot if they could not be taken prisoners. I certainly had, from all I heard, very serious apprehensions for my friends. I do not remember that Cuthbert Grant said anything particular on the morning he went away.

[This excerpt from Bryce's book is followed by an excerpt from Bell's book on the Selkirk settlers.]

THE AFFAIR OF "SEVEN OAKS."

The following account of the affair of "Seven Oaks" is taken from *The Selkirk Settlement and Settlers* by Mr. C.N. Bell, F.R.A.S., a member of the Society.

On Governor Semple's return to Fort Douglas from visiting the inland posts of the Hudson's Bay Co., in June, 1816, he again assumed direction of affairs, which had been temporarily managed by Colin Robertson. That he did not altogether approve of the management during his absence is learned from the testimony of an eye-witness, yet living, in the person of Donald Murray, who informs me that Robertson was in great disfavor with the Settlement and Hudson's Bay Co. officials, and when, on hearing of the probability of an attack by the Northwesters, he started for York Factory in a boat, taking Duncan Cameron, a prisoner, he insultingly hoisted a pemican sack as an ensign instead of the British flag which was the usual one used on such occasions. Word was received at the settlement that the Northwesters were determined to destroy both it and the settlers. On the 17th June, Peguis, chief of the Swampy Indians, residing in the district about the mouth of the Red River, waited on Governor Semple to offer the services of his men, some seventy in number to assist in protecting the colonists. This proffered assistance was declined with thanks by Semple, who did not foresee the occurrences of the succeeding two days. Alex. Macdonnell sent a party of about sixty Canadians and half-breeds with a few Indians, mounted on horseback and bearing some provisions, across by land from the Assiniboine to the Red River, the route followed taking them along the edge of the swamps, about two miles out on the prairie from Fort Douglas, and from that point gradually drawing nearer to the main highway, which is now the northern continuation of Winnipeg's

Main street, until it joined the latter at a spot known as "Seven Oaks," on account of the seven oak trees growing there, within a hundred yards or so south of a small coolie, now called Inkster's creek. One half of the Metis had arrived at the coolie and passed on to Frog Plain (Kildonan church prairie), taking two or three settlers prisoners to prevent their giving the alarm, when the remainder were discovered by a sentinel, placed in the watch tower of Fort Douglas, with a telescope. He immediately gave an alarm, and Governor Semple left the fort with a small party of company's servants to intercept the Metis, whom he met at Seven Oaks as they arrived at the highway. Semple had by this time been joined by some of his servants and officials, so that he arrived on the scene with about 28 companions.

It is difficult to get at the exact truth of what followed this meeting of the rival traders. A host of affidavits are on record made by men on both sides, who, while agreeing in the main particulars, disagree as to details. However, herewith is given a version of the affair emanating from each side.

Two Accounts

The first is an affidavit made by John Pritchard, who had been in the service of both the XY and Northwest companies, but in 1816 was a resident of the Selkirk settlement. He was the father of the Rev. S. Pritchard, and grandfather of Rev. Canon Matheson, of this city.

On the afternoon of the 19th of June, 1816, a man in the watch-house called out that the half-breeds were coming. The governor, some other gentlemen and myself looked through spy-glasses, and I distinctly saw some armed people on horseback passing along the plains. A man then called out: 'They (meaning the half-breeds) are making for the settlers,' on which the governor said: 'We must go out and meet those people; let twenty men follow me.' We proceeded down the old road leading down the settlement. As we were going along we met many of the settlers running to the fort, crying, 'The half-breeds! the half-breeds!' When we were advanced about three-quarters of a mile along the settlement we saw some people on horseback behind a point of woods. On our nearer approach the party seemed to be more numerous, on which the governor made a halt and sent for a field piece, which, delaying to arrive, he ordered us to advance. We had not proceeded far before the half-breeds, with their faces painted in the most hideous manner, and in the dresses of Indian warriors, came forward and surrounded us in the form of a half moon. We then extended our line and moved more into the open plain, and as they advanced we retreated a few steps backward, and then saw a Canadian named Boucher ride up to us waving his hand and calling out, "what do you want ?" The governor replied, "what do you want?"

To which Boucher answered, "we want our fort." The governor said, "Go to your fort." They were by this time near each other, and consequently spoke too low for me to hear. Being at some little distance to the right of the governor, I saw him take hold of Boucher's gun, and almost immediately a general discharge of fire arms took place, but whether it began on our side or that of the enemy, it was impossible to distinguish. My attention was then directed to my personal defence. In a few minutes almost all our people were

EITHER KILLED OR WOUNDED.

Captain Rogers, having fallen, rose up and came towards me, when, not seeing one of our party who was not either killed or disabled, I called out to him, 'For God's sake give yourself up!' He ran towards the enemy for that purpose, myself following him. He raised up his hands and, and in English and broken French, called for mercy. A half-breed (son of Col. William McKay) shot him through the head, and another cut open his belly with a knife with the most horrid imprecations. Fortunately for me, a Canadian (named Lavigne), joining his entreaties to mine, saved me (though with the greatest difficulty) from sharing the fate of my friend at that moment. After this I was reserved from death, in the most providential manner, no less than six different times on my way to and at the Frog Plain (the headquarters of these cruel murderers). I there saw Alexander Murray and his wife, two of William Bannerman's children and Alexander Sutherland, settlers, and likewise Antony McDonnell, a servant, were prisoners, having been taken before the action took place. With the exception of myself, no quarter was given to any of us. The knife, axe or ball, put a period to the existence of the wounded; and on the bodies of the dead were practised all those barbarities which characterize the inhuman heart of the savage. The amiable and mild Mr. Semple, lying on his side (his thigh having been broken) and supporting his head upon his hand, addressed the commander of our enemies, by inquiring if he was Mr. Grant; and being answered in the affirmative, 'I am not mortally wounded,' said Mr. Semple; 'and if you get me conveyed to the fort, I think I should live.' Grant promised he would do so, and immediately left him in the care of a Canadian, who afterwards told that an Indian of their party came up and shot Mr. Semple in the breast. I entreated Grant to procure me the watch, or even the seals, of Mr. Semple, for the purpose of transmitting them to his friends, but I did not succeed. Our force amounted to twenty-eight persons, of whom twenty-one were killed and one wounded. The governor, Captain Rogers, Mr. James White, surgeon, Mr. Alexander McLean, settler, Mr. Wilkinson, private secretary to the governor, and Lieut. Holt, of the Swedish navy, and fifteen servants were killed. Mr. J.P. Bourke, storekeeper, was wounded, but saved himself by flight. The enemy, I am told, were sixty-two persons, the greater part of whom were the contracted servants and clerks of the Northwest company. They had one man killed and one wounded. The chiefs who headed the party of our enemy were Messrs. Grant and Fraser, Antoine Hoole and Bourassa; the two former clerks and the two latter interpreters, in the service of the Northwest company.

Boucher's Story

The above declaration and the following are published in a book entitled *Statements Respecting the Earl of Selkirk's Settlement, etc.*, written by Selkirk's relative, a Mr. Halkett, a director of the Hudson's Bay Company committee, and it is from this source that most historians have drawn their information relating to the Selkirk side of the case.

The man named Boucher, mentioned by Pritchard in his affidavit, was taken as a prisoner to Montreal, and while there made the following declaration, on the 29th of August, 1816, before a justice of the peace:

Voluntary declaration of Francois Firmin Boucher, accused on oath of having, on the 19th of last June, killed at the colony of the Red River, twenty-one men, among whom was Governor Semple, says: 'That he did not kill any person whatever; that he was sent, four days before the death of Governor Semple, by one of the partners of the North-west Company, Mr. Alexander McDonell, from Portage la Prairie, to carry provisions to Frog Plain, about three leagues lower than the fort at the Forks of Red River. That he and his companions, to avoid being seen by the Hudson's Bay settlers, passed at a distance from the Hudson's Bay fort. That, with a view of weakening the Hudson's Bay party, the Bois-Brules wanted to carry away some of the Hudson's Bay settlers—and, assisted by the deponent to interpret for them in English, they went and carried one off. That, as they proceeded towards Frog Plain, they observed a group of Hudson's Bay people—upon which a certain number of the men in the service of the North-west Company, called Bois-Brules, joined the deponent and his companions. That these, thinking the Hudson's Bay people meant them harm, because they advanced with their muskets in their hands, the Bois-Brules wanted to fire on them; but the deponent opposed their doing so. That at last he advanced alone to the Hudson's Bay party to speak to them, and came so near Governor Semple, that the latter took hold of the butt end of the deponent's gun, and ordered his people to advance; that they, not obeying him, and the deponent saying that if they fired they were all dead men, Governor Semple said that they must not be afraid, that this was not a time for it, and that they must fire. Immediately the deponent heard the reports of two muskets fired by the Hudson's Bay people. That at this moment the deponent threw himself from his horse, still holding the mane, and that the horse being afraid, dragged him in this manner about the distance of a gun shot, where he remained. That, from the moment when he was thus carried away by his horse, the firing became general between the people of the North-west and the

Hudson's Bay. That the fire was begun by those of the Hudson's Bay. That the men in the service of the North-west Company were about sixty-four in number (of whom thirty were at the beginning of the firing), assembled for the purpose of taking the Hudson's Bay fort by famine. He is uncertain by whose orders, but supposes it was by the chiefs, that is, Mr. McDonnell, Mr. Grant, Antoine Hoolle, and Michael Bourassa. That he heard Mr. McLean enjoin them to avoid a meeting with the Hudson's Bay people. That after the firing was over he saw a Bois-Brule named Vasseur near Governor Semple, then wounded in the knee and arm, who was taking care of him, and who, notwithstanding, had taken his belt or sash, his pistol and his watch, and afterwards carried them away. That he himself had at the moment saved one Pritchard from being killed, and also Francois Deschamps and several other Brules wanted to kill him.

After the Fight.

Many of the settlers are of the opinion that the first shot fired was by Lieutenant Holt, whose gun went off by accident, thus precipitating the conflict. In all, twenty-one persons were killed, the remaining eight escaping into the woods, which at that time extended from the highway to the river bank, and making their way to Fort Douglas, one or two swimming the Red River and passing up the east side until opposite the fort. It is to be noticed that only one actual settler was killed.

At the fort all was confusion, the settlers—men, women and children—crowding into the houses within its walls. Mr. Bourke managed to regain the fort with the cannon and a small remnant of the men he took out, and the tale they told struck terror into the hearts of all, who expected an attack would be made immediately by the Northwesters. An anxious night was passed, but no attack came, the Bois-Brules having a wholesome dread of the cannon possessed by the colonists.

John Pritchard had been taken as a prisoner to the camp ground of the main body of the Metis, which was situated where the Kildonan ferry landing now is, I am informed by Mr. Donald Murray, whose parents had also been taken prisoners on their farm, two lots above that point, on the morning of the tragedy. He begged of Cuthbert Grant, the leader, to be allowed to go to Fort Douglas. After obtaining permission from Grant, he met with a refusal from the rest of the party; but after giving a promise to return, and agreeing to bear a message to the fort people that they must leave the next day for Lake Winnipeg, he was allowed to depart. Grant accompanied him as far as "Seven Oaks," where the bodies of the killed lay upon the ground, but as it was after nightfall when he passed there, he was spared the sight of the horrible scene.

Arriving at Fort Douglas, he informed the settlers that the Metis demanded that the colonists should depart, and had promised that if all public property was given up to them, they would give a safe escort to the people and allow them to take all their personal effects. Two other parties of North-westers were daily expected to arrive in the Red River, one coming from the Saskatchewan and the other from Lake Superior, and it would be necessary to send some of the Bois-Brules with them to explain the position of affairs.

The colonists at first refused to agree to the terms of capitulation, and Sheriff McDonnell, who was in charge of the settlement, decided to hold to the fort as long as the men were inclined to protect it. In the morning, however, after they had more fully considered their situation, the settlers concluded to depart, and after several visits of the sheriff to the Metis camp an arrangement was agreed on.

How the Indians Acted

A number of Indians under Peguis were camped on the east side of the river and took no part in the troubles, but their sympathies were plainly with the colonists. They went out the morning after the engagement and brought in the bodies of the killed, or as many as could then be found, for a small number, I am informed by eye-witnesses, were concealed in the heavy brush in the vicinity, as wounded men had crawled into thickets and there died. Mrs. Kaufman, who yet lives in Kildonan east (since died, 1892), informs me that she saw the Indians bring in the dead bodies to Fort Douglas with carts, and that Governor Semple and the doctor were buried in board coffins, and the others wrapped up in blankets, the whole number being interred in a grove of trees on the south side of the creek southwest of the fort, and quite near the spot whereon now stands the residence of ex-Mayor Logan. She says the body of one man was naked, the clothes having been stolen before the Indians found it. Mr. Donald Murray also informs me that when the burial took place, Chief Peguis stood near by, with the tears streaming down his face, and he repeatedly expressed his great sorrow at the sad occurrences taking place. Donald Murray states positively that all these bodies were removed some years after to St. John's Church graveyard, but he is not now able to locate the site of their re-interment. He remembers distinctly that on the morning the settlers handed over the fort to the Metis, all the ammunition for the cannon was carried down to the river and thrown into the water from the end of a boat moored in the stream.

[After these excerpts, an anonymous reporter—presumably Bell—describes the rest of the ceremony.]

THE "SEVEN OAKS" MONUMENT.

The Manitoba Historical and Scientific Society, in pursuance of its aim of marking the historic spots within their territory with suitable monuments, had in view the erection of a stone on the site of the affair of "Seven Oaks," a spot near the highway, which is a continuation through Kildonan of Main Street, Winnipeg. In 1890 the Countess of Selkirk, the widow of the last Earl of Selkirk, who was the son of the founder of the colony, visited Winnipeg, and offered to erect, under the auspices of the Society, a monument of the battle. This generous offer was gladly accepted, and a site was given by Miss Inkster, sister of Sheriff Inkster, for the purposes of the Society. In 1891 the monument, prepared by Mr. Samuel Hooper, of Winnipeg, was placed in position, and the Society, with a large company, proceeded to the unveiling of the monument on the 19th of June, the anniversary of the battle.

THE UNVEILING.

The ceremony of the unveiling of the "Seven Oaks " monument in Kildonan took place on the afternoon of June 19th, and was well attended by old settlers of that vicinity and also by citizens of Winnipeg. Lieutenant-Governor Schultz and party drove down in four carriages. With His Honor were Mr. John MacBeth, President of the Historical Society; Col. Villiers and Col. Howard. In another carriage were Mr. C.N. Bell, Corresponding Secretary of the Society, Lieutenant Williams, and Mr. Ernest Phair, His Honor's private secretary. The ladies of the party were Mrs. Schultz, Mrs. Chief Justice Taylor, Mrs. Howard, Mrs. MacBeth, Mrs. W.J. Tupper, Mrs. Jellyman, of Chicago, Miss McDonald, and Miss Mair. The old families of the Red River settlement were represented by Messrs. Archibald Pritchard, Sr., Wm. Fraser, Norman Matheson, Hector Sutherland, Donald Sutherland, Robert Sutherland, Angus Polson, Geo. Munroe, Jno. Bruce, Robert MacBeth, Sheriff lnkster. Miss Inkster, who gave the site for the monument, was among the ladies present. On the platform were the Lieutenant-Governor, Messrs. John MacBeth, C.N. Bell, Chief Justice Taylor, Mr. Justice Dubuc, U.S. Consul Taylor, Canon Matheson, Col. Villiers, and Col. Howard. Among the others noticed on the grounds were Messrs. G.F. Carruthers, C.P. Brown and Mrs. Brown, James Porter, W.D. Russell, T.C. Keenleyside, Dr. Phillips, Prof. Laird, J.T. Huggard, Archer Martin, and W.F. Henderson. The Proceedings were opened with an address by the President of the Historical Society, Mr. John MacBeth, who spoke as follows :—

THE PRESIDENT'S ADDRESS.

Your Honor, Ladies and Gentlemen,—We have met together to-day to unveil a monument, to mark one of the historic spots in our country. Before proceeding further, I, as President of the Manitoba Historical and Scientific Society, wish to tender to the council and members of that body my grateful thanks for doing me the honor of electing me to the honorable position of president. No one more fully appreciates the fact than I do, that my election to preside over a society composed of so many learned and scientific gentlemen as is the one I have just referred to, was not made on account of my fitness for this honorable position, but entirely intended as a delicate compliment to the old settlers of this country by my colleagues. I would be indeed ungrateful if I did not here publicly tender my thanks to the members of the Manitoba Historical and Scientific Society, for thus honoring the old Selkirk settlers, by electing one of their number, humble and incapable though he may be, to preside on this occasion. On the 19th of June, 1816, just 75 years ago, an unfortunate conflict took place between the rival trading companies, the Hudson's Bay and Northwest, in which Governor Semple and twenty men fell. Without entering into the causes which led to this lamentable affair, the Manitoba Historical and Scientific Society are simply erecting this monument to mark, as I said before, a historic spot. I wish here publicly to express the thanks of this Society to her Ladyship the Countess of Selkirk, who, many of you will remember, visited this country and this spot a short time ago, for generously furnishing us with the necessary funds for erecting this monument. I also wish to tender, on behalf of the Society, our grateful thanks to Miss Inkster, who kindly donated to us the land on which this monument stands. I wish also, on behalf of the Society, to thank His Honor the Lieutenant-Governor for his kindness in consenting to unveil this monument; and for myself, as president, to thank him for his kind attention and assistance on this occasion. I cannot conclude these few remarks without expressing the thanks of the Society to the Messrs. Hooper, who made and erected this monument, for their promptness in the execution of their contract. Before proceeding to the unveiling ceremonies, Mr. C.N. Bell, our energetic and capable corresponding secretary, and ex-president, will read a brief sketch of the events commemorated by the monument.

A HISTORICAL SKETCH.

Mr. C.N. Bell was next called upon. *[The beginning of Bell's speech largely repeats his earlier account of Seven Oaks. He then describes the monument itself.]*

... [T]his monument is erected by the Manitoba Historical Society;

by means of the generous aid granted by the present Lady Selkirk, to mark the spot on which was enacted a tragedy, which forms one of the most salient points in the history of the Red River Settlement, for the unfortunate occurrence led to the peaceful solution of all the artificial ills that distressed the first agriculturists, who first proved to the world the fertility of the lands of the Red River Valley of the North.

The Historical Society have long desired, and had in view, the marking of several historical sites, such as the Seven Oaks, Fort Douglas and Fort Gibralter, and have been enabled through the kindness of Lady Selkirk to make this beginning. The work of the Society, in this direction however, will not be completed until a suitable tribute is paid to the intelligence, energy and patriotism of La Verandrye, and the self-sacrificing French-Canadian discoverer and explorer of this province, by the erection of a stately and handsome monument, bearing on its face some record of his life's work.

THE GOVERNOR'S SPEECH

The Lieutenant-Governor *[John Schultz]* was then asked to address the assembly and unveil the monument. He said:—

Mr. President and Members of the Historical Society, Ladies and Gentlemen:

You have heard from authoritative sources to-day all that relates to the monument before us, and upon that subject I need not touch; but the present seems to me to be an occasion when we should all acknowledge the value of the services which have been rendered to the people of this province and of the Dominion by the Historical Society of Manitoba and it is to their great credit that what we see to-day is only one of the many instances I might refer to, where their aid has been of the greatest value in giving permanency to those portions of the history of this country which, already dimmed by time in the memories of living men, are in danger of passing into the realm of vague tradition, or of being wholly lost.

I have been requested by the President and Council of this Society, on the anniversary of the event, to unveil the monument which commemorates it; and while there may be differences of opinion as to the causes which led to the combat and loss of life these stones record, yet everyone present who is familiar with the early history of this country will agree with me that, even apart entirely from these events, this monument stands upon historic ground, and the Society, in determining the site to mark the battle of Seven Oaks, which extended from the grove which gave it its name to near Fort Douglas, was wise, I think, in placing it near this great highway, which traversing as it does this province from north to south and east to west, is but the enlargement of the trail which connected the great northern waters and woods, the home of the Chippewyan and Cree, with the vast prairies of the south and west, where dwelt, differing in language only, the divisions of that great and warlike nation, the Dakotahs. I have said that this road, whether as Indian trail or King's highway, in old or more recent times, is indeed historic. . . . Truly this is an historic place; and from the spot where I now stand could once have been seen nearly all of the old historic strongholds of the Hudson's Bay, the North-west, and the XY Companies. From it may still be seen places made memorable by the good works of the Rev. Mr. West, Bishops Anderson and Provencher, the Rev. John Black, and other devoted men; within view are the residences of Hon. John Inkster, the father of our worthy sheriff, a member of the old Council of Assiniboia, and that of my brave and valued old friend, Hon. Robert McBeth, also a member, and the father of the President of our Historical Society whose instincts of hospitality were not to be thwarted by the knowledge that confiscation and worse might follow his shelter of a hard-hunted friend; and I see all around me here worthy children of such worthy sires, the descendants of those pioneer Selkirk settlers whose tale of sorrow, suffering and danger always evokes sympathy and wonder. Mr. President, we are, if I mistake not, near the place where the first plow turned the first furrow—presage of peace, plenty and prosperity—on the eastern verge of that vast prairie which extends to the Rocky Mountains; and having suitably marked the scene of battle, let us bury with the foundation of this monument the feuds, jealousies and strifes of the past which it recalls, and remembering that English and Irish, Scandinavian, German and the descendants of the gallant

Gauls and Gaels, as well as those of mixed blood, who have figured so prominently in the annals of this country, are now, by the mandate of our Queen, of one country and one people; and while still heirs of the unsullied patriotism and the invincible courage of our colonial and provincial ancestry, and proud of the heroic past, wherein English vied with French in the defence of their common country, we are Canadians all, from the Atlantic to the Pacific, and we may look forward with that hope which is justified by the immensity and value of our resources, by the law-abiding, moral and religious character of our people. If we be true to our God and ourselves in the great trust He has imposed upon us, endeavoring to avoid those strifes of race and creed which it was a great part of the life work of the great Canadian who now, amid the sorrow of the nation, sleeps with his fathers at Cataraqui *[a reference to Sir John A. Macdonald who, having died two weeks earlier, was buried at Cataraqui Cemetery in Kingston]*, to reconcile, we may be the builders of a nation forming part of an empire greater than any world has yet seen; and upon this continent to be a Canadian citizen may be even a prouder boast than was that of the citizen of an ancient empire, less great than is ours now, "Civis Romanus sum." Mr. President, I have spoken too long, and will now proceed to execute the duty with which your council has entrusted to me; and in the name of the contributors to this memorial, in the name of the president, officers and members of the Historical Society of Manitoba, I unveil this monument, which marks the scene of the battle of Seven Oaks, in the hope that when these rocks are seen from the historic path near which it is placed, and from the railway which passes close by, types in themselves of the change from the old to the new, it will be remembered that as nature has clothed with verdure this spot, once wet with blood, so should we, except as matters of historic interest and record, clothe with forgetfulness all animosities, jealousies, bitternesses and strifes, and turning to the fair prospects before us as an united people and nation, thank Almighty God that the sad past is indeed past, and implore His blessing upon our efforts for a brighter future.

At the close of his remarks His Honor unveiled the monument, the act being greeted with general applause. The monument is of native Selkirk stone, and the workmanship a credit to the designer, Mr. S. Hooper. It stands nine feet six inches in height, and its size is four feet at the base. On the top is carved a wreath of flowers. The inscription is on the west side, facing Main street. On the upper portion are carved the words, "Seven Oaks," and beneath is the inscription: "Erected in 1891 by the Manitoba Historical Society, through the generosity of the Countess of Selkirk, on the Site of Seven Oaks, where fell Governor Robert Semple and twenty of his officers and men, June 19th, 1816."

The ceremony of the unveiling was followed by several short addresses.

Rev. Canon Matheson spoke as follows: "As a native of Manitoba, and one born within a few rods of this historic spot, I have been asked to say a few words on the occasion of the unveiling of this monument. Three-quarters of a century ago to-day my grandfather took part in the unfortunate conflict which occurred on the banks of this ravine, and was one of the few who survived that sad and fatal day in the annals of the Red River colony. He owed his life to the clemency and intercession of a friendly French-Canadian, and his record of the affair, known as Pritchard's narrative, is perhaps the most accurate which we possess to-day. As the adopted son in the home of that grandfather, I well remember what a close friendship was cherished and maintained to the relatives of that French Canadian for his kind deed to the head of our family in this land. Being, then, one of the direct descendants of a family so intimately connected with the history of the event which we mark to-day, my nature would be impervious to all sentiment were there not something stirred up in my breast by the ceremony of this afternoon. My feeling is one of thankfulness, and that thankfulness is of a three-fold nature. I am thankful, first of all, that we natives can claim such close kinship with the distant past of a country which is destined to have such a glorious future. I am thankful, in the second place, that a wise Providence overruled the disunion of that past, and so soon welded the discordant and oppressing elements of those early days in a community of a happy, contented and self-reliant people. It was well, perhaps, that our colony was thus at its inception baptized in struggle. It tended to make those pioneer fore-fathers of ours staunch men, staunch and true to lay broad and deep the foundations of that God-fearing little community in which it was our privilege to be nurtured. Our present is a consequence of that past. We live to-day under the grateful shade of the tree which our forefathers planted. We reap in peace to-day the harvest, the seeds of which they sowed in toil and blood.

"In the third place I would thank the members of the Historical Society and the Countess of Selkirk; I would thank them on behalf of the natives of the country, if I might be permitted to do so, for rearing this monument to perpetuate the memory of an event in our country's history. This is indeed a pleasing evidence of their interest in and of their close identification with the history of their adopted country.

"I will say no more, as there are other representatives of those con-nected with the event we commemorate who may wish to say a word or two. As I look around me, however, a thought comes to me. This monument erected in the faith in which it is my privilege to minister, and standing in my pathways I go around with the message of peace which passes all understanding, will be a constant reminder to me of what we owe to the God of our fathers who has spoken His peace to this land, which was once the warpath of the plumed and painted sav-age of our plains. "Seven Oaks," once the scene of a battle bitter in its cruel intent, is now the scene of a battle benign in its benevolence, the scene of a contest in the civilities of a cultured life, the arena for the display of those amenities of social life which make it the meeting place, not of hostile factions but of hospitality's friends, the rendez-vous where old times keep ever green the memories and friendships of the past, and where new-comers receive a warm welcome to the land of their adoption."

U.S. Consul Taylor remarked that he attended this interesting oc-casion with the assurance that he should enjoy the luxury of being a listener to President McBeth, Governor Schultz and Secretary Bell, and not a haunted man, oppressed by an engagement or a call to speak. Still he would endeavor to second what has been so well said of two

Selkirk ladies. Firstly, he referred to Cicely Louisa, Countess of Sel-kirk, and the last of the title he regretted to add, whose visit to the Selkirk Settlement, now Manitoba, in 1889 was a most interesting event. The consul was present on two occasions, a Sunday service at Kildonan church and a garden party on the site of Fort Douglas, now the residence of ex-Mayor Logan, and when the representatives of the colonists of 1812-16, (actual colonists in the instances of Matheson, and a Bannerman, and a Polson) were presented to her Ladyship her personal knowledge of every family was most wonderful. It was his privilege to be present with Mr. and Mrs. John Fraser at the anniver-sary of their marriage fifty years before, it being the first union of children born in the colony on the Red River. The Historical Society owes to her Ladyship the suggestion and the fact of the present memorial of Fort Douglas, and its site is the appropriate donation of Miss Mary Inkster of "Seven Oaks," a descendant of the sterling Norse element of the Orkney Islands—that invaluable portion of the popu-lation of Central Canada which is native to the soil in the names of Bannatyne, Norquay, Inkster, Clouston, Polson and others equally and honorably memorable. Yesterday—18th of June—was marked by a Norse demonstration—a kindred event in the ethnology of Mani-toba. The Icelandic element of the Province, 5,000 strong, assisted by influential deputations from Minnesota and Dakota, including two representatives in the Legislature of North Dakota, celebrated by an imposing procession and exercises the inauguration of self-government in Iceland, 1,017 years ago. The oldest historic Scandinavian stock has found its new home in the great prairie ocean of Northwest America, and so is destined to be repeated in this new world the story of the bold Northmen of yore—the sons of Thor—who rolled the conquests of the Teuton to the gates of Imperial Rome and gave new and wholesome life to the civilization of Europe. So might it be on the American continent.

Judge Dubuc spoke of himself as being, not a descendant of the old settlers, but one of the pioneer settlers of the new generation, he hav-ing come here twenty years ago in the month of June. He had been glad to find a very fine country and the people very hospitable. He said he had been glad to hear the references to the first white man who had come to this country, and referred to the fact that the foundation of a monument to La Verandrye had been commenced in St. Boniface.

Col. Villiers and Col. Howard were called upon to speak, and in a few words they expressed their pleasure at being present, and congratulated the Society on the completion of its enterprise.

Cheers were then given successively for the Queen, the Governor-General, the Lieutenant-Governor, and (at the call of his Honor) for the Historical Society and Lady Selkirk.

Transaction No. 43, read in the season of 1891-1892.

John McBeth, c. 1885

JOHN McBETH

(B. 1854)

JOHN McBETH WAS PRESIDENT OF THE HISTORICAL AND Scientific Society from 1891 to 1893.[1] In his speech, delivered at the unveiling of the Seven Oaks Monument at the beginning of his term, he makes a modest and, at the same time, very revealing comment: "No one more fully appreciates the fact than I do, that my election to preside over a society composed of so many learned and scientific gentlemen ... was not made on account of my fitness for this honorable position, but entirely intended as a delicate compliment to the old settlers of this country by my colleagues."[2]

The "old settlers," by which is meant the Selkirk Settlers and their descendants, possessed a special status at this time. George Bryce and other writers had established them as simple but noble yeomen farmers, the vanguard of civilization in the heart of the wilderness. McBeth assumes, probably correctly, that his membership in this charter group has qualified him for the job of president. That he graciously accepts this as his due demonstrates that he, at least, agrees with the role Bryce assigned to the Selkirk Settlers. While McBeth seems to genuinely regret the passing of the world of his youth and its replacement with the more complex society of Manitoba in the 1890s, his portrayal of the Red River colony as a sort of Arcadia, where simple, happy farmers

---

1. McBeth's name was also sometimes spelled MacBeth and McBeath.
2. "Seven Oaks," *Transactions of the Historical and Scientific Society of Manitoba*, No. 43, 1891-92, p. 25.

lived a life of peace and contentment, probably owes a lot to George Bryce's writing. This theme was carried to almost ridiculous extremes in Frank Larned Hunt's "Britain's One Utopia," published about ten years later as *Transaction* No. 61.

John McBeth, like Samuel Pritchard Matheson, came from a family that had become very successful in the context of the Red River Settlement. Born in 1854, John McBeth was one of ten children of the Honorable Robert McBeth and grandson of Alexander McBeth, the patriarch of the family that came to Red River with the third contingent of Selkirk Settlers in 1815. One of his younger brothers was the Reverend R.G. McBeth, a prolific writer of western Canadian history and biography, and one of his sisters married the famous John McKay, the Métis trader and buffalo hunter. John's father, Robert McBeth, was a prosperous farmer and general merchant in Kildonan, who transported goods for the Hudson's Bay Company between York Factory and Fort Garry. In the following *Transaction*, John McBeth describes how men would pay off their debts to general merchants like his father by working for them on long freighting trips from Hudson Bay. Robert McBeth was also a magistrate and Justice of the Peace, and sat on the Council of Assiniboia. He was famous for having hidden John Schultz in his house after Schultz escaped from captivity in Upper Fort Garry in 1870, an act that Schultz acknowledged with gratitude in his Seven Oaks speech.

John McBeth was elected as the Conservative MLA for Kildonan and St. Paul's in 1884 and 1886. He died relatively young, perhaps from tuberculosis,[3] and little evidence remains of his career and life. However, like all the Red River residents of his generation, he is an interesting transitional figure in that he was a teenager at the time of Confederation and grew to maturity in the rapidly changing world of Manitoba in the 1870s and 1880s. His account of Red River life "in the good old days" is, therefore, partly based on stories told to him

---

3. A photo of McBeth in the Provincial Archives photo collection bears an undated, handwritten annotation: "died of TB."

"by gentlemen personally cognizant" or by "gentlemen who have witnessed the scenes," rather than upon his own recollections.

He does call upon his own memories, and gives his listeners a perhaps unintended glimpse at the racial prejudice that was a part of Red River life, when he describes slipping out of the house to avoid having to kiss "our dusky lady friends": Aboriginal women who came to visit on New Year's Day. Since at least one of his uncles had married a local Aboriginal woman and McBeth had many mixed-race cousins, his anecdote is one he likely would not have told in a different setting.

In John McBeth we hear an authentic voice of the old Red River Settlement, but the voice of one who, like Archbishop Matheson, successfully made the transition to the new Northwest that was born with Confederation.

Social Customs and Amusements
of the
Early Days in Red River Settlement

ONE OF OUR EARLIEST RECOLLECTIONS OF FESTIVITIES (and they were of such a boisterous character as to make a lasting impression on my mind) was the return of the boatmen—as they were called—from York Factory. A short description of this interesting and at that time very necessary personage may not be out of place, although most of you are familiar with the character, but few present have seen him in his pristine glory. The boatman, voyageur or tripman, as he was variously called, belonged to that class of settler who did not farm sufficiently to make them independent of the Hudson's Bay Co. or general merchant. The trips to York Factory were two in the year, known as the summer and the fall trips. These were made for the purpose of bringing goods landed at York by the Hudson's Bay ships which brought cargoes of supplies for the interior, including the Red River. These boatmen were generally engaged during the winter preceding the voyage. If a man ran short of anything and had not the money wherewith to purchase, or something to exchange for the commodity required, he went to the Hudson's Bay company's store or to some general merchant or freighter and got an advance and agreed to pay for the same by going to York. He was then bound to be ready to start about the first of June. In a crew of eight men there was generally found one who furnished fun for the others or who, from some peculiarity, was made the butt of the party. There was generally a fiddle or two in the crowd and lots of men who could play it. I am told by gentlemen personally cognizant of the fact, that in one instance there was a boat's crew, where the fiddle was passed down from the steersman to the bowsman and every man in the boat could play it. It was said on those trips when a flat stone was found it was at once utilized as a ball room floor, and each man in turn "hoed it down" to the enlivening strains of the fiddle. When the different brigades met at York Factory and whilst waiting for their cargoes, I am told by gentlemen who have witnessed the scenes of boisterous hilarity and continued festivities that it simply (to use a purely original phrase) "beggars description". Upon their return to the Red River and immediately upon unloading their boats, a goodly supply of the "ardent" was broached and they proceeded to make "Rome howl". It was generally looked upon as a way (a little noisy if you like) they had of celebrating a safe return from a more or less dangerous and perilous voyage.

OLD TIME UNIONS

In these early days people were "married and given in marriage", and I believe the custom prevails even in our times of greater advancement and enlightenment; but O, what a different affair a wedding in the old times was to those of the present day! At the time of which I speak, a marriage license cost the large sum of thirty shillings (about $7.50). As there were very few Rothschilds or Vanderbilts in the country then (although many have appeared on the scene lately, especially during the "boom"), economy was practiced, and the good old fashioned custom was resorted to of publishing the bans. You will pardon me if I digress for a second. I used the words "thirty shillings" a moment ago, and they remind me of a story told me by that prince of genial and social old timers, the late lamented Honorable John Norquay. The incident, which actually occurred, was this: In the early days the currency was pounds, shillings and pence, and when at the time of the transfer it was changed to dollars and cents, it was sometime before the old settlers could master the new system. For instance, a certain woman was asked to sell a wavey, several of which her husband had just brought home, and she was offered fifty cents a piece for them. She indignantly rejected the offer, stating emphatically that she could not take less than one and six pence apiece for them, which sum of course was readily and cheerfully given to the intense happiness and delight of the worthy dame. The purchaser you will observe was ahead a cool 12 1/2 cents on each bird he bought. Now to return to the subject. A wedding in the olden times in the Red River settlement was not the tame affair of the present day. It did not consist in orange blossoms, ushers, a wedding breakfast, congratulatory speeches, wedding presents and last but not least, the orthodox honeymoon trip. A wedding breakfast they certainly had, and several of them for that matter, and dinners and suppers galore. When such an important event took place in the settlement the friends and relatives of both the "high contracting parties" were invited. The mode of invitation differed from the present style. Instead of sending out a card something like this:—

"Mr. and Mrs. Smythe request the pleasure of your company at the marriage of their daughter Mary Aramenta Jane to Mr. Fred Augustine Horatio de Jones, on Wednesday, the 15th of February, 1893, at 12 o'clock, noon, at St. John's Cathedral."

they adopted a surer way, especially considering the postal facilities of the times. The father of the bride generally went personally from house to house and extended the invitation to those he wished to have. I am told that sometimes the bride and one of her bridesmaids did the inviting. This custom certainly did not obtain within our recollection. The festivities generally commenced the day before the solemnization of the marriage (which usually took place on a Thursday). Eating, drinking, but principally dancing was the order. On the eventful day proper the happy couple drove to church, accompanied by a long procession of invited guests in carreols and cutter, beautiful horses all bedecked with wedding-favors, etc., and every "gallant" accompanied by a "partner". Some times, it is said, "partners" were scarce, and sometimes some young belle was not a little embarrassed by the importunities of her several admirers to accompany them to the marriage. She had, however, to make a choice, often weeks before the event, and although she must necessarily overwhelm several with disappointment and grief she might safely be trusted (as now) to choose the right one. I have a very distinct recollection of only succeeding in getting a "partner" for a wedding (the last of the kind we attended) at Prince Albert, some years ago, after four or five unsuccessful attempts; and at that time I was just about that age when I thought—well; that I was not a very bad looking fellow.

The return of the marriage party or procession was generally made the opportunity for the young men to give an exhibition of the speed of their horses (and they had splendid horses then) and the men with the slowest invariably brought up the rear at the finish. There was one invariable rule in these drives and that was that no one would dare pass the bridal party in the race, as to do so would be to commit a breach of etiquette which would neither be overlooked nor forgiven. We have now arrived

AT THE HOUSE

of the bride's parents which was always used for the feast. The house of a neighbor was always cheerfully given up for the dancers (all unnecessary furniture—including beds sometimes—were bundled out), and now in very truth the fiat went forth, "on with the dance, let joy be unconfined". These festivities have been known to go on with unabated vigor and joyous hilarity for three days and three nights. It is true they were rather hard on moccasins, but people very often provided themselves with more than one pair, so when one was worn out a new pair was ready. But the dance went on until there was nothing but was worn out except the dance floor, and sometimes there was very little of that left. Some may perhaps think that the mocassin part of this account over drawn, but I can assure you seriously that I am, if anything, under the mark. Of course, you must understand that when I use the word "dancing" I mean "dancing": not the dances of modern days; no, instead of pianos and orchestras we had the good old fashioned fiddle, and always plenty of able and willing hands to play it. Instead of the effeminate, easy going and dreamy waltz, we had the always exciting and lively "Red River jig," which required not only skill to dance but lots of endurance as well; instead of the modern cotillion and quadrille we danced the ever reliable old Scotch reel or reel of four, and instead of the somewhat lazy and languid lancers we danced the ever popular and swingy old eight-hand reel.

The next important step with the marriage festivities was the "kirking". On the Sunday immediately after the marriage the bride and bridegroom, accompanied by the groomsmen and the bridesmaids, drove to church, their horses still flying the many colored ribbons used on the wedding day, and the bridal party themselves all arrayed in their wedding habiliments. They all sat together and were, of course, the cynosure of all eyes in the church, and it is pretty safe to opine that the clergyman would have to use considerable lung power and do a good deal of "desk pounding" to attract the eyes of his flock from this particular seat to himself; and I fancy that the dresses, bonnets, etc. of the bride and bridesmaids would be chief topic of conversation after church instead of the sermon. The bridal party all dine together that day at the house of the bride.

Now you may perhaps imagine that this would end the festivities, but not so. The bridegroom is still at his father-in-law's, and he must be brought back to the paternal roof, and the new daughter must be welcomed right royal. The day fixed for the groom to take home his bride (always to his father's house where he lived whilst preparing his own home) was Tuesday. It was now the turn of the parents of the groom. They invited, in the same way as before, all their relatives and friends to celebrate the arrival home of their daughter-in-law. It is now the same old story: fiddle, "jig" feasting and making merry, generally till sunrise the following morning, when all go home, put off their wedding garments, and go about their daily work as if they had been peacefully slumbering all night instead of passing a sleepless one, enjoying to the fullest the giddy dance.

During the winter months private parties were frequently given, and as everybody knew everybody they were much more enjoyable than some of the larger and more formal parties of the more recent times.

An "at home", a "five o'clock tea", and the modern "card party" were unknown, as was also a "reception day". Instead of having some stated day in the week for receiving calls or visits, as we called them, every day was a reception day. When one lady wished to visit another she simply went when it was convenient for her to do so, and always found the latch string on the outside of the door. She invariably found the lady on whom she was calling at home, if she was not out, but never found her out when she was at home. I was told by a lady a short time ago that the words "at home" had two meanings, one of which was "not receiving". I of course took her word for it and did not worry over looking through different lexicographies to ascertain if the words really had two meanings.

Christmas day in the Red River settlement was not very well observed, but New Year's Day was the day that was kept. It was a great day, a red letter day, in fact, especially for the aborigines. Every Indian who had a flint lock gun had it loaded up, and it was a very common thing for settlers to be disturbed about daylight on New Year's morning by a volley of musketry outside the door. This was the way our dusky brothers ushered in the day that would be to them one of continual feasting.

After this preliminary the Indians would divide themselves into squads and start on their visits, calling at every house on their way and getting something to eat at each place. If they could not eat all that was given them a receptacle was always at hand in which the remnants were stowed away to be discussed later on. The settlers always prepared beforehand for their numerous callers of this class. . . .

The 24th of May was always a great day in those old Red River times. People would gather at Fort Garry from Lake Winnipeg to Portage la Prairie, and as far up the Red River as Pembina and St. Joe across the line. We had no military manoeuvres, but horse racing was the whole sport. We have on many occasions ridden races from the fort down what is now Main street, but was then only a trail, to about where we are now standing. *[Although the location for this lecture is not mentioned in the printed version, meetings of the society usually took place in the council chamber in City Hall.]*

There was very keen competition in the different events, and every race was won on the merits—the best horse invariably winning the race. There was very little gambling at these events and pool selling was unknown. Neither was there any "jockeying", "pulling horses" or "selling races". There was always much satisfaction among those who took an interest in horse races to know that if their favorite did not win he was at least fairly beaten.

We knew nothing about Dominion Day, but I can well remember when the 4th of July was celebrated by our American friends then resident in Winnipeg, the proper salute was fired and the day generally observed with horse racing and other sports. . . .

CONCLUSION

Your patience must be now fully exhausted and I will not further try it, but will conclude by reading a short poem written by Wm. Gerrond, Esq., lately of High Bluff, but now of Prince Albert. Mr. Gerrond was bard of the Portage la Prairie St. Andrews society and was always ready with a poem to read on St. Andrew's day. Many of his efforts were of very considerable merit, but when he expressed the ideas of an old settler in poetry, on the old and new order of things in this country, he certainly did it well. Before reading the poem I may explain that there are perhaps some present who will not understand the words "me whatever", which occur three times in the poem was, and is yet, a very common expression amongst the natives of this country and they really mean "for my part". For instance instead of saying "For my part, I'm going to the fort," he would say "Me whatever, I'm going to the fort." With this explanation I will give you the poem.

WHAT WAS AND IS AN OLD SETTLER'S IDEA

Oh! For the time that some despise,
At least I liked them, me whatever,
Before the transfer made us wise,
Or politics made us clever.

Then faith and friendship, hand in hand,
A kindly tale to all were telling,
From east to west, throughout the land,
Contentment reigned in every dwelling.

'Twas then we all in corduroys
Would travel to the church on Sunday
And listen to the good man's voice,
And do as he had said on Monday.

Our women too, both wife and maid,
Had lovely tresses for a bonnet,
A goodly shawl upon the head,
Was all she ever put upon it.

Then gold was scarce, 'tis very true,
But then it was not much we wanted,
Our artificial wants were few,
And we were happy and contented.

But now alas the times are changed,
At least I think so, 'me whatever,'
And artificial wants are ranged,
And piled in heaps along the river.

Our women's thrown away the shawl,
And got instead a showy bonnet
With many a costly falderall
Of feathers, silk and lace upon it.

Our men despising corduroys
In broadcloth grace the church on Sunday,
And then go home to criticize
And do as they've a mind on Mondays.

Our good old faith's supplied with doubt
And friendships killed by speculation;
And sweet content is driven out
And grumbling envy fills her station.

Oh for the time that some despise,
At least I liked them, "me whatever,"
Before the transfer made us wise,
And politics had made us clever.

Transaction No. 44, read January 24, 1893.

JOHN C. SCHULTZ
(1840-1895)

THIS PAPER, DELIVERED NEAR THE END OF HIS LIFE WHEN John Schultz was a successful man, established and wealthy, a senator, and the Lieutenant-Governor of Manitoba, is a reminiscence of his first journey to Manitoba in the 1860s, when he was little more than a boy. He paints a fascinating picture of travel at the time, including such details as how to pack and travel in a Red River cart. He also gives us a glimpse of himself as a raw greenhorn, new to the country and making all the mistakes that greenhorns make. Schultz comes across in this lecture as an amusing, engaging man, quite unlike the difficult and irascible person portrayed in many historical accounts.

John Christian Schultz is a fascinating and contradictory character, who played a central role in the founding of Manitoba and had great influence in shaping the young province. Lady Aberdeen, the wife of the Governor General, recorded during a visit to Winnipeg in 1895 that Schultz and his wife had been "intensely unpopular,"[1] and Sheriff Colin Inkster, on reading the complimentary description on Schultz's tombstone, remarked, "What a pity we knew him." The source of this bad feeling can be found in Schultz's attitudes and actions during his early days in Red River when he was the aggressive and single-minded leader of those who advocated the acquisition of the Northwest by Canada. His antagonism toward and opposition to

---

1. Lovell Clark, "A History of the Conservative Administration 1891-96," PhD thesis, University of Toronto, 1968, p. 953.

John C. Schultz, in Lieutenant Governor's uniform, c. 1892

Riel's government are well known to anyone familiar with the Resistance of 1869-70. What is not so generally known about him is the gradual softening of his attitudes later in life.

Schultz was born in 1840 in Amherstburg, on the Detroit River in Upper Canada, to a Norwegian father and an Irish mother. When he was six, his father abandoned the family. Nevertheless, the young Schultz acquired an education and, working to support himself, studied medicine at Queens and Victoria College in Coburg. He did not graduate with an MD but this did not stop him from practising medicine in Red River when he settled there in the early 1860s. It was common for doctors on the Canadian and American frontiers not to have medical degrees; Schultz at least had some training.

Schultz quickly became more interested in business than in medicine and, during the 1860s set out to make his fortune. He began buying real estate, eventually controlling large tracts of the City of Winnipeg. He became the partner of his half-brother, Henry McKenney, who operated a store and fur-trading business. By the later 1860s the partners became embroiled in a bitter dispute and McKenney had Schultz jailed. Schultz's wife and friends broke into the jail and released him, an act of lawlessness that added to the animosity toward him in the colony.

In spite of the fact that he and the other Canadians at Red River were a minority, Schultz was able to influence events through the *Nor' Wester*, the newspaper he acquired in 1865. The paper was fierce in its condemnation of the Hudson's Bay Company and tireless in its support for union with Canada.

During the time of the Provisional Government of Louis Riel, Schultz proved to be a determined and dangerous opponent of the Métis president. Even after the collapse of the Provisional Government and the triumph of his viewpoint, Schultz continued to hound Riel. During his years as an MP, Schultz seconded a motion expelling Riel from the Commons and supported another banishing him to the US. But he also took what was, given his attitudes toward the Métis, an unexpected interest in the welfare of the Aboriginal population of the west, consistently speaking in favour of more fairness in their treatment.

He also advocated measures to preserve the dwindling buffalo herd of the Northwest.[2]

Schultz was appointed to the Senate in 1882 and became Lieutenant-Governor of Manitoba in 1888. He was knighted in 1895, shortly before his death. He continued to champion the cause of western Aboriginal people and, during the crisis over the status of French as an official language in Manitoba's government and school system, he worked to gain concessions for the French-speaking Roman Catholics.

Given his animosity toward Riel and the Métis in the 1860s and 1870s, these later actions are surprising. Equally surprising are the provisions of his will, which, if his wife had predeceased him, would have left one-third of his estate for "the technical education of mixed-blood people and Métis in Manitoba"; and one-third for hospitals, mainly for the "half-breed and old resident population of this province."[3] Whether he was motivated by remorse or by a more mature view born of his advancing age, his later life does in some degree compensate for the extremism of his youth.

Schultz's last years were marred by chronic illness, and he finally died of a hemorrhage of the lungs in Mexico in 1895. His wife, Agnes, continued to live in Winnipeg until her death in 1929. She was a social and community leader, and left an estate of close to half a million dollars, all of which was bequeathed to local charities.

---

2. Clark, "A History," 952.
3. Ibid., 954.

The Old Crow Wing Trail

PRESIDENT, LADIES AND GENTLEMEN.

It had fallen to my lot to have seen and traversed, with the exception of part of one, all the summer and winter roads which, many years ago, connected the Red River or Selkirk settlement with the outer world, and they may be enumerated as follows:

1. The old North West Company's route, from the mouth of the Kaministiquia through Shebandowan, Lac des Mille Lacs, the beautiful lakes and streams of the height of land between Superior and Lake Winnipeg to Rainy Lake, the lovely river which drains it into the Lake of the Woods, that later second river which bears its waters to Lake Winnipeg, which with its rapids, chutes and falls is, I think, unsurpassed in beauty by any river of Laurentian Canada.

2. The Hudson's Bay York Factory route, too well known to need any description, and of which I have only seen a part.

3. The Breckenridge Flats route, skirting the west bank of the Red River to near where it receives the name at the junction of the Sioux Wood and Ottertail rivers, and crossing the Red River at Georgetown or Abercrombie to traverse to the Ottertail Ford the flats which gave the route its name, and

enter the rolling lake-dotted Country which lay between it and St. Cloud on the Mississippi, 80 miles above St. Paul.

4. The winter monthly mail carriers' dog train route of the old days, which crossing the Red River at Fort Pembina, sought for shelter and night encampment the skirting of Minnesota Woods at the sources of the eastern effluents of the Red River, as far as Red Lake, crossing which on the ice it traversed many of the small lakes which form the extreme headwaters of the great Mississippi down to Leech Lake, and thence southward, passing through mazes of small lakes and through the hunting grounds of the "Pillagers," to the junction of the Crow Wing with the Mississippi River, and then down the east bank of that stream to Fort Ripley, Sauk Rapids and St. Anthony, to St. Paul.

5. The military stage and early Red River steamer route, which connected St. Paul with Fort Garry in 1860.

6. The Dawson route, which cut off the laborious navigation of the Kaministiquia River by a road to Lake Shebandowan, using thence the old water route of the North West Co. with dams on several streams, better landings and improved portages to the Lake of the Woods and the North West Angle, from which a road had been cut to St. Anne and St. Boniface, thus saving the broken navigation of the Winnipeg River, the crossing of Lake Winnipeg, and the ascent of the Red River.

7. The old Crow Wing Trail, opened in 1844 by a few adventurous spirits under direction of William Hallett, who, having been attacked by the Sioux on their way to St. Paul by Lac Travers and St. Peter, sought safety in returning by this route, many miles of which had to be cut through the woods.

Of these seven routes of travel I have, Mr. President, ladies and gentlemen, chosen the last-mentioned because, unlike most of the others, it may not be traversed today. The ploughshare of the Minnesota settler has obliterated its once deeply marked triple track, and even where, like the old buffalo paths of South-western Manitoba, these may in some places be distinguished, the fence of the old and the new settler bars the way.

Another reason may be found in the fact that over it I made my first prairie journey, that from one of its encampment I saw the last herd of buffalo ever seen east of the Red River, and that though I am about to describe it as seen by me in a peaceful journey late in the fall of 1860, I was to traverse it again when comparatively disused during the year of the Sioux massacre in Minnesota, as the only hope of reaching Fort Garry from St. Paul, where I then was, when a camp fire was out of the question, each river-ford and bluff of timber to be avoided, and a stealthy Indian tread to be fancied in the rustle of every leaf.

Coming up from Kingston in the spring of 1860 by way of the lakes to Chicago, one railway only was then in existence in the direction I wished to travel, its termination being Prairie-du-Chien, on the Mississippi. From this point the only connection to St. Paul, then a large frontier town and trading post, was by steamers built for the navigation of the upper Mississippi, and well do I remember my first look at these extraordinary boats; accustomed as I was to seeing the vessels used on the great lakes, where strength and solidity is required, they seemed frail to absurdity in contrast. The supports of the upper deck, scarcely heavier than the trellis work of grape vines, were called stanchions; and I discovered that two inch oak was considered heavy planking for these extraordinary craft. The boiler was on deck, the four feet of hold not of course having room for it, and the power was conveyed to an immense wheel at the stern, which, extraordinary as it looked to one accustomed to the heavy side wheels and screws of the steam craft on other waters, was yet found to serve an admirable purpose when approaching the shallows and sand bars in the upper part of the river.

No ordinary rule of navigation seemed to be followed in the running of these steamers; and watching everything with the curiosity and interest of nineteen, I especially marked the method in which the "heaving of the load," which was ordered from the wheel-house, as we approached some shallow navigation, was carried out by the mate on the fore-deck. That functionary first seated himself near the bow, with his legs hanging over the unbulwarked deck, and in this position, with a ten-foot pole, the lower four feet of which were painted alternately red and white, he plunged it into the water announcing as he drew it up "three feet full;" plunged again, he announced "three feet scant;" another effort brought "two-and-a-half feet;" then the bell rang and the steamer's speed was decreased, and when "only two feet" was announced, the order was given to "back her." Her bow was then pulled towards another part of the bar, and when "two feet full" was announced as the result of the next effort, the bell was rung "go ahead," and the steamer "North Star" wriggled with an eel-like motion, which set the glasses jingling in the cabin, and made one feel as though riding an hippopotamus, over the deepest part of the bar, when "two-and-a-half feet," "three feet," "three-and-a-half feet," were announced in quick succession, followed by another dip of the pole which, passing beyond the four foot mark, brought the announcement from the mate, who rose at that moment to put away his pine lead-line, "no bottom."

Fine weather, and the beautiful scenery along the banks of the upper Mississippi, made the trip a pleasant one, and brought us safely to St. Paul; Minnehaha was visited, and the Falls of St. Anthony, as well as the beautiful and historic promontory, then crowned by Fort Snelling; then came the question of the remainder of the journey, over 650 miles, which lay between that city and Fort Garry.

The first stage line had just been given the contract for the carriage of the mails to the then remote military outpost of Fort Abercrombie, with a bonus large enough to induce the contractors to agree to the stipulation demanded by the government, that the mails should be carried in "overland" coaches with four horses; and these military conditions facilitated my traversing that part of the journey. Shortly before this Anson Northrup, a well known Upper River steamboatman, had brought a small steamer, named after himself, during the spring flood up to near the head of the Mississippi River, and from there had portaged the machinery and the boat, in sections, over to the head waters of the Red River, and the boat, which had been rebuilt and christened the " Anson Northrup," was then lying at Georgetown, the Hudson's Bay Company's temporary transportation post, 45 miles north of Abercrombie.

The journey on this stage was a pleasant one; the beautiful Minnesota lakes and rivers, on which temporary stage stations had been built, lent a great charm to it, which all have felt who have in summer traversed this route. At Georgetown, so named after Sir George Simpson, I inspected the craft which was to take us by the river about 500 miles to Fort Garry. It was a miniature edition of the Mississippi steamer, but there was an ominous look about the wheel-house, however, which was on all sides heavily protected by four inch oak planks, which the captain did not allay by saying "Of course you have your gun along with you." Further investigation shewed an arrangement by which cord wood for fuel could be so piled while the vessel was steaming on her course as to protect the lower deck from bullets. The good-natured engineer also shewed me a contrivance by which, at a moment's notice, he could turn a stream of hot water and scalding steam upon any body of Indians who might strive to take possession of the boat in case it should accidentally strike the bank, or land for additional fuel. All this was very new, very strange and very attractive to a young fellow who had only heard of such matters from incidental reading of Indian wars and forays, and when further explained, it appeared that the Red Lake Indians, after further thought, had become dissatisfied with the conditions of the treaty made with them by Governor Ramsay, of the then Territory of Minnesota, and proposed to prevent whites passing through or occupying their country till a new arrangement had been made. . . .

A detention of two weeks at Georgetown waiting for some small portions of machinery, however, saved us from difficulty with the Indians, none of whom we saw on our guarded passage down the river, they having probably gone back to their hunting grounds near Red Lake.

Pembina was reached, then only half a dozen houses; the boundary line was crossed, then Fort Pembina, (the Hudson's Bay Company's wooden stockade) came in view. Thirty miles below we reached the first of the Red River settlements, the inhabitants congregating on the banks to see the strange steamer passing; and it was with intense interest that we reached at last the bend of the river which disclosed the twin-towered cathedral of St. Boniface; another bend, and Fort Garry came in view; a straight run along the present course of the Winnipeg Rowing Club, was traversed, when, turning up the Assiniboine to land where Main Street bridge now is, the groves, church and tower of St. John's could be seen across the almost blank intervening space; and the steam whistle once belonging to a very much larger steamer, which had been blowing almost continuously for the previous half hour, brought, I think, what must have been very nearly every living human being for two miles around to the sloping bank where the steamer landed. Ascending this bank, Fort Garry, so often heard of, was inspected; and even then time and an imperfect foundation had left cracks in the stone walls. It seemed, however, a place which a very few men could hold against a number unprovided with artillery; for the bastions were pierced on all sides, not only for small arms, but cannons were mounted at each embrasure. The front gate was massive, like the front wall, which faced towards the Assiniboine, and was entirely flanked and protected by bastion projections so that there was no chance for any force unprovided with artillery to make a rush on the gateway. This gate, however was only open on special occasions, the business gate of the Fort being on its eastern side, and was simply a sallyport, where more than two men could not enter abreast. Passing down this side of the Fort was the King's highway, which led off in a northerly direction and was continued to Lower Fort Garry, or the "Stone Fort," and thence to the Peguis Reserve and the two Sugar Points. No building whatever was built upon this road; the houses of William Drever, the two of Andrew McDermott's, A.G.B. Bannatyne's, that of the Ross', Logan's, Bouvette, Brown and Inkster, being, where the land admitted of it, on the banks of the river, some distance to the east.

I have said that the Cathedral of St. Boniface then possessed two towers, which have been made familiar to the whole of this continent by the beautiful description of the poet Whittier in the "Red River Voyageur." The Cathedral Church of St. John also possessed its tower, (a square and very massive one), and my first Sunday in the settlement found me one of its occupants during the morning service; and I noticed on the bordered wainscoting which extended up some height above the pews the plain evidence, on its paint work, of the extreme height, and of the gradually decreasing of the waters of the flood of 1852. From near its gate could be seen the residence of the Right Reverend Dr. Anderson, then Bishop of Rupert's Land; a building very little changed, except outwardly, built solidly of logs, and now the residence of His Grace the Primate of all Canada; and between the Church and this house stood the then closed College of St. John.

During my summer's stay I had visited the Peguis Reserve, the King's Highway which led to the Sugar Points of Mapleton, its southern border, crossing then as now the Image Plain; had seen the Kildonan Church, the Middle Church and that of St. Andrew's, and visited the Stone Fort; had seen St. James and Headingley Churches, crossed the White Horse Plains, where I saw its fine church; traversed "Le Grand Marais" to Poplar Point with its church, High Bluff and its place of worship, and that of the Portage, all monuments of the earnest zeal and tireless efforts of Archdeacon Cochrane. I had seen the chiefs of far off tribes who had come to Fort Garry to trade, had laughed with our own Crees and Ojibways, who stood on the bank, at the unsuccessful attempt of two Plain Crees to cross the Red River in a bark canoe, these children of the prairie, whose home is on horseback, having no use for nor acquaintance with the paddle; had seen the Plain hunters come back with their load of pemmican, dried meat, and the flesh of the buffaloes last seen by the returning brigades; had eaten of the Marrow fat and Berry pemmican, and oh, greater gustatory joy than all else, had partaken of the delicious hump, the odor and taste of which are still fresh in my memory after three and thirty years. The falling leaves and autumn tints of October 1860 reminded me, however, that I must leave for the winter this land of plenty and promise; and as the steamers had long since ceased to run, I began preparing for the trip which I am about to describe.

This road or trail, called by those at this end of it "The Crow Wing Trail," and at the other "The Old Red River Trail," was one which had been used for many years; and while our Metis and Crees were at war with the Sioux, it was considered both safer and shorter than the one on the west side of the River, until Fort Abercrombie was built; and even then was often used, as being less open to prairie fires, with better wood for encampments and high gravelly ridges to render part of it at least almost as good as a turnpike road. Its drawbacks were the many streams, eastern effluents of the Red River, which had to be forded, some of them, like the Red Lake River, being after heavy rains very formidable obstacles to loaded or even light carts. It was a favorite land route with Sir George Simpson, who died the year I first traversed it; and James H. McKay, his trusty and trusted voyageur, known to the English and French settlers as "Jeemie," and to the Sioux as "Jimichi," who was to become a member of the Legislative Council of Manitoba on the recommendation of Governor Archibald, was proud of the fact that always on the tenth day of their start from Crow Wing at the stroke of noon from the Fort Garry bell he landed Sir George at the steps of the Chief Factor's House. Relays of horses enabled him to do this, rain or shine; and the slightest stoppage in muskeg or stream found McKay wading in to bring Sir George on his broad shoulders to dry land.

Fortunately for me, a more experienced head than mine had chosen the horses, selected the cart and saddle, and suggested the outfit for the journey; and, though I found soon after starting, that there were wrinkles in ramp and travel that experience only can teach, still I acknowledged my indebtedness to my friend, and proceed to enumerate the outfit which he deemed sufficient to land me and the Canadian friend, who was to accompany me, safely at Crow Wing; and I give these in the order of their importance. Two Red River ponies, who disdained oats and had never eaten of aught save prairie grass, dry or green, " Blackie" and "Bichon," both good types of their hardy class, short barrels, sturdy legs, long manes, and tails which touched their fetlocks; different in disposition, however, Blackie having a bad eye and uncertain temper, with a disposition to smash things with his hind legs, which would have been fatal to a buggy, but was energy thrown away on a cart, when one knew how helpless he was with a clove hitch around the root of his tail with one end of a short piece of shaganappi, the other end of which was tied to the front cross bar of the cart, the eight or ten inches distance between the attached ends affording but little scope for the exercise of powers such as Blackie undoubtedly possessed. This peculiarity was not the only one of Blackie's, which would have placed him second to Bichon in this narrative, had he not some qualities useful indeed in time of trouble. He had a practice of trying to bolt when his harness was loosed, to escape the inevitable hobble without which Blackie, whose leadership Bichon, the tractable and gentle, always followed, would have left us on the Prairie to our own devices more than once; and even with these, shaganappi obstructions to his rapid locomotion he made time fast enough to make his capture, till his stomach was full, a very difficult matter. Though bad in these respects, he was good in others; for the swamp must be deep that he could not pull a cart through; and the bank of a stream just forded must have been steep and slippery indeed that Blackie's unshod feet could not scramble up. Bichon, the patient, would do his best and, failing, would lie down in the one or slide back to the bottom of the other. So that as we are apt, after many years, to remember the good and forget the bad, I have given the first place in this, I fear, rambling narrative, to Blackie; though I acknowledge gratefully that it was on Bichon the obedient's back that I explored the bog or essayed the river crossing when the one was likely to be bad or the other deep. So much for the horses. The saddle was simply a tree, strapped on over a blanket, which was easier on the horses than the Indian saddle; and the cart harness the dressed buffalo skin one of the time, with the collar and hames in one piece, short traces to iron pins in the shafts, to which also were attached the hold backs, which were the broadest and heaviest part of the harness. Shaganappi reins and a bridle with no blinkers completed the simple but efficient equipment.

Items Nos. 1, 2, 3 and 4 being now described, I come to an

important one, No. 5, the cart, the popular impression of which now is that it was a ramshackle, squeaky affair, with wheels five feet high, each one of which dished outwardly, so that the fellow looked as if about to part company with the spokes awl hub; and those who have seen them as curiosities at an Exhibition wonder if the wood had shrunk, which left a loose opening where felloe joined felloe in the queerly dished wheel, or whether indeed the fellow who made these joints had been quite himself when he completed this wooden monstrosity, which had not a scrap of iron on or about it. Queer looking they undoubtedly were, as compared with the present trim buggy, though the squeak is a libel as applied to a lightly loaded travelling cart, which has been fairly treated by the application of the scrapings of the frying pan to its axle; yet no vehicle, I verily believe, which has been used before or since, was so suited for the traversing of a country where, in one day, it might have to travel over, with its three-inch-wide wooden tire, a shaking bog, a miry creek, a sandy shore, or a boulder strewn path up steep hills. At a cost of two pounds sterling, in the old days, one became the possessor of a vehicle, the high wheels of which made it easy to draw, the great dish of the wheels made it hard to upset, while the loose jointed felloes saved the wheel from wreck, by closing and yielding when a rock was struck in a deep river crossing, or the hidden stump in a newly cut trail was encountered. A very haven of rest wert thou, O cart, on the prairie, when, the long day of travel ended, a large square of canvas thrown over you made a tent before a camp fire better than any other, and an ark of safety when the swollen river was too deep to ford; thy wheels off and under the box, with the same square of canvas about all, thou wast a boat made in ten minutes, in which two travellers, with their belongings, might paddle or pole from shore to shore in safety, leading the swimming horses behind.

My excuse for thus apostrophising my Red River cart as a sentient being is that, like Blackie, it had tricks of its own which puzzled the uninitiated. Attempt to ride in it in any way that one is wont to do in a civilized vehicle, and it soon *rattled* (if I may use a modern expression) its occupant, who found himself, to a musical accompaniment of frying pan and tin kettles, trying alternately to preserve himself from being pitched onto the pony, having his right or left ribs cracked against the side rail, or turning a somersault over the tailboard of the cart. No, there is only one way to ride in a cart with ease and pleasure, and that is seated in front on its floor, with your legs hanging down near the horse's tail. If you are luxurious, tie a broad piece of shaganappi from rail to rail to support your back, put an extra folded blanket under you, sway your body slightly with Blackie or Bichon's jog-trot, and you need not envy the occupants of a coach and four. N.W., better known as "Commodore," Kittson appreciated this fact and never would in any of his later prairie trips ride in any other way or in any other vehicle.

As there is only one way to ride in a cart, so there is only one way of stowing its accessories; the most important of which is your half-sized axe. Put into the cart by a green hand, this useful implement becomes an engine of destruction; cuts into your packages of tea, etc., ruins your blankets and jolts along till its long handle reaches far over the tail board, and an extra jump tumbles it on to the trail, to delight the heart of the first Indian who passes, but to cause you to be extremely sorrowful when you have to make camp with a jack-knife, or replace an old axle. No, the axe should take no risks, and must have a leather socket for its head and a strap for its handle, and both outside the cart on one of the side boards. The gun is the next in importance; and for that, too, there is only one way, if you are not to risk shooting yourself or your companion. The butt must rest near your seat on the left side, the barrels in a loop to the top rail at an angle of 45 degrees, this arrangement, while making its carriage quite safe, enabling you to seize it quickly while yet the prairie chicken or duck is passing.

Not so dangerous as the two former, but infinitely more difficult to manage are the frying-pan, with its long handle, and the copper and tin kettles, to put the one loose into the cart was to blacken and smear all its contents; while the kettles, after a preliminary row-de-dow, would speedily part with their bales and lids, batter themselves into uselessness against the sides, and then jump out bodily on to the track. No, having tried many ways with kettles, I have come to the conclusion that only when inside one another and lashed securely below the centre of the axle, where they may jingle in peace, are they to be circumvented. As for the frying-pan, having been so often entirely beaten in attempts to muzzle one, I have long ago given up any thought of rendering innocuous that, jingling, banging, crooked, perverse but indispensible adjunct to prairie travel.

The cart cover I have incidentally mentioned; this must be large and light, so as to completely envelope the cart, either as a tent or boat, and is preferable to a tent for light travelling, as it saves the carriage of pins and poles, may be used by the tired traveller much sooner at night, and may be folded in the grey dawn by the still half-asleep voyageur without tripping over pegs or ropes.

As prairie chicken and duck were abundant, the substantials for the trip were as follows:—Pemmican (marrowfat if possible) 20 pounds, hard biscuit, 30 pounds, tea, sugar, butter and salt; a little flour, to make the "Rubbiboo" assume a bulky appearance when Indians had to be breakfasted or dined, their mid-day entertainment being generally avoided by giving them a biscuit each, and keeping on ourselves with a lunch of pemmican "au naturel;" a pair of blankets each, a couple of buffalo robes, then costing 12 shillings sterling each, our clothes in a couple of waterproof bags, and Lo! the expedition was complete.

The voyage proper did not commence till Pembina was reached, for the traveller who brought the latest news and could speak a little French was always sure of the best they had in the way of bed and board at any of the houses of the Metis, whose settlement extended then half way to Pembina. One's horses too were always included in the generous hospitality, and Blackie and Bichon ate of the sweetest of the recently mown prairie grass. The second night was invariably passed at Pembina post, where the H. B. officer in charge (a predecessor of an esteemed member of our Society, Chief Factor Clark), extended similar hospitality on a better scale, and saw you safe on to the ferry in the morning. We had arrived at Pembina, had eaten buffalo steak for supper, had slept in a civilized bed, had porridge for breakfast, followed by buffalo steaks again, the first helpings of which were taken from the bottom of the liberal pile, to give point to the worthy master's standing explanation, that the Company's cooks always put the best at the bottom, I suppose for their own delectation after their master's meal was over. Our worthy host's close scrutiny of our horses and equipment seemed to be satisfactory save that he insisted on his present of a little dried buffalo meat, which he said went far when you met Indians, and on learning that it was my first essay at prairie travel, urged me to take a young Indian part of the way to put us on the right track. This was a damper, for the trail on the east bank was in full view, going up from the ferry landing, and the line of the Red River skirting woods, through which it had been cut, could be distinctly seen, and so while middle age experience on the bank expostulated and advised, youthful ignorance and over-confidence at the horses' heads on the ferry thanked and assured, till the ferry touched the opposite bank, up which Blackie quickly sprang, anxious to be away from his floating footing, which yawed and jerked in the passage across. Alas, when was ever the confidence of the young justified as against the experience of their elders? The tracks, triple marked, were plain enough till the outer limit of the skirting woods was reached, and then they began diverging like the ribs of a fan, but as they all led through a low savannah, ignorance, to wit, myself, assumed that they would converge again on higher ground, and so the best marked of them was followed.

It was noticed that the trail we had chosen was a circuitous one, if we were to reach by it the first camping place on the bank of the "Two Rivers," but we supposed that to be due to the necessity of reaching higher ground; doubts, however, about it were set at rest after a couple of hours' travel, by its ending abruptly at the hay stack behind a willow bluff which had concealed it. There was nothing for it but to return and essay another track, which brought us to where hay had been cut and carted away; a third venture having failed, and the day being far spent, we gladly availed ourselves of the services of a Metis boy, who piloted us to where we could see the aspen bluff near the ford of the first river we had to cross. "Experientia docet" generally when too late; and the day ended with tired horses, and only a short part of a day's journey traversed. The two rivers, with their muddy, miry banks and bottoms, were crossed at dusk, for it is a rule in prairie travel always to encamp at the further side of the stream, that the morning's start may be made with dry clothes and fresh horses; and while Blackie and Bichon are recruiting their energies on the rich grass of ungrazed savannah land, let me give a brief account of the character of this old trail from Pembina to Crow Wing, the low savannah country dotted with willow bluffs, such as I have mentioned, and which is drained by the two rivers, extends from Pembina to the Tamarc River crossing, about thirty-five miles from Pembina; and the traveller, after fording this, the Middle and Snake Hill rivers, all branches of one stream, enters upon a country of fine gravel ridges, running in the main north and south, with a growth of aspen willow and balsam poplar flanking them, the delicate catkins, buds and leaves of which in the early spring make them look like a long avenue where the landscape gardener has been at work. This extends nearly all the long way from the Snake Hill to the Sand Hill River, where the old gravel ridges of former lakes trend off too much to the east, and the trail crosses a high dry prairie which is fairly good for travel, but yet is unlike the voyageur's paradise I have just described, and I may as well explain why. The three essentials of prairie travel are wood, water and grass; and the swamp-flanked, tree-bordered ridges I have described furnished these in their perfection. Ducks and prairie chicken constantly flying up, good encampments anywhere to right or left of track, safety from prairie fires, which cannot run in such a country, and the best of pasturage till the snow falls, for the ponies; while on the other hand the dry level prairie affords no safety from the mad rush of the fierce fires its now dried herbage, save the objectionable one of starting another to your leeward; there are long stretches between watering places, wood only on river banks, and no shelter from any preliminary canter which old Boreas may choose to take before he settles down to his winter's pace; and as it was the 18th of October before we started on our journey, the beautiful Indian summer might or might not last us through our trip.

Level high treeless prairie was to be traversed thence to the Red Lake River and far beyond it till the Wild Rice was reached, and there the country changed, with heavy boulders on the hills and multitudes of small lakes fringed with small oaks; this continued to Detroit Lake, a beautiful sheet of water, now, I believe, a pleasure and health resort, some of its gravel hills being then distinguishable for miles by the high stages bearing the bodies of the dead, from which fluttered pieces of red and blue cloth; and near them the remains of food placed for the spirit's early journey to hunting-grounds, which the Ojibways must have thought good indeed if better than near this very spot, which afforded the best an Indian could desire of all the deer and fowl of that beautiful lake district; where every stream teemed with fish, and buffalo once were plentiful low down on the river which bears their name only three days journey away. The trail followed at the edge of the water this beautiful lake for nearly two miles and the ponies chose to walk in the shallow water to cool their unshod feet, sorely tired by our hasty crossing of many leagues of burnt prairie to reach where grass could again be had. We had reached this lake late at night, and already Blackie and Bichon were eating, as if for a wager, of the rushes and rich grass above the sand line on its shore; when a kettle of tea, a few biscuits and some dried meat being disposed of, weary limbs sought rest. Where should we sleep? Why, what could be better than a bed on this clean white sand, which the last high wind has piled up as if for that special purpose ? Hurriedly the cart was drawn over the highest, finest and softest ridge, and then a blanket and to sleep. How easily and softly the sand yielded till it made a bed like a plaster cut; no downy couch equalled it; and yet when morning dawned it was another case of "experientia docet." No, I have since that night slept on the axe-hewn planks of a frontiers-man's floor, on the prairie, in a canoe, on smooth Laurentian rocks, and I give each and all the preference to soft white sand, no bed more unyielding when it has you in its embrace; and no wonder my friend and I woke with a feeling as though we had been kicked all over by Blackie, and resolved to sleep anywhere or to sit up all night, rather than sleep in sand again. . . .

Crow Wing, a frontier trading village, was reached at last, fifteen days' journey for the four hundred miles; and we fared sumptuously on fried bacon and many triangular cuts of apple pie. . . .

Crow Wing was the point to which from St. Paul the masters of brigades frequently teamed with wagons a portion of their cartloads to save the heavy sand road down the eastern bank of the Mississippi. At Crow Wing the carts were finally loaded, it being a work of thought and care to so apportion the cart-loads that one should not carry all the heavy goods and another all the light; where, also, the cart covers of raw beef or buffalo hide securely fastened on and the long slow journey commenced, the money not spent at St. Paul was generally got rid of here in necessaries for the trip of over a month, and in presents for the loved ones at home.

One part of the equipment of a number of carts in a brigade was a long and strong rope for river crossings and soft places which a light travelling cart traversed safely with an extra spurt on Blackie or Bichon's part, but which were formidable obstacles for loaded carts, especially at the steep bank of a slippery and muddy river crossing. In such places the ox, strange to say, was better in the miry bottom and the horse the better for the steep bank; for the cloven hoof parted in the mire, giving a better footing to aid his patient and great strength; while the horse's hoofs gave him a better hold on the slippery bank; both needed aid however when a deep slough was reached or streams of the kind I have mentioned had to be crossed; at such places, if not very bad, the rope was attached to each cart as it came up and five or six of the men at the further end aided the struggling ox or horse just at the right moment; but when the bog or slough was very bad indeed, then the animals were taken out to find their own way over, while the whole force of brigade men pulled the loaded cart through.

Many a thousand tons of freight have been carried over this road, and a brigade frequently meant hundreds of carts; on the tall trip they generally went down light, the buffalo robe catch having been carried in closely compressed bales of ten robes each by the spring brigades, the arrival of which in St. Paul was an event not only to the fur-buyers, but to the people of the place, who lined the side-walks as the long train of squeaking, fur-laden carts passed through, and English half-crowns and sovereigns were to be had at almost any of the shops, all of which eagerly sought the Red River trade.

It is time however that I came back to our own experiences of travel, some of which were amusing afterwards, but very puzzling and annoying at the time. One of these was the crossing of the Red Lake, the largest river on the route. A winding track through large elm trees had brought us down to its brink, and here we could see the deep tracks of loaded carts straight over the gravel shore and into the water; directly opposite were similar tracks on the other side. It seemed all right, though the ford was at a place where the water ran very swiftly indeed. Pursuing our usual plan, Bichon with the saddle tried the ford, but the water was soon above his breast. He was brought back, and the tracks going in and coming out closely inspected again to see if it was straight across. Tried on foot with a long pole to keep from being swept off my feet in the rapid, the water was soon breast high. What could be the matter? Surely where loaded carts could go so shortly ago we might easily pass; and there had been no late rains to swell the river. Searching back to the top of the bank we could find no diverging track to another part of the river, and yet it was clearly a case of swim to cross it here. Tired with the effort, the horses were allowed to graze, and tea was made, after which the essay was made to cross the river on foot at a point further up, where broken water seemed to show shallowness, and it was while essaying this that I found the secret of the ford. The carts had indeed entered straight into the water at the foot of the sloping bank we had descended, but, once in, they had turned up-stream to make the crossing in a horse shoe fashion which brought them out directly on the opposite side, where again a sloping bank formed the best path for ascent and descent.

Many minor difficulties at other places were the rewards of inexperience, and, pleasant as the trip had been, it was a relief when it was over, the ponies placed in careful hands for the winter, the cart and harness stowed away, and St. Paul was reached, early in November. . . .

Transaction No. 45, read in the season of 1892-93.

MARION BRYCE
(1839-1920)

MARION BRYCE WAS BORN MARION SAMUEL ON A prosperous farm in Kirkliston near Edinburgh, in 1839. She was educated privately. After living for a time with her family in Newry, in Ireland, she immigrated to Toronto to become the principal of Mrs. Birnie's Ladies School. She married George Bryce in 1872 and moved to Manitoba. The couple had only one child, who died in infancy.

Mrs. Bryce had a small private income that enabled her to employ servants and freed her to lecture in French and German at Manitoba College. She wrote many papers on historical subjects and was recognized for her scholarly work when she was elected a Fellow of the Royal Society.

She was, with her husband, one of the first eleven members of Winnipeg's Knox Church, the first Presbyterian church in the city. Because she was a minister's wife and because of her own interests and abilities, she became heavily involved in charitable work. She was well liked by her co-workers, "being at once dignified and wise and easy to get on with."[1] Her charitable work established her as a community leader and she was one of a handful of women with an entry of her own in the 1912 *Who's Who in Western Canada*. She was, at various times, president of the Christian Women's Union, the board of the Old Folks Home, Middlechurch, the Winnipeg section of the Council of Women, the McCall Mission, and the Women's Mission

---

1. *Legislative Library Biography Scrapbooks*, Number B7, pp. 98 and 99.

Association; and vice-president of the Winnipeg Women's Canadian Club and secretary of the Victorian Order of Nurses.

Mrs. Bryce's lecture reveals the astounding level of public charity in Winnipeg in its first two decades, a time when it was not a large or particularly wealthy city. She documents the enormous and essential role played by women in establishing and maintaining charitable institutions. It is clear that far from being demure ladies of leisure, Winnipeg's women were eager to roll up their sleeves and make right what was wrong in their young community.

The Winnipeg Lodging and Coffee House, opened November 1898

The Charitable
Institutions of Winnipeg

———•———

IN GIVING A HISTORY OF THE CHARITABLE INSTITUTIONS of Winnipeg, we naturally begin with the oldest and most important, viz.: the Winnipeg General Hospital. Anyone examining the public edifices of our city is sure to have his attention drawn to a group of buildings belonging to the hospital, occupying a block between McDermot and Bannatyne Avenues, and west of Nena. A closer examination of these buildings and their uses will show that the Winnipeg General Hospital, like the City of Rome, was not built in a day. Building after building has been added, according to the requirements of our city and Province, and we are pleased to think that we have such a memorial of the advancement of medical science in our midst. The oldest of the group of buildings was opened to receive patients in 1881 but earlier records show that the hospital had a history of twelve years' duration previous to that date.

The Winnipeg General Hospital was organized December 13th, 1872, and its Act of Incorporation was passed May 14th, 1875. The board of management applying for the Act were George Young, Gilbert McMicken, W.N. Kennedy, Rev. W.A. Clark, Thos. Lusted, G.B. Spencer, A.G.B. Bannatyne, J.H. Ashdown, Stewart Mulvey, A.G. Jackes, J.H. O'Donnell, Jos. Royal, J.H. McTavish, and W.G. Fonseca. Drs. O'Donnell, Jackes and Lynch were the medical men chiefly associated with the hospital in the earlier period of its history.

Anyone who remembers Winnipeg in those early years as a mere village, with its new population, mostly young men, constantly being added to from the East, its crowded boarding houses, its imperfect buildings, hastily erected to accommodate new arrivals, the absence of sanitary arrangements and the prevalence of typhoid fever, can speak of the necessity for an hospital even at that stage of the city's existence. Yet it was not one of the new arrivals who was the chief benefactor in this matter, but one who had come to Red River when a mere lad, and who had spent most of his life there, the Hon. A.G.B. Bannatyne. The first building used for hospital purposes was on the banks of the Red River, somewhere near the foot of Lombard Street. The second was a log house in Point Douglas, rented from the late Hon. John Norquay. The imperfections of both these buildings soon convinced the hospital board that they must arise and build. The Messrs. McDermot and Bannatyne donated the present hospital site, afterwards enlarged, and a building was erected on it in 1875, which was occupied as an hospital until 1882. During the financial struggles of this early period the hospital board was more than once indebted to the ladies of the city for substantial aid. As early as 1873 a bazaar was held under the auspices of Mrs. Bannatyne for the benefit of the hospital.

In the fall of 1877 the increasing demands upon the hospital having brought it into financial difficulties, a meeting of the ladies was called and a statement of its affairs laid before them. The secretary treasurer showed that the hospital's annual cost of maintenance was about $4,000, to meet which there was: The local Government grant, $1,250; city grant, $500; Dominion Government, for patients, $250; Hospital Subsidy, $300; private patients, from $300 to $400, leaving a large deficit to be made up from uncertain sources. The hospital was at the time $700 in debt for maintenance. The ladies willingly came to the rescue. The city was divided into districts, two ladies being appointed to canvass each. A generous response was made to their solicitations, and in this way about $1,200 was raised. Later on the ladies held a bazaar, or, as it was called, an apron festival, by which $400 more was realized.

About the same time a small addition was made to the hospital, costing $150, the whole of which sum was kindly donated by Mr. Moberly, a contractor, then in the city. Such are a few of the facts looming through the mists that usually obscure the dawn of history.

The years 1882 and 1883 were, perhaps, the most progressive in the history of the General Hospital. In the boom years the city had grown with abnormal rapidity and the resources of the hospital were inadequate to meet the increasing demands upon it. Something had to be done to place its affairs on a firmer footing.

The Act of Incorporation was amended in 1882 . . . removed the limit of property that could be legally held by the corporation. It also empowered the directors to raise money by mortgages. The life membership fee, which had heretofore been $50, was now raised to $100 and the name changed to Life Governor. The annual fee, which had been $4, was increased to $10.

FINANCES

In January, 1881, the Dominion Government, which had, in former times, been rather stingy in its dealings with the hospital, passed an order in council, authorizing the payment of 60 cents per day for each immigrant patient treated. At the time of which I speak this was quite a source of revenue to the directors, over $18,000 having been paid during the two years.

In 1883 the Charity Aids Act passed by the local Government secured to every hospital approved by the Governor in Council payment of 25 cents per day for every free patient treated. The City Council twice increased its grant during these two years. The original annual grant of $500 was first advanced to $1,200 and again to $5,000. A by-law at the same time was passed, giving the city representation of one on the board of directors for each $5,000 given. At the present day the grant is $10,000. The municipalities began to send in contributions more regularly, and Hospital Sunday became an established fact, although it has always been difficult to have all the churches make their collections on the same Sunday.

Perhaps the most pleasing event during these two years was the establishment in 1883 of the suggestion of Mrs. W.G. Dennison, of the Women's Hospital Aid Society, the object being to supply the hospital with bedding, clothing and other necessary comforts. Although the ladies of the city had somewhat fitfully taken an interest in the hospital from time to time, and by donations had supplied its wants, the organization of this society not only assured a more regular supply of household necessaries, but also, a careful supervision of the same, and was a great relief to the board of directors.

BUILDINGS.

The hospital building which had been in use since 1875, had during the boom years been found quite inadequate to the growing requirements of the city, and in 1881 a temporary location and building in Point Douglas had been purchased from the Dominion Government at a cost of $5,000, to be used until the old building could be moved from the hospital site and a new building erected. In addition to subscriptions of citizens to the building fund, the board received from the Hudson's Bay Company $2,000; from the C.P.R. a similar amount and from the City Council a special grant of $5,000. A mortgage loan of $25,000 was incurred. After the usual troubles and vicissitudes attending on building operations at that time, the new hospital, costing $63,115.95, represented at the present time by the general and administration buildings, was opened 13th March, 1884, and was a great boon to the sick and suffering, as well as to the attendants, as the Point Douglas building, although roomier than the old hospital, was not even so well suited for hospital purposes, and on account of an outbreak of smallpox within its walls in May, 1882, the patients had to be accommodated in tents on the prairie around it. . . .

MORE RECENT YEARS.

In approaching more recent years it seems unnecessary to enter into the details of the hospital's history, as its printed records are available, and yet even a sketch would be incomplete without reference to the main features of advancement. The hospital building was no sooner completed in 1884 than the directors began to see that in the interests of medical science the work of the hospital would have to be extended. But, burdened as they were with a mortgage debt, for a large amount of which some of them had become personally liable, it could not be expected that they would immediately add to their responsibilities.

The Jubilee years of Her Most Gracious Majesty, Queen Victoria, always bring showers of blessings, and of these showers a good many drops are sure to descend on the Winnipeg General Hospital. In 1887 the directors of the hospital made an appeal to the public for a jubilee fund wherewith to discharge the complete debt on the hospital property. The response to the appeal amounted to $14,062.95, which not only wiped out the debt, but left a considerable balance in the hands of the directors to undertake whatever extension might be thought most desirable.

SCHOOL FOR NURSES.

The hospital had, up to this time, been indebted to outside sources for its supply of nurses, but in order that the nursing staff might be increased and a number be available for sending out to city and country, a school for nurses was opened in 1887. To provide proper accommodation for these nurses when off duty, a home was found to be a necessity. This home became an established fact in November, 1888, and its occupation left a considerable amount of room in the hospital to be used for the accommodation of patients. The directors had also a maternity hospital in course of erection in 1888, which was finished in December of that year. This branch of medical work had, since 1883, been under the care of a society of ladies, called the Christian Women's Union. At this stage it was almost necessary, for the completion of the nurses' course, and that of the medical students, that it should be under the direction of the hospital authorities. The members of the Christian Women's Union were quite willing that it should be so transferred. Indeed, the proposal came from their side.

An operating theatre and a disinfecting kiln was also added to the equipment of the hospital in 1888; and a separate and roomy ward was set apart for the treatment of children. The latter was fitly named the "Brydges Memorial Ward for Children," in memory of Mr.

Brydges. It was for the purpose of formally opening this ward that Mr. Brydges had gone to the hospital on the 16th February, 1889, when he so suddenly died. During the same year, 1889, the hospital and the board sustained another great loss in the death of the president, the Hon. A.G.B. Bannatyne, who had been in ill-health for several years.

The enterprises of 1887, even with the help of grants, left the board once more in debt, but by 1891 this was all paid off and they were ready to undertake further extension. The next important building undertaken was an isolated hospital for infectious diseases, as the general building had now become too crowded to allow of wards being set apart for this purpose. This building was finished and ready for patients on the 26th January, 1893, and the following year increased accommodation for nurses was added in connection with it. There is but one more building to speak of, that called the Victoria Jubilee Addition, at present in course of erection to the West of the main building, and connected with it by a corrider. This building will be devoted altogether to surgical cases, and will contain a roomy and well lighted operating theatre. To meet the expenses of this handsome addition to the hospital the Provincial Government and the City Council have each granted $10,000; $2,000 from Mr. W.W. Ogilvie is available, and it is hoped that the general subscriptions will bring the sum up to $50,000. Of the lesser but very important equipments of the hospital—the two ambulances, for example—there is scarcely time to speak.

The hospital has always had a plentiful supply of water from its own flowing wells, pumped into the building by steam power. It also has its own plant for electric lighting. . . .

THE WOMEN'S AID SOCIETY HOSPITAL.

This society has already been mentioned in connection with the General Hospital, and it is to the hospital that it owes its allegiance. It was organized in 1883, the annual membership fee being $2. Its object was to supply the hospital with bedding, clothing and other necessary comforts. The first officers were: President, Mrs. Aikens; Vice-Presidents, Mesdames Brydges, Pinkham, Denison and Pitblado;

Secretaries, the Misses Mingaye and Drever; Treasurer, Miss Mingaye. Committees were also appointed for various kinds of work.

In order to enable the society to make a good beginning the store-keepers of the city supplied goods at very reasonable prices, and Dr. M.T. Hunter generously paid for these goods to the amount of $500. Thus the newly erected hospital was well stocked with all the needed bedding and linen. Since that time the society has had a very prosperous career. Having no buildings of its own, it has had to be indebted to friends for a place in which to convene. For a number of years Mr. Sprado has allowed the society to hold its monthly and committee meetings in one of the dining rooms of the Manitoba Hotel. The recent fire rendered this society homeless for the time being, but it is hoped that soon again it will be found in comfortable quarters.

For a number of years the society raised its funds chiefly by entertainments, an annual ball being given for the benefit of the hospital, but the sentiment of many of its supporters was found to be in favor of direct giving, and it was resolved in 1892 that in future the society should depend more for its income on the extension of its membership fees, and other larger or smaller subscriptions.

This plan was so successful that it seems to have been adopted by the society as its permanent source of revenue. Occasionally the funds are augmented by the proceeds of entertainments, but these are usually proferred to the society by their promoters.

When a new building has been added to the hospital the draft upon the resources of the Aid society is larger than at other times, as the members have not always limited themselves to the ordinary provision expected of them, but have helped considerably with other furnishings. We may take 1897 as a normal year, when the cost of articles supplied by the society amounted to $948.55. Two of the members, Mesdames Bell and Sprague, collected money during the jubilee year for a new ambulance, as it was necessary to keep one for infectious cases.

The presidents of this society have been Mesdames Aikens, Lynch, Pinkham, Farrell, F.W. Harris, Ewart, Street, Blanchard, Adams, Somerset Aikells, Drewry, Moffat, and Mrs. H. Bell, at present in office.

Secretaries: The Misses Mingaye and Drever; treasurers: Miss

Mingaye, Mrs. Macfarlane; secretary treasurers: Miss Ailkens, Mesdames Eden, J.G. Moore and Mrs. E.M. Wood, at present in office.

THE CHRISTIAN WOMEN'S UNION.

The Christian Women's Union owes its origin, in March, 1883, to a few devoted women whose strong desire was to bring together women of different Protestant denominations and varied predilections and to unite them in some important work in which they could all be interested. The proposed work naturally took the form of work among women. A mass meeting of the women of the city was called and met in the old court house near the site of the present City Hall, an ancient landmark that has since disappeared. A board of management was chosen with Mrs. Galton, sister of Mrs. W.R. Mulock, as president, she having been one of the leading spirits in the movement.

Collectors were appointed to raise funds and the city was divided into districts for this purpose. In order to receive a Government grant an Act of Incorporation was applied for early in 1894 under the name of the Christian Women's Union of Winnipeg. The Act was passed by the Legislature in April of that year and a grant of $500 was given, now $250. The annual fees are $3.00; life membership, $50. The ladies applying for this Act were Mrs. Mary E.J. Aikens, honorary president; Mrs. Catherine Rowe, president; Mrs. Eleanor Whitla, vice-president; Miss Mary Jazdrowski, treasurer; Mrs. Annie Monk, corresponding secretary; Mrs. Jemima Irwin, recording secretary; Mrs. Marion Bryce, 1st directress; Mrs. Matilda Lynch, 2nd directress. The first work undertaken was a home for young women earning their living in the city and absent from their own homes. The old Bannatyne residence on the river bank, with its grounds extending from Bannatyne to McDermot St. was rented for the purpose of the home, which was opened in the spring of 1883.

This institution was afterwards moved to a smaller house on Hargrave Street, but it was not taken advantage of by those for whom it was intended—it rather seemed to attract the idle and incompetent—so in a short time it was thought advisable to have it closed. In the meantime, with the glad approval of the leading physicians of the city, the society had opened a Maternity Hospital in the Bannatyne building. The hospital was not designed only to benefit the class usually styled unfortunate, but also poor married women who were destitute of comforts in their own miserable shanty homes at that time so common. There were also private wards for ladies coming from the country and from distant towns for the advantage of good medical skill and nursing. The Bannatyne building having been sold, the maternity hospital was moved in September, 1884, to a large house formerly occupied by Sheriff Armstrong, at the foot of May Street, Point Douglas, and in 1886 it was again moved to the adjoining roomy house, the former residence of the late Major Morice.

These frequent changes of residence shewed that the board were never altogether satisfied with the hospital quarterrs, and indeed, they were always painfully aware that their accommodation came far short of the requirements of modern science. Although among nearly 200 adult inmates they were so fortunate as never to lose a single case by death, yet two slight outbreaks of fever warned them of the risk to life they were running. They felt the necessity of erecting a proper building, but the medical men began to see in the state of advancement of our city, and in the interests of the Medical College it was time for the Maternity Hospital to be placed under the sheltering wing of the General Hospital. The union quite agreed with them, and towards the end of 1887, after the second fever outbreak, the Maternity Hospital was closed and this chapter of the history of the Christian Women's Union came to an end.

Previous to this, on the 1st January, 1885, in a small building adjacent to the Maternity Hospital, the Children's Home was opened by the Christian Women's Union. It was primarily for the benefit of the little ones born in the hospital that the home was intended, but other needy children were admitted. The family soon outgrew the narrow limits of the premises, and in April of that same year the home was moved to a more commodious house on Assiniboine Avenue, foot of Hargrave Street. In September, 1896, it was again transferred to a larger building on Portage Avenue.

When the Children's Home was removed to a distance from the

Maternity Hospital a separate committee was appointed from the members of the C.W.U. for its management, and this was a stepping stone to its finally becoming an independent institution.

Those whose hearts went out to work among the children applied for and obtained from the Legislature an Act of Incorporation as the board of management to the Children's Home, June, 1897.

After the Children's Home had been removed from under its care, and the Maternity Hospital had become an adjunct of the General Hospital, the C.W.U. had a breathing space. There was one phase of work open to them akin to their former hospital work and springing out of it, but it was feared that this would not carry with it public sympathy. They hesitated, but there was money in the treasury, over $1,000, and they felt that they should without delay put it to some useful purpose.

That the corporation was so wealthy came about as follows: From the opening of the Maternity Hospital there had been admitted from time to time patients from the immigrant sheds. The General Hospital authorities, it was understood, were paid at the rate of 60¢. a day for each immigrant patient placed under their care and the board of the Maternity Hospital concluded that they should be paid at the same rate for each immigrant woman sent to them, and the bills were made out accordingly. Year after year these accounts were disputed by the Dominion Government, but finally the sum amounting to $900, was paid, just when the society seemed to require it least.

It was not long before the C.W.U. became convinced that it was their duty to open up a refuge for women. The Maternity Hospital had served the double purpose of an hospital and a refuge and now the members of the union felt that an industrial home was needed for the kind of inmates that were likely to come under their care. But the inconveniences of a rented house for the purposes of the home determined the union to build, so as to have room for industrial branches to occupy and improve the inmates. The money on hand enabled the board to pay ready cash for the spacious lots now occupied by the home. It is an ideal site on McDermot Ave., West of Kate Street, as the work is so closely connected with that of the General Hospital.

In 1889 the union was chiefly engaged in canvassing the city for the means to erect the present building, which is evidence in itself that a generous response was met with. The last installment of a mortgage debt upon the property was paid in 1895. In March, 1891, the new home was opened with a reception given to a large gathering of friends. Since that time it has been found very suitable for the work with a few improvements made from time to time. As since the opening of the Salvation Army Rescue Home the more degraded cases are not admitted to the C.W.U. home. It is suitable as a refuge for aged poor women as well as for respectable married women coming to the city for medical care, indeed, there are no hard and fast lines drawn with regard to admission, excepting several very necessary ones in the by-laws; each case is considered when the application is made. The home shelters about sixty inmates during the year. Such is a brief sketch of the history of the Christian Women's Union. It has sometimes been in financial and other difficulties, but a kind providence has always helped it over hard times. The presidents were Mesdames Galton, Rowe and Bryce; vice presidents, Mesdames Whitla, Lynch, Wesbrook, Somerset and O'Loughlin; secretaries, Mesdames Irwin, Doupe, J.B. Monk, (Dr.) Rerr, (Dr.) Orton, Culver, C.H. Campbell, J. McBride, Atkinson and McClenaghan; treasurers, Miss Jazdowski, Mrs. M.T. Hunter and Mrs. (Dr.) Clark. The present officers are: Patroness, Mrs. Patterson; Hon. president, Lady Schultz; president, Mrs. George Bryce; 1st vice-president, Mrs. J. B. Somerset; 2nd vice-president, Mrs. J. M. O'Loughlin; recording secretary, Mrs. A.V. McLenaghan; corresponding secretary, Mrs. J.J. Roy; treasurer, Mrs. A.W. Clark; financial secretary, Mrs. Wm. Bathgate; Sunday service, Mrs. George McVicar. The C.W.U. has a Government grant of $250 and a civic grant of $300.

THE CHILDREN'S HOME.

Nothing appeals so strongly to the hearts of the benevolent as work among poor children. To smooth the path of life for little footsteps will surely earn the blessing of Him who said, "Suffer little children to come unto me, and forbid them not, for of such is the kingdom of heaven."

It has been already said in the sketch of the Christian Women's

Union that the Children's Home was commenced by that society in 1885, and conducted by it until 1887, when it became independent and obtained an Act of Incorporation of its own. Those who applied for this Act were the following officers: Mrs. Sarah McKilligan, first directress; Mrs. Georgina Smith, second directress; Mrs. Ella Ross, third directress; Mrs. Agnes Culver, secretary; Mrs. Lizzie Hunter, treasurer, and others to the number of thirty constituting the board of management. The annual membership fee was $3; the fee for life membership, $25.

The board was given power to contract with a parent placing a child under its care for absolute control of the child, unless the parent by paying a yearly amount towards its maintenance shows a desire to retain possession of his or her child. The children to be admitted into the home are boys under 6 years of age, and girls under 14, more or less destitute. Children over whom the board of management has absolute control are, if possible, given for adoption, and it may be of interest to know the terms on which adoptions are made:

> When a person makes application for a child, two certificates of character, one from a clergyman and the other from a justice of the peace, are required to be furnished. Three months are generally allowed for approbation and, if everything is satisfactory, an indenture, in duplicate, is signed by the contracting parties. The children must be well clothed and sent to school for a certain number of months in the year. Payments of five dollars per year are required until the child is 10 years old; fifteen dollars when the child shall have attained the age of 16 and twenty dollars when the child is 18 years of age. This sum is payable to the child by the corporation, when the guardianship of the home ceases. A written annual statement of the condition and welfare of the child is also required, so that the children are never lost sight of by the home, during their years of minority.

The three buildings in which the children had successively been housed had all been found comfortless and inconvenient and at last, after much discussion as to a proper location, a very fine lot and private residence on River Avenue, Fort Rouge, was purchased in 1888. The house was almost rebuilt and extensively added to and when it was opened to receive the little ones there was a mortgage debt of $3,000 upon it. This was a somewhat daring venture, but the promoters had great faith in the love of mankind for little children. Additions both to the lot and building have been made from time to time, and some years ago a pavilion was built on the grounds so that the children may be shaded from the sun when at their play. In the Jubilee year, 1897, a stone foundation was put under the home and a new kitchen and boys' dormitory were added.

In the home there is only room for 55 children, and it is nearly always filled to its utmost capacity. The children of school age attend the public school in Fort Rouge, and their teachers give a good account of them. They also accompany Miss Hynd, the matron, to divine service.

Almost ever since the home was removed to Fort Rouge Mr. E.E. Stephenson has conducted Sunday School there with his able coadjutor, Miss Nixon, and some other assistants. The Children's Home board have been most fortunate in their matron, Miss Hynd. Her loving, prayerful care and her individual study of each child has transformed a mere public institution into a true home for the little ones.

So many young children unable to do much for themselves necessitates the keeping of a staff of domestics, so that the institution is an expensive one, but it has the sympathy of the public and is well supported. Through the kindness of friends, too, the little ones never fail to have a merry Christmas time, and delightful sleigh rides during the winter, as well as their little picnics in the park and free rides on the street cars during the summer.

The chief difficulty the board has had to encounter has been the payment of the debt on their property, but this is now in a fair way of being discharged. They have still a mortgage of $3,000, but they have $2,000 in their building fund, and when the other thousand is reached, the Children's Home will have a very valuable property without incumbrance.

Since the Act of Incorporation the officers have been: Patronesses, Lady Schultz and Mrs. Patterson; Lady Taylor, 1st directress, still in office; Mrs. A.M. Patton, at present acting directress; 2nd and 3rd directresses, Mesdames Taylor, Fisher, Cowley, Wesbrook, Patton, Hart, Ewart. Mrs. Culver, secretary now in office; Mrs. Naim, assistant secretary. The board suffered loss in the death of its first treasurer, Mrs. M.T. Hunter, and of its second treasurer, Mrs. Jas. Fisher, when they had held office but a short time. Mrs. Wickson has been treasurer since 1889. The society has a grant of $500 from the Government and $500 from the City Council.

THE PRISONERS' AID ASSOCIATION.

was organized in 1890. Its object was to attend to the spiritual welfare of the prisoners of both sexes in Winnipeg during the period of their incarceration and to seek their reformation in every possible way, to provide for their comfort and to promote their interests on their discharge from prison, and to seek the improvements of prisons and police stations when found to be necessary.

Shortly after the organization of the association an Act of Incorporation was asked for and obtained. This Act applies only to the City of Winnipeg and at the next sitting of the Legislature an amendment to the Act will be asked for extending the operation of the association to the Province of Manitoba.

The first officers were: Rev. Mr. Davis, President; Mr. W. R. Mulock, treasurer; Mr. Thomas Gill, secretary. The Rev. C.C. Owen is the present president. This association has a small Government grant.

ABERDEEN ASSOCIATION.

The formation of the Aberdeen Association was suggested on October 19th, 1890, in the first address given by the Countess of Aberdeen before a Winnipeg audience. During a trip taken by Lord and Lady Aberdeen through Southern Manitoba, they were struck by the lonely aspect of the prairie homes and the dearth of reading matter everywhere apparent seemed to them a great privation, particularly for those who had been well educated and accustomed to read. The result of Lady Aberdeen's words on this subject was the formation of the parent branch of the association, at a meeting called on November

12th, 1890, at the Clarendon Hotel, where a number of ladies undertook to supply the lonely homes of the Northwest with instructive and entertaining literature, Lady Taylor was appointed president.

The task of supplying the whole of the Northwest with reading matter was found too much for the Winnipeg ladies to attempt and there are now twelve branches of the association throughout Canada, with headquarters in Ottawa. Even the literary resources of Canada were found too limited for the required supply, and a branch association was formed in England, with the Marchioness of Dufferin and Ava as president, and with free rooms in the Canadian Institute, London. Through the influence of Lady Aberdeen, the association is indebted to the post office authorities, the Dominion and Allan lines of steamers, and the Canadian Pacific and Grand Trunk railways for free transportation of parcels. The English railways give half fare rates.

But it is the work of the Winnipeg branch that we have chiefly to sketch on this occasion. The local Government have kindly given the use of rooms in the Lands Titles Office for the reception and distribution of literature and from 300 to 400 parcels are sent out monthly. The secretary keeps up a correspondence with the recipients of this literature and sometimes the description of the loneliness of prairie life given in the letters received by her are truly touching.

The association endeavors as far as possible to consult the taste of the different readers, and sometimes the senders are startled by such an instance as the following, which shows the necessity for the circulation of pure literature in our country. A young girl who had requested some reading to be sent to her home was asked by letter what kind of literature the family enjoyed most. She replied that they preferred sensational stories of the Jesse James type.

THE LITERATURE MOST USEFUL
TO THE ABERDEEN ASSOCIATION.

Weekly and monthly religious and church papers and periodicals of all denominations, in good condition; agricultural, scientific and technical journals of the current year only; fashionable papers of the current year only; good magazines of any date, in good condition.

Sets of magazines in consecutive numbers for the year are most valuable. Sunday School papers of all denominations for teachers and scholars, Christmas annuals and pictures, children's books of all kinds, standard works of history, biography, travel and fiction, all good books, French, German and Scandinavian and Gaelic literature for applicants speaking those languages; daily papers are not required on account of their transient interest only. The denominational periodicals are sent to the charge of the different clergy in the Northwest to be judiciously distributed by them.

In the Jubilee year, 1897, packets of seed from the Experimental Farm, Ottawa, were sent through the association to its readers so that their homes might be beautiful by the growth of trees and flowering plants. A portrait of Queen Victoria, also sent through the association, now graces many of these homes on the plains.

The income of the association is derived from fees and subscriptions. The outlay for twine and wrappers amounts to quite a large sum during the year. Officers: Lady Taylor, president; Mrs. Wickson, acting president; Mrs. Kirby, secretary; Miss Thomson, treasurer; Mrs. Wm. Clark, acting treasurer.

THE FREE KINDERGARTEN ASSOCIATION.

The Free Kindergarten Association, founded in 1892, gathers the poor children at the north end of the city into their school room in the old Swedish Church, Ellen Street. In the place of liberty to run about the streets, something good has to be given, so the ragged and hungry little ones are clothed, fed and provided with pleasant occupation of acknowledged educational value.

The work of the association is based upon the principles laid down by the founder of the kindergarten system, Frederick Freobel, and the promoters believe that the proper education of children during the first seven years of their lives does much to reduce poverty and crime in any community.

But the members of the Free Kindergarten Association do not limit their benevolent work to the children alone. They get acquainted with the homes of the little ones, visiting the mothers, tending the sick among them, and organizing mothers' meetings for their improvement. Special classes for sewing are held both for the mothers and little girls, and sometimes the members invite the mothers to a tea, a kindness that is much appreciated by these poor overwrought housewives. With the help of some of the gentlemen of the city Boys' Brigades have been recently organized in connection with the work, one for the smaller and one for the bigger boys. Already some signs of improvement are noticed among the rougher lads. The services of Miss Barnett, the principal, have been invaluable, both in the school room and outside. She has the faculty of gaining the hearts both of the children and the mothers.

Miss Barnett has the assistance of two pupil teachers in her work. The school has an average daily attendance of sixty children. Some people think that when the kindergarten system is introduced into the public schools the work of this association will no longer be necessary, but this is quite a mistake. The Free Kindergarten members practice a kind of charity that would be quite outside the duties of the teachers in the public schools. The work of the association has been of great value among the foreign elements of our city. This association depends for its revenue on fees and subscriptions and many a weary step the members have to take in the interests of their sometimes empty treasury. We may imagine the joy of these ladies, when two years ago they became possessed of a piano at a moderate price. The City Council has promised a small grant ($100) for this year, 1899. The presidents have been: Mrs. Dexter, Mrs. Fisher, Mrs. Godfrey Parker and Mrs. R.H. Bryce at present in office. Secretaries: Miss Colby (Mrs. Cook), Mrs. R.H. Bryce, Mrs. T.J. McBride, Mrs. Atkinson, Mrs. Chown, Mrs. Jardine, at present in office. Treasurers: Miss Dolly Maguire (Mrs. Hughes), Mrs. W.L. McKenzie, Mrs. Capt. Robinson, at present in office.

THE WINNIPEG LODGING AND COFFEE HOUSE ASSOCIATION.
This association for work among men was commenced by Holy Trinity Church in 1893, during the curacy of the Rev. J. Page. It was designed to provide a cheap boarding place for industrious men, and

also to induce the idle to become industrious. The principle of the association is to give no assistance without some equivalent in work or payment. A small building was rented in 1893 by Mr. Page and Capt. Graburn, with accommodation for about twelve men. A large building was rented in 1894 and soon after the work outgrew the bounds of a parochial undertaking, so that it deserves a notice in a sketch of the public charities of Winnipeg. In order to place the institution on a broader basis a joint stock company was formed in 1898, with shares of $10 each.

A substantial brick building was erected by this company on Lombard street, with a roomy wood yard for the employment of the men. The building was opened on the 1st of November, 1898. This lodging and coffee house, as it is called, is expected to be self-supporting, indeed, it is now more than paying its way so it may soon be removed from the list of Winnipeg charities. These men have to pay for their beds 10¢. and 15¢, for their meals 5¢, 10¢, 15¢, according to quality, making it possible to obtain 3 meals and a bed for 25¢ a day. The new building has accommodation for 100 men. Since its opening it has had not less than 55 men sleeping there and sometimes it has over ninety.

The mission hall in the building is rented at $12.50 a month. Holy Trinity Church still looks after the spiritual welfare of the men and rents the mission hall for the holding of Sunday school, night school, Gospel services, etc. Mrs. Scott acts as deaconess in connection with the mission, and does untold good in a quiet way by relieving suffering and distress of all kinds. The association is desirous of having a lay worker to live in the building, and look after the spiritual welfare of the men. In the meantime this duty is taken in turn by some member of the brotherhood of St. Andrew, interested in the mission. Chairman of the association, Mr. J.H. Brock; secretary, Mr. H. Whitla; treasurer, Mr. E.H. Taylor.

SALVATION ARMY.

This body has been doing good work in Winnipeg since the early eighties, and it has at present two charitable institutions, a Rescue Home for Women, at 486 Young Street, and a Shelter for Men, 686

Main Street, with a wood yard, corner of Princess and Fonseca Street, in connection with the latter, for the employment of the men. The Rescue Home is also of the nature of an industrial home. As the Salvation Army does not publish any annual report of their institutions it is difficult to obtain information as to the means employed by them or the result of their work, but there is good reason for our faith in beneficent nature. The Rescue Home has a Government and civic grant.

THE DOOR OF HOPE.

Since its establishment in the city the Women's Christian Temperance Union has engaged with great diligence in endeavoring to "rescue the perishing." Its latest enterprise is the Door of Hope. This institution was opened about two years ago under the auspices of the union, but recently it has been handed over to a managing board of ladies of the city. An experienced trained matron, Miss Boland, a short time ago came from New York to take charge of the home, which is situated at 168 Bannatyne Avenue. Its object is the reformation of the inebriate women we so frequently read of in the press reports of the police court and station.

The Door of Hope has met with a severe loss by the recent death of Mrs. George C. Mills, a most devoted temperance worker and one of the chief promoters of the institution. The work of this institution is still in a tentative state, but we trust that its success will soon be assured.

GIRLS' HOME OF WELCOME ASSOCIATION.

The work of this association is designed to serve the double purpose of providing a good class of domestics for our community and of securing a shelter and protection for girls of that class coming without friends to the country. It also affords a boarding place for girls from the city or country when temporarily out of situations. A girl arriving at the home for the first time is allowed her board for 24 hours, afterwards she has to pay at the rate of $2.50 a week.

The home owes its origin to Miss Fowler from London, who generously furnishes $500 a year for three years and also her personal superintendence for the same length of time. The work of the home is conducted in harmony with the home of the National Emigration Society of Montreal. The board of directors consist of 36 ladies with an advisory board of gentlemen. Miss Fowler, who is sacrificing so much, naturally has an important voice in the management. The membership fee is $1.00, the Government grant $500. The chief difficulty the association has is to get a good class of domestic to come to the country. The members do not like to run the risk of furnishing the passage money, but in the short time the home has existed, it has been, and in future it ought be, useful in connection with the Government immigration. The association does not yet possess a building of its own and as the present roomy house on Assiniboine Avenue, allowed free of rent by the Hudson's Bay Company, is only for a summer residence, it is at present closed until the opening of the spring immigration. The officers are: President Mrs. Parker; vice-president, Mrs. W. H. Adams; secretary Mrs. Bole; treasurer, Mrs. Crotty.

THE CHILDREN'S AID ASSOCIATION.

In 1898 the local Legislature passed a statute called "An Act for the Better Protection of Neglected and Dependent Children." To insure the carrying out of this Act, an association was formed in this city called the "Children's Association," and this is the youngest of our city charities. By the enactment, this association may be empowered by county court judge or magistrate to take possession of any destitute orphan children, or any child that is being ill-used neglected or corrupted by its parents or guardians. The word "child" applies in this Act to any boy under 14 or any girl under 16 years of age. The association is thus constituted guardian to such child.

The children are first taken to a temporary shelter on Mayfair Avenue, Fort Rouge, which has been rented by the association and furnished at the expense of the Government and City Council, where they begin to learn the advantage of being clothed, fed and kindly treated. As soon as possible foster homes are got for them at a distance from their former evil environment, so that they may be likely to grow up respectable and useful citizens of the state. Since its recent commencement, the association has had 24 children under its care, 5 have been adopted and 7 placed in foster homes or otherwise provided for, and 11 are now in the shelter. The demand from the country for children is far greater than the supply. As the association is carrying out the enactment of the Government and also relieving the City Council of onerous burdens, liberal grants from each are expected. President, Mr. Daniel McIntyre; secretary, Dr. Blakely; treasurer, Mr. W.M. Johnstone.

WOMAN'S COUNCIL.

Most of the Women's Associations are affiliated with the local Council of Women of Winnipeg, organized by Lady Aberdeen. At the annual meeting of the council short accounts of each society are read and the members have thus an opportunity of getting interested in each other's undertakings.

OTHER CHARITIES.

It is not within the scope of this paper to give an account of the temporary work of the city relief committee or the benevolence and charity of the different organizations of the Freemasons, Oddfellows, Foresters, United Workmen and the like, which in their active charity or their bequeathment and other benefits do so much to relieve suffering. The latter are private charities, and their reports are not accessible. The benevolent Scottish and other national associations are helpful in relieving the necessities of their poor and needy fellow countrymen, but their work does not require buildings and so, though it is very real, it is not easily seen.

Time forbids to notice the work of ladies' charitable societies, young people's associations and other bands of Christian workers connected with the churches. These are all doing excellent service, and exemplify one of the truest works of a living Christianity, which is to "remember the poor," and to "visit the fatherless and the widows in their affliction."

Transaction No. 54, read February 1st, 1899.

Catching wild pigeons, 1857

GEORGE ATKINSON

(D. 1913)

GEORGE ATKINSON WAS A WELL-KNOWN TAXIDERMIST and naturalist, who lived in Portage la Prairie. He had come to the west from Toronto around 1881, settling first in Port Arthur, where he began working in his field, and where he wrote one of his first scientific papers, a study of the turkey vulture. He came to Winnipeg in 1883 but after four years moved west to Portage la Prairie, a better location to study the bird life of the prairie.

He prepared specimens for museums in eastern Canada, the United States, and Europe, and wrote books, pamphlets, and magazine and newspaper articles about the birds of his district. Many people interested in learning about western Canadian birds visited his store in Portage. Behind this establishment he kept an aviary, where he studied the behaviour of captive birds.

Atkinson died tragically in June 1913 while making an annual trip by boat to observe birds along the Assiniboine River from Brandon to Portage. He had what was thought to be an epileptic seizure, fell overboard, and was drowned. His body was never found.

In this paper, one of several he presented before the Historical and Scientific Society, he records one of the great ecological disasters of the nineteenth century: the destruction of the passenger pigeon. Of particular interest is Atkinson's description of the research techniques he employed in establishing when the bird was last seen in Manitoba.

A Review History of the
Passenger Pigeon of Manitoba

———•———

IF WE WERE AT ALL INCLINED TO DOUBT THE FACT THAT in nature's economy one immutable law is that the stronger shall prey upon the weaker or that despite alleged enlightenment and advanced appreciation of moral responsibility, man, who is made head of creation, has in his consideration of all other forms of life failed to rise above the animal nature of making all weaker and less resourceful creatures subservient to his dominating will, to kill at his pleasure, to enslave for his convenience or to deny the right to life for the gratification of an autocratic whim. If, I repeat, we were in doubt that these conditions were existent we would but have to peruse for a time the natural history of the world for conclusive evidence to dispel all doubt.

Yet while the biological history of any country records the decrease and disappearance of many forms of life due to just or unjust circumstances, it remains for the historical records of North America to reveal a career of human selfishness which may be considered the paragon. Within four centuries of North American civilization (or modified barbarism) we can be credited with the wiping into the past of at least three species of animal life originally so phenomenally abundant and so strikingly characteristic in themselves as to evoke the wonders and amazement of the entire world. And sad to relate, so effectual has been the extermination that it is doubtful if our descendants a few generations hence will be able to learn anything whatever about them save through the medium of books. While herein again we shall be just subjects of their censure for having manifestly failed to preserve in history's archives any material amount of specific information.

The earlier settlers landing upon the Atlantic coast between New-foundland and the Carolinas found them in possession of armies of great auks and the few scraps of authenticated history which we now possess disclose a most iniquitous course of wanton slaughter and de-struction which ended in the complete extinction of the bird over sixty years ago. Yet in the face of this destruction there remain but four mounted specimens and two eggs in the collections of North America to-day while but 70 skins remain in the collections of the entire world.

If possible more ruthless and inhuman was the carnage waged against the noble buffalo, the countless thousands of which roaming over virgin prairies excited the wonder and amazement of the entire sporting and scientific world, and which, to-day, are represented only in zoological parks where all individuality will eventually be lost in domestication. While the greater portion of our literature dealing with them is so exaggerated and so fantastically interwoven with fiction with a view of creating author heroes that its scientific value is almost nil.

Co-incident almost with the passing of the buffalo we have to record the decline and fall of the passenger pigeon, the subject of this paper. A bird which aroused the excitement and wonder of the entire world during the first half of the last century because of its phenomenal numbers.

A bird also which stood out unique in character and individuality among the 300 described pigeons of the world and which won the admiration of every ornithologist who was fortunate enough to have experience with it living or dead. Yet withal not exempt from the op-pression of its human foe who has been instrumental through inter-ference with its breeding and feeding grounds and through a continued persecution and ruthless slaughter for the market, in reducing the species almost beyond hope of salvation which now rests upon the possibility of a few isolated pairs unauthentically recorded, still remaining which may be able to perpetuate the species. Should these fail the species is doomed to be one of the past.

The passenger pigeon, the species under observation, was first described under the genus Columba or Type Pigeons, but subsequently Swainson separated it from these and placed it under a genus Exctopistes because of the greater length of wing and tail.

Generically named Ecopistes—meaning moving about or wandering, and specifically named Migratoria, meaning migratory, we have a technical name implying not only a species migrating annually to and from their breeding ground but one given to moving about from season to season selecting the most congenial environment for both breeding and feeding.

Audubon especially remarked of this species that the food supply was a much greater factor in regulating their movements than was the temperature and that they would appear in one district for a time and disappear from it as soon as the food supply became inadequate, and we can readily appreciate how rapidly the supply would become exhausted in the most productive districts with the demand upon it necessary to supply the immense multitudes of the birds recorded for the first half of the last century.

It would appear that the birds followed the line of the Mississippi Valley, spreading eastward to the line of the Alleghany mountains, northward into Ontario and up the Red river Valley to the very shores of Hudson's Bay, selecting locations for nesting accommodation for colonies aggregating from thousands to millions as the food supply guaranteed. With all the knowledge we have possessed of the inestimable multitudes which existed during the early part of the last century and with their decline begun and noted generally in the later sixties and early seventies, we still find that no steps whatever were taken to prevent their possible depletion and few records of any value are made of the continuance or speed of this decrease and not until the last decade of the century do we awake to the fact that the pigeons are gone beyond the possibility of a return in any numbers. When a few years later reports are made that pigeons still exist and are again increasing scientific investigation shows that the Mourning Dove has been mistaken for the pigeon or that the Band-tailed pigeon of California is taken for the old Passenger pigeon and so we have continued since the early nineties investigating rumours of their appearance from all over America, North and South, and the West Indian islands, but all reports point us to the past for the pigeon and some other species under suspicion.

I doubt very much if the historian desirous of compiling any historical work would find himself confronted with such a decided blank in historical records during an important period than that confronted in the compilation of a historical record of the Passenger pigeon within any district which it formerly frequented during the period from about 1870, when the decline was first noted, to 1890, when the birds had practically passed away. In this matter Mr. J.H. Fleming, of Toronto, in writing me, says: "The pigeon seems to have gone off like dynamite. Nobody expected it and nobody had prepared a series of skins," and to this I can add that no one seems to have made any series of records of the birds from year to year. Since their disappearance, however, things have changed; everybody is alert for pigeons, and everybody has a theory, but beyond affording subject of social conversation or awakening a recital of old pigeon experiences from the old timers, these rumors and theories seem to return to the winds from whence they came.

The latest theory advanced to me by a correspondent is the possibility of some disturbance of the elements in the shape of a cyclone, or a storm striking a migrating host in crossing the Gulf of Mexico and destroying them almost completely. This is a plausible theory but I am unable to conceive how such immense hosts of pigeons as are recorded up to 1865 could possibly have met with sudden disaster in this manner even in the center of the gulf without leaving some wreckage to tell the story and such is not recorded. . . . Personally I am inclined to cherish my original contentions that the continued disturbances of the breeding and feeding grounds, both by the slaughter of the birds for market and by the dissipating of the original immense colonies by the clearing of the hardwood and pine forests of the United States and Eastern Canada compelling these sections of the main column to travel further in search of congenial environment, curtailing the breeding season and I have no doubt frequently preventing many from breeding for several seasons. While the persistent persecution and destruction for the market was in no way proportionately lessened in the vicinity of these smaller colonies as long as a sufficient number of the birds remained to make the traffic profitable. It can at once be seen that this continued drain upon these smaller colonies when other conditions were becoming more difficult for the birds to contend with would be instrumental in depleting the entire former main column to a point when netting and shooting were no longer profitable and the remnant of these colonies having to run a gauntlet of persecution over their entire course of migration to and from winter quarters and to such proceeding there could be but one result, and that the one we now face, extermination.

Of those records made during the pigeon's day, as we might call it, the earliest we have are those made by a Mr. T. Hutchins, who was a Hudson's Bay Company trader operating for some 25 years in the district adjacent to Hudson's Bay, during which time he made copious notes of the birds frequenting that district, which were afterwards published by Pennant in his *Arctic Zoology* in 1785. He says in part:

> The first pigeon I shall take note of is one I received at Severn in 1771, and having sent it home to Mr. Pennant, he informed me that it was the migratoria species. They are very numerous inland and visit our settlement in the summer. They are plentiful about Moose Factory and inland, where they breed, choosing an arboreous situation. The gentlemen number them among the many delicacies the Hudson's Bay affords our tables. It is a hardy bird, continuing with us until December. In summer their food is berries, but after these are covered with snow they feed upon the juniper buds. They lay two eggs and are gregarious. About 1756 these birds migrated as high as York Factory, but remained only two days.

In a report issued 1795 Samuel Hearne also reports the birds abundant inland from the southern portion of Hudson's Bay, but states that though good eating, they are seldom fat.

The first provincial record, that made by Sir John Richardson in 1827, in which he says: "A few hordes of Indians, who frequent the low floods districts at the south end of Lake Winnipeg, subsist principally on the pigeons during the period when the sturgeon fishing is unproductive, and the wild rice is still unripened, but further north the birds are too few in numbers to furnish material diet."

I presume he means further up Lake Winnipeg's shores, since Hutchins and Hearne both reported them common nearer Hudson's Bay.

From this time until the later fifties and the early sixties no records are available for the present province of Manitoba, but it will not be out of place here, for the sake of comparison as well as for the benefit of those of us to-day who, having heard some of the stories of our fathers and grandfathers of the phenomenal pigeon flights and rookeries, and because of not having seen, are unable to conceive of such stories being other than the fanciful yarns of a declining intellect, to record some of these seemingly incredulous and exaggerated records by those devoted two ornithological pioneers of America, Wilson and Audubon. . . .

[Atkinson then quotes at length from Audubon and the American naturalist Alexander Wilson, including Wilson's description of a flock of over two million pigeons that was a mile wide.]

When I decided to attempt the preparation of a review of the history of the pigeon in Manitoba, I felt that having had practically no experience with the bird myself I should have to depend upon the reports of representative pioneers of the country for my facts as to the numbers of the birds formerly found here, and the period of their decline and disappearance. I accordingly drafted a series of questions which I submitted to these gentlemen, and I have to tender them all my sincere thanks, as well as that of the scientific world, for the ready responses and the conciseness of the information received.

I shall quote here from the replies received.

One of the earliest residents I find is Mr. George A. Garrioch, of Portage la Prairie, who says:

I was born in Manitoba, and came to Portage la Prairie in about 1853. I was then only about six years old, and do not remember very much about the pigeons at that time, but as long as I can remember they were very numerous.

They passed over every spring, usually during the mornings, in very large flocks, following each other in rapid succession.

I do not think they bred in any numbers in the province, as I only remember seeing one nest; this contained two eggs.

The birds to my recollection were most numerous in the fifties, and the decline was noticed in the later sixties and continued until the early eighties, when they had disappeared. I have observed none since until last year when I am positive I saw a single male bird south of the town of Portage la Prairie.

Mr. Angus Sutherland of Winnipeg in reply to my interrogation, states:

I was born in the present city of Winnipeg and have lived here for over fifty years. The wild pigeons were very numerous as far back as I can remember. They frequented the mixed woods about the city, and while undoubtedly many birds bred here, I remember no extensive breeding colonies in the province, and believe the great majority passed farther north to breed. About 1870 the decrease in their numbers was most pronouncedly manifest, this decline continuing until the early eighties, when they had apparently all disappeared, and I have seen only occasional birds since, and none of late years.

Mr. W. J. McLean, formerly of the Hudson's Bay Company, and at present a resident of Winnipeg, sends me some valuable information which supports my contention regarding the influence of food supply. He states:

I came to the Red River Settlement in 1860 and found the pigeons very numerous on my arrival and that they had been equally numerous for some years previous. The birds came in many thousands and great numbers of them bred in the northeastern portion of the province through the district north of Lake of the Woods and Rainy Lake, where the cranberry and blueberry are abundant, and these fruits constitute their chief food supply as they remain on the bushes and retain much of their food properties until well on into the summer following their growth. They also feed largely on acorns wherever they abound. The first decline I noticed was about the early seventies and 1877 was the last occasion on which I saw any numbers of the birds, when I encountered large flocks of them passing northwesterly from White Sand river near Fort Pelly. This was on a dull drizzling day about the middle of May, and I presume they were then heading toward the Barren grounds district, where the blueberry and cranberry are again very abundant.

Mr. E.H.G.G. Hay, formerly police magistrate of Portage la Prairie, now of St. Andrew's, reports:

I came to the country in June, 1861, and found that the pigeons were abundant previous to my arrival. To give you an idea of their numbers a Mr. Thompson, of St. Andrew's, some mornings caught with a net about 10 feet square as many as eighty dozen, and in the spring of 1864 I fired into a flock as they rose from the ground and picked up seventeen birds.

The birds were mostly migratory in what is now known as Manitoba and mostly all would go further north after the seeding season, and I never heard of any extensive rookeries such as one recorded for the east and south. The few that bred here frequented mixed poplar and spruce. They seemed most numerous in the sixties and began to show signs of decreasing about 1869 or 70 and by 1875 they had all disappeared and I have only seen an occasional bird since.

Mr. William Clark, of the Hudson's Bay Company, Winnipeg, informs me:

"The first place I remember having seen pigeons in Manitoba was at White Horse plains (St. Francois Xavier) in 1865, where they were very numerous, many of them breeding in the oak trees in that district.

"Two years after this I went to Oak Point on Lake Manitoba, but do not remember the birds there nor since."

Mr. Charles Boultbee, of MacGregor, Man., replies as follows:

> I have resided in Manitoba since 1872 and have taken pigeons as far north as Fort Pelly in the fall of 1874, but know nothing of them previously. In our district they usually made their appearance in the fall and fed upon the grain. I never found them nor did I ever hear of them breeding in the province in any numbers.
>
> They continued fairly numerous until about 1882, at which time we had to drive them from the grain stooks, but they then disappeared and only stragglers have been noted since.
>
> None of the flocks noted in Manitoba in any way approached those recorded for the east and south for numbers.

There is no doubt that many other reports could have been secured, but as all seem to tend toward the one conclusion, I shall save time and space by summarizing that information at hand.

Some months ago I made a statement in an article written for local interest to the effect that Manitoba never was the home of the wild pigeon. By this I meant that because of unfavourable breeding and feeding conditions within the province, only the smallest percentage of the enormous flocks recorded for the south and east could possibly exist here. The records here collected support me in this contention so far as that proportion of the province west of the Red River is concerned, but the record of Sir John Richardson tends to show that favourable conditions must have existed immediately south of lake Winnipeg, through what he calls a low lying district, and where we can assume cranberries and blueberries were abundant, as they were through the district subsequently reported by Mr. McLean to the east and north-east of this district. There is no doubt that the difference in the character of the country east of the Red River from that of the west would present more favourable conditions for the birds, but with all it has not in one case been shown that the birds nested in colonies approaching the size of the famous eastern and southern roosts, and reports seem rather to show that those which bred within the province were more generally scattered over the country, at the same time being numerous enough to guarantee the shooter and the netter to pursue a profitable traffic in the birds. All evidence seems to show that large numbers passed through the province to and from the northern breeding ground, possibly that recorded by Hutchens near Hudson Bay and westward, and that they were excessively numerous up to about 1870, when they began to decrease. This decline continued until the middle eighties, when they were practically all gone, and with the exception of a few stragglers none have been seen since while as to the latest authenticated records, I quote from notes in my former pamphlet on "Rare Bird Records":

> The beautiful specimen I have been able to secure for illustration herewith is loaned me by Mr. Dan Smith of Winnipeg, who shot it in St. Boniface, south-east of the Cathedral, in the fall of 1893, and so far as I have been able to discover is the last authentic record for the vicinity of Winnipeg, while the only specimen I was ever privileged to handle in the flesh in Manitoba was collected at Winnipegosis on April 10, 1896, and sent me to be mounted. It was a male specimen in the pink of condition in every way. No other specimen was noted with it, and no authentic records have been made in Manitoba since then.

I have since that time expended much effort in following up rumors of the bird's presence in various districts with a view to locating a breeding pair. Not alone have my desires been to secure and preserve a skin or mounted specimen, but with the possibility of locating a breeding bird and securing the bird alive or securing the eggs while fresh to assist in the salvation of the pigeon in a partially domesticated state, since the only specimens now living in captivity are those owned by Professor Whitman, of the University of Chicago, who in writing me says:

My stock seems to have come to a complete standstill, having raised no young for the last four years. The weakness is due to long inbreeding, as my birds are from a single pair captured about 25 years ago in Wisconsin. I have long tried to secure new stock, but have been unsuccessful. A single pair would enable me to save them, for they breed well in confinement.

I have crossed them with ringdoves, and still have three hybrids but as these are infertile there is no hope of even preserving these half-breeds alive. Of all the wild pigeons in the world the passenger pigeon is my favourite. No other pigeon combines so many fine qualities in form, color, strength and perfection of wing power.

I am enabled, through the kindness of Prof. Whitman, to exhibit a photograph of one of his younger birds taken in his aviary in Chicago.

Transaction No. 68, read March 2, 1905.

SIGTRYGGUR JONASSON
(1852-1942)

IN 1901, WHEN HE DELIVERED THIS PAPER BEFORE THE SOCIETY, Sigtryggur Jonasson was an established businessman and intellectual who could speak with greater authority than anyone about the history of his countrymen in Canada.[1] He participated in the events he is describing, which deal with the Icelanders' attempts to establish colonies in Ontario.

Jonasson was the first speaker who came from neither the English nor French communities to be invited to speak to the society. The talk marks a new departure for the society: the beginning of an openness to non-British immigrant groups and their history, which would become fully developed in the post-World War II years, when the society helped publish a series of histories of Manitoba ethnic communities. In the comments made after his talk and recorded at the end of the *Transaction*, we see evidence of the different attitude of Anglo Canadians toward the Icelanders among the various immigrant groups. They are praised as being "good settlers." Because they were from northern Europe, they were seen as being not very different from the Orkney, Scots, and English settlers, and, according to the racial hierarchies subscribed to by many Canadians at the time, more desirable than immigrants from other areas. This view of the Icelanders was made clear nearly ten years before, at the unveiling of the

---

1. For a biography, see *Sigtryggur Jonasson* (Winnipeg: Manitoba Historic Resources Branch, 1984).

Seven Oaks Monument, by the US Consul James Taylor, who spoke about the thousand-year history of democracy in Iceland and how the "Sons of Thor" brought "wholesome life to the civilization of Europe." [2]

Sigtryggur Jonasson was one of the founders of the Manitoba Icelandic community, and was called by some the "Father of New Iceland." He was born in Iceland and at fourteen went to work as secretary in a government office. At the age of twenty he left his homeland and immigrated to Ontario, where he engaged in various businesses. Like educated men in other immigrant groups, he became an immigration agent for the Ontario government and his activities are described in this paper.

In 1875, working with the Presbyterian minister John Taylor, Jonasson organized a group of Icelanders to travel to the shores of Lake Winnipeg, reaching what is now Gimli on October 21. From that small beginning, the flourishing Manitoba Icelandic community of today has grown. Jonasson continued to play an enormous role in building the colony. He started the first Icelandic language paper in North America, *Framfari* (*Progress*), and edited it for a time. His businesses, a sawmill and the steamer *Victoria*, provided badly needed paid work for the settlers.

In time he moved from Gimli, settling first in Selkirk, to run his shipping company, and later in Winnipeg. In the city, he took the lead again, establishing another paper, *Logberg* (*Tribune*), and editing it until 1901, and setting up an insurance and real-estate business. He helped finance the building of the first Icelandic Lutheran church in Winnipeg and became the first Icelandic Canadian to enter provincial politics when he was elected to the Manitoba Legislature. As a Liberal, he represented the constituency of St. Andrews, and was later joined by his cousin, B.L. Baldwinson, who sat on the opposite side of the chamber as a Conservative.

In 1906, Icelandic farmers were having problems marketing their

---

2. "Seven Oaks," *Transactions of the Historical and Scientific Society of Manitoba*, No. 43, 1891-92, p. 37.

cattle and Jonasson organized a Livestock Marketing Cooperative. The venture unfortunately went bankrupt and the backers, including Jonasson, were ruined. He never recovered financially from this business failure. He died in 1942.

Sigtryggur Jonasson, c. 1874

The Early Icelandic
Settlements in Canada

———•———

THOUGH ONLY A LITTLE MORE THAN A QUARTER OF A century has passed by since the Icelanders began to settle in Canada, yet it is somewhat difficult to gather up certain facts which appear to me absolutely necessary to embody in a paper of this kind, in order to make it of some real historical value.

Before taking up the main subject of this paper—the Early Icelandic Settlements in Canada—I think it is proper to touch on certain events which led up to the founding of these settlements. And in this connection it is necessary to explain that one of the difficulties in framing this paper is the fact that the writer had a considerable share in matters connected with the first Icelandic settlements in Canada.

It naturally suggested itself to the writer that he should leave himself entirely in the background, but he, himself, being one of the actors in the drama, it seemed impracticable to ignore the fact altogether.

The information that the writer had some share in the matters he has undertaken to record may also be of some importance, inasmuch as it makes clear that he is not altogether depending on material furnished by others—is not merely dealing at second hand in this matter—but has personal knowledge of most of the facts recorded.

With reference to the events, then, which led up to the establishing of Icelandic settlements in Canada, I think it is not out of place to mention, that as far as known, no emigration had taken place from the Island of Iceland from the time the Norsemen first began to settle there, in the year 874, until in the sixth decade of the nineteenth century, when two or three small parties emigrated to South America (Brazil). In saying this I, of course leave out the emigration to Greenland towards the close of the tenth century—whence it is claimed that the Icelandic colonists made several expeditions to the east coast of Canada in the beginning of the eleventh century. I am, of course, only referring to modern times.

Thus it will be seen that the great emigration-wave of Europe did not strike the historical island, bordering on the Arctic circle, until after the middle of the nineteenth century.

In the spring of 1870 four young men left Iceland for North America, landing in Quebec on the 19th day of June. They, however, went through to the United States, to Wisconsin, and settled there. They are considered the first real Icelandic immigrants to North America, although it is known that a few persons from the Westman Islands (a short distance off the south coast of Iceland) had been proselyted by Mormon missionaries and gone to Utah some years earlier. The next year (1871) a small party left Iceland and went through to Wisconsin, and in 1872 another small party (a little over a dozen persons) also went to Wisconsin. These few who had so far emigrated were, however, both from the southern and northern districts of Iceland, and some of them wrote letters to their friends at home, describing this rediscovered country in rather glowing terms, so that the news spread among the people on both sides of the island at the same time. Some of these letters were published in a fortnightly newspaper, issued in the chief town in the north of Iceland, during the winter of 1872-3, and then people in that part of the island began to talk in earnest about emigrating on a considerable scale, and to gather up whatever information they could about the different parts of the North American continent.

The writer, then a young man of twenty, followed this movement with great interest from the very first, and in the summer of 1872 started on a voyage of discovery all by himself, landing in Quebec in September, 1872.

When the writer left home, he had not made up his mind in what part of this vast continent he would try his luck, only that he would go to Quebec and see some of Canada to begin with. But on board the steamer which brought him across, he became acquainted with an elderly Scotchman from Ontario, who had gone home to Scotland on a visit and was returning to Canada. This gentleman gave the writer advice on two heads in particular: First, not to drink any of the St. Lawrence water without mixing a "wee drop" of whiskey with it, and second, to go to Ontario, assuring the writer that that province was the finest part not only of Canada, but of the whole North American continent!

Whether or not the writer followed the Scotch gentleman's advice regarding the first point, he did not feel any bad effects from the St. Lawrence water, but he followed his advise as to the second point and stopped in Ontario—in the south-western part of the province—and did not regret it.

The writer (who is, as far as is known, the first Icelander that settled in Canada) wrote some letters to friends in the north of Iceland during his first winter in Ontario and gave his impressions of the province, which were favourable. Whether this had anything to do with directing attention to Ontario is not clear, but it is a fact that Ontario was discussed at a meeting held at the port of Akureyri, in July 1872, by the first large party of emigrants which left Iceland. The intending emigrants discussed their destination at that meeting. Some advocating settling as near the Atlantic coast as possible—in Nova Scotia or New Brunswick—others advocating Ontario, and some advocating the Western States, particularly Wisconsin, where some of their countrymen had already settled, as stated above.

The result of these deliberations was that it was decided that the whole party, numbering some 180 souls, should—with the exception of a few who had relations and friends in Wisconsin—go to Ontario in a body. . . .

[Jonasson then describes the first two years of Icelandic settlement in the Muskoka and Parry Sound districts of Ontario, where the available land was not very good for farming.]

In the summer of the same year (1874) word came across to the effect that a large party of immigrants was expected from Iceland, in the course of the season, and that there was a likelihood that they would go to Nova Scotia. The Icelanders at Rousseau *[Ontario]* discussed the matter thoroughly, and from the knowledge they had gained about Canada at large, they came to the conclusion that they would rather advise this expected party to come to Ontario than go to the Maritime Provinces.

The result of this was that the Agent of the Ontario Government at Rousseau induced the Government to send the writer to meet the steamer which was expected to carry the party across and land it at Halifax. Consequently the writer did go to Halifax and waited there some weeks, until he got word from Quebec that the steamer—the old St. Patrick, of the Allan Line—was bringing the party direct from Iceland to Quebec. The writer then went to Quebec and met the ship there, she arriving on the 23rd day of September with 365 Icelandic souls on board. A few of the immigrants were determined to go to Nova Scotia and were consequently sent there, but most of the party came on to Toronto.

Many of these immigrants were poor and required employment to support themselves and families. It was therefore decided to send the whole party—except some single men and women who could get employment elsewhere—to a village called Kinmount, some 50 miles back from the town of Lindsay, a new railway—the Victoria Railway—being under construction between these two points.

The writer went to Kinmount in advance with an Agent of the Ontario Government, to make certain arrangements for the reception of the immigrants, and when the news spread that a large party of Icelanders was coming there, to settle in the vicinity, the people of the quiet little village were considerably excited. Everybody was asking what kind of people these Icelanders were; whether they were peaceable; how they looked, etc. One lady was particularly anxious to know of the Agent how the Icelanders looked, and asked him if they were not Eskimos. The writer was standing at the Agent's side at the time—a much younger and a good deal better looking man than now—when the Agent—who was possessed of some humor—pointed to the writer and said: " Behold a specimen of an Icelander!" The lady changed the subject of the conversation.

The party was then moved to Kinmount, and the men were employed on the railway during most of the winter, but owing to some financial difficulties work was suspended, which left the immigrants in a sad plight. There was enough "free grant" land in the vicinity of Kinmount, but upon being examined next spring, with a view of settling some of the party on farms, it was found to be no better than the land in the Muskoka and Parry Sound districts, so very few cared to take up land in the vicinity of Kinmount. . . .

As already stated the Icelanders at Kinmount were in a sad plight, and the idea was uppermost in the minds of most of the Icelanders in Ontario to move to the Western States as soon as they could. At that very time people in Ontario were becoming interested in Manitoba, and a movement was beginning thither. A gentleman by the name of John Taylor, who lived not far from Kinmount, then had a conference with the Icelanders in that locality and offered to go to Ottawa and try to interest the Dominion Government in helping the Icelanders to establish themselves in the Canadian Northwest, and this offer was thankfully accepted. Mr. Taylor then went to Ottawa and had an interview with some of the Dominion ministers in reference to the scheme of settling the Icelanders in the Northwest, but the ministers seen were rather dubious about these people, as desirable settlers— and reluctant to take up the matter.

Lord Dufferin was the Governor-General of Canada at that time, and it so happened that he had, as a young man, come up to Iceland on a cruise into the Polar seas, and had seen the Icelanders at home. He has told of his impressions of Iceland, and her people in his famous book *Letters from High Latitudes*.

Mr. Taylor then saw Lord Dufferin, and it is an open secret that he interested himself in the scheme of settling the Icelanders in the Northwest and interceded with his ministers. This is, amongst other things, proven by the words he used in one of his speeches when he visited the Northwest in the summer of 1877. He said to the Icelanders: "I have pledged my official honor to my Canadian brethren that you will succeed"—and the writer believes that the Icelanders have redeemed the pledge of their noble friend.

Pursuant to the arrangement made by Mr. Taylor at Ottawa, the Icelanders at Kinmount held a meeting on May 30th, 1875, and chose delegates from amongst themselves, for the purpose of visiting the Canadian Northwest and reporting upon it as to its fitness as a future home for the Icelanders. The delegates selected were: Mr. Skafti Arason, now one of the wealthiest farmers in the Municipality of Argyle; Mr. Christian Johnson, implement dealer at Baldur; Mr. Einar Jonasson, now residing in the village of Gimli; and the writer. The delegates started for the Northwest on July 2nd, accompanied by Mr. Taylor, going by way of Milwaukee. There they were joined by Mr. S. Christopherson—now a successful farmer residing at Grund, Manitoba—as a delegate on behalf of the Icelanders in Wisconsin, and then the party proceeded to Moorhead, Minnesota, that being the nearest railway point to what was generally known as Fort Garry. From Moorhead the delegates proceeded down the Red River by one of the old sternwheel steamers, landing at Fort Garry—Winnipeg—on the 16th day of July 1875, which is the date on which the first Icelanders set foot on Canadian soil in the Great Northwest.

The delegates were at once favorably impressed with the Red River country, although it did not look very inviting in the neighborhood of Winnipeg at the time they arrived, the grasshoppers having eaten up almost every green thing. After having seen the country round Winnipeg and made enquiries about the different sections within a radius of one hundred miles or so, the delegates decided to go to Lake Winnipeg and examine the west shore of that vast inland sea. Their reasons for fixing on that part of the country were as follows:

1. They thought that the grasshoppers would not be as likely to do damage to crops in that region as on the prairie; 2. There was abundant building timber and fuel in that section; 3. There was a waterway from that section to Winnipeg; 4. There was abundance of fine fish in the lake; 5. A large tract of land could be obtained there as an Icelandic reserve without interfering with other settlers; 6. The main line of the Canadian Pacific Railway was supposed to cross the Red River at the present site of the town of Selkirk, and would not be far from a settlement on the southwest shore of Lake Winnipeg.

The delegates proceeded to Lake Winnipeg in a York boat, supplied by the Hudson's Bay Company, and had for a guide the late Mr. Joseph Monkman from St. Peters. After examining portions of the west shore of Lake Winnipeg, as far as time would allow, and finding that the soil was of good quality, they selected there a site for an Icelandic colony, commencing at the southern boundary of township 18 and running north along the shore a distance of 36 miles—together with Big Island—and christened the tract selected "New Iceland," the same being now included in the Municipality of Gimli.

After returning to Winnipeg, the delegates drew up a report of their observations and advised their countrymen in Ontario to come to the Northwest. Three of the delegates then went east—two remaining in Manitoba—and presented the report to the Icelanders at Kinmount, who, after due deliberations, decided to move to "New Iceland" in a body that same fall, although it was a risky thing on account of the lateness of the season.

Consequently a party of about 250 Icelanders from the vicinity of Kinmount left for the Canadian Northwest on the 21st day of September, this number being considerably increased on the way by additions from other parts of Ontario and from Wisconsin. The party went by rail to Sarnia and there took a steamer to Duluth. Thence the party went by rail to the Red River and came down that highway of those times on a steamer and barges. Quite a few of the party, mostly single people remained in Winnipeg, but the bulk made as speedy preparations as possible to go to "New Iceland."

The party secured a number of so-called flatboats, on which they loaded themselves and their supplies, and started from Winnipeg, for Lake Winnipeg, on October 17th. The current carried the fleet down to the mouth of the Red River, which was a very slow sail, occupying four days. According to an arrangement made with the Hudson's Bay Company their steamer, the "Colville"—the only lake steamer at that time—took the fleet of flatboats in tow at the mouth of the Red River on the morning of the 21st of October, and pulled these frail craft without any serious accident to Willow Harbor—15 miles from the mouth of the river—and the fleet landed there at the sand bar which protects the north side of the harbor, close to the present site of the village of Gimli, on the afternoon of the same day, at 4:30 o'clock.

Although it froze up a few days after these plucky pioneers landed at Willow Bar, they managed to build themselves log shanties and pull through a long and extremely severe winter.

Thus was the first and largest Icelandic settlement in the Canadian Northwest formed—a settlement which, in spite of several misfortunes in its early days, now contains some 2,500 prosperous people.

Transaction No. 59, read March 22, 1901.

Michael Sherbinin in 1907

MICHAEL SHERBININ
(1856-1940)

THIS PAPER WAS PRESENTED BEFORE THE SOCIETY AT A time when Ukrainians in Winnipeg and Manitoba were the victims of a great deal of persecution and racism. The author, Michael Sherbinin, is certainly one of the most interesting of the thousands of newcomers flooding into Manitoba during the first decade of this century. A Russian count from what is now Ukraine, he lived in this province from 1901 to 1911. He was a follower of Leo Tolstoy, the great Russian author, pacifist, and Christian anarchist whose worldview idealized the simple life of the Russian peasant. Sherbinin became a Protestant and worked for the Protestant Religious Tract Society, which in Imperial Russia was sufficient grounds for exile to Finland.

In 1901 Michael Sherbinin was brought to Canada by a Quaker group to be a teacher among the Doukhobors, a religious sect that had also been persecuted in Russia. They settled in the Rosthern area of Saskatchewan with the help of Count Tolstoy, among others. When he first arrived in Winnipeg, Sherbinin lived with Cyril Genik, another educated Ukrainian living in the city. He went to Saskatchewan as a Presbyterian missionary and teacher among the Doukhobors until their autocratic leader, Peter Veregin, arrived and forbade them to go to Sherbinin's school.

Back in Winnipeg, Sherbinin taught English and other subjects to young Ukrainian student teachers and ministers at Manitoba College. With the help of his wife, he established a non-denominational mission, The Stranger's Rest, on Schultz Street, between Magnus and Burrows. There, Mrs. Sherbinin helped young Ukrainian mothers adapt to life in Canada, providing a day care and teaching sewing. The Sherbinins operated a boy's training school where such skills as boot repair were taught to enable immigrant boys to earn a living. With J.S. Woodsworth, Sherbinin held non-denominational prayer meetings.

In 1908, two years after delivering the paper reprinted here, Sherbinin broke with the Presbyterian Church because he was accused of being a socialist who lured some of his young Manitoba College students to move to the socialist Shevchenko Hall. He quarrelled with some of his former patrons, including Charles Gordon, the minister of St. Stephen's Presbyterian Church. Writing as Ralph Connor, Gordon used Sherbinin as the model for the character Michael Kalmar in his novel *The Foreigner*. Sherbinin was stung by the insulting portrayal of Ukrainians in Gordon's book.

Experiences such as this one motivated Sherbinin to try to break down barriers between immigrants and the English-speaking majority in Winnipeg. In the 1909 Christmas issue of the *Tribune*, he celebrated the cosmopolitan diversity of Winnipeg, taking an imaginary walk along Main Street from Portage Avenue to the Canadian Pacific Station, making positive comments about all the different nationalities one might see along the way. Many Canadians felt that people like the Ukrainians were just too alien to ever fit in and Sherbinin probably had this in mind when he wrote: "It is wonderful when one comes to think of it how the west swallows up all these people that come into it, and how in a few years they have dropped much of their former nationality and taken on so much of the Canadian in its place."[1]

In another newspaper piece he pleaded for fair treatment of Ukrainian men looking for work, offering to find workers for anyone who sent him requests.[2] He described the heart-breaking case of a Ukrainian who had followed a man delivering firewood all day, looking for a job splitting logs. No one would hire him because he was a "foreigner."

---

1. *Winnipeg Tribune*, December 18, 1909, p. 46.
2. *Manitoba Free Press*, March 18, 1909.

In these newspaper pieces, Sherbinin tried to counter prejudice with rational argument, and appealed to simple human kindness. In this *Transaction*, Sherbinin provides his audience with a brief, and somewhat romantic, history of Ukraine. By emphasizing the "common ground" between the histories and even the languages of Ukraine and Britain, Sherbinin is making his case for Anglo-Canadians to accept the newcomers from eastern Europe.

While he lived in Winnipeg, Sherbinin also produced a "Christian Catechism," the first Ukrainian language book published in Canada, and the "Handbook of the Ruthenian Language," which was very much in demand among language learners.

In 1911 his wife's poor health led the Sherbinins to leave Winnipeg for Chicago. He lived and worked there until his death in 1940.[3]

---

3. For a biography of Michael Sherbinin, see George Knysh, *Michael Sherbinin in Winnipeg: A Preliminary Study* (Winnipeg: Ukrainian Academy of Arts and Sciences in Canada, 1994).

Galicians Dwelling in
Canada and Their Origin

IN STUDYING A NEW PEOPLE IT IS GOOD TO KNOW BOTH wherein they differ from us and also wherein they are like us.

It seems to me that although both methods of studying a nation are useful, the second one or the one where we look into the common ground that a people has with us, is more interesting and gratifying. By beginning a study from all points of similarity between us and a new people, we will see that the points wherein that people is unlike us, will gradually be reduced and partly even vanish away.

We would dwell on the people commonly called here Galicians, known also under the more scientific name of Ruthenians (or Little Russians).

The Ruthenian language belongs to the same family of languages as English, French, Latin, Greek, Gaelic and Welsh, that is to the Aryan family of languages. The Encyclopaedia Britannica tells us that Aryan means honorable and noble. . . .

SIMILAR TO ENGLISH

In traveling over a settlement of Slavic people we would be astonished to find from 5 to 800 words which have some similarity with English, Latin, French and Welsh.

"Andrey ore ploohom"

would mean: Andrew plows with the plough, where "ore" reminds us of Latin "arare" to plow and of "arable" land in English. "Marina pase hoosy" means: Mary feeds the geese. "Tomko pase swyni" means: Tom feeds the swine. Pasty means to feed or to tend a flock and therefore pastor means pastyr in Ruthenian. "I am the good shepherd" sounds: "Ya yesm pastyr dobry" in Ruthenian.

Surely the ancestors of the Ruthenians and of those who speak the English tongue spoke languages much similar to each other. We need not consult many books to find the truth of it. Take for instance such phrases as this: "Bystra struja rushila cherez dolynu." It means: The boisterous stream rushed over the dale. "Pohanskij hetman lezhav prosterty pered tzarem" means: The pagan chief lay prostrate before the tzar (or the king, which means practically the same thing).

And to change the subject into one more idyllic:

How would that phrase sound in Galician:

"The sister is sitting a while in the garden and is plaiting a garland from roses, periwinkle and tulips."

"Sestra sydyt' hvylu oo horodi i plete girlandu z rozh, barvinku i tuli-paniw."

Then we ought not to be astonished in seeing a common ground which both languages have in words handed down to them by the Christian religion such as Angel, Archangel, Apostol, Kleric (Cleric), Parochialny, Episcop, Presveeter (Presbyter), Diakon (Deacon), Eucharistia, Christiane, which sound almost alike in both languages. . . .

THE AGE OF VIKINGS

And now here we will recall some interesting events which England and the duchy of Russ, from which these Galicians spring, had in common.

You will remember that the first Danes or Northmen who came to England made their first incursions in 789. About that time the Northmen came to the north of France and imposed their power on Normandy. These incursions of the Northmen continued all through the IX Century and we know that the wave of these Scandinavian Vikings, whom some historians call pirates, broke against England, France, Paris, Sicily, Naples and other lands.

It is these very Northmen who reigned in England as Danish kings from 1014 to 1044, and then under the name of Normans from 1066 to 1104, who settled also in Iceland in 861 and in Russia in 862. They wore the some coat of mail; the same pointed helmets, and spoke the same language, probably with a few distinctions of dialect.

These Northmen would impose their rule on the nations whom they subdued; sometimes they would share the power along with the assembly of the people as in the Republic of Novgorod in Russ or Russia of today; sometimes they would form a corps d'elite or a praetorian guard of more powerful rulers as in the instance of Constantinople, and would help these monarchs in their campaigns against other powers. . . .

The conception of an unbroken succession of princes ruling in Russia's towns and duchies is wrong, as in the eleventh, twelfth and thirteenth centuries Russia had several republics with more or less developed rights.

The chief republics were those of Novgorod and Pskov. Novgorod was a flourishing town belonging to the Hanseatic League and inhabited by many foreign merchants.

This powerful republic, which styled itself as "the Lord, the great Novgorod," was annexed to the principality of Moscow by John III in 1478. It was sacked and crushed by John the Terrible in 1570, who brutally murdered several of its citizens.

Among the Slavs of the Russian principalities two opposite tendencies were continually at work; the tendency to aggregation and national unity and the tendency to dispersion and independence.

A centripetal tendency characterizes the North, or Russia, while the tendency to independence or a centrifugal force is dominant in the South or in Oukraina.

NO DISCRIMINATION, OBEY!

The ideal of Russia is to yield to the will of the majority, to the power of the prince, to have the individual will drowned in the Will of the ruler. A Russian carries that principle so far that with him obedience, subordination, and, if necessary, patient endurance, is the greatest virtue. To this principle everything else is sacrificed. Motto: Obey and don't discriminate. The will of the individual is often crushed before the will of society or state. This is the centripetal ideal of Russia.

INDIVIDUAL FREEDOM.

On the other hand, what ideal do we see in Oukraina? A love of liberty, respect of individual opinion, and that craving for individual freedom is so great that sometimes, if carried to an extreme, it weakens the welfare of the community. The Little Russian, or Galician, can stand for his opinion. He can sometimes hold it with a rare obstinacy, and he will stand for his convictions. He is bred in an atmosphere of comparative freedom.

Ruric's great-grandson, whose old Norse name, Valdemar (Ruler of the Sea), was corrupted into Volodimer and Vladimir (972-1015), embraced Christianity and married the daughter of a Greek Caesar. Valdemar, who had been a cruel and sensual heathen prince, is told to have undergone a thorough change after his conversion. He became mild, hospitable, thoughtful and spent much in charities.

This prince is called Vladimir the Great by his people, and his name has been woven into the folklore, as a successor of the pagan divinities whom he destroyed.

Although the title of kniaz, which these rulers bore, is translated by prince, we are entitled to interpret it as king, as it is practically derived from the Scandinavian konung or king.

One of Vladimir's descendants, worthy of the name of king, was Yaroslav the Wise, 1116-1154. He edited the Code of Laws. He occupied a glorious place among the princes of his time. His sister Mary was married to Casimir, King of Poland; his daughters also became the wives of kings; Elizabeth of Harold the Brave, King of Norway; Anne of Henry I, King of France; Anastasia of Andrew I, King of Hungary.

Of his sons, Vladimir, the eldest, is said to have married Githa, daughter of Harold, King of England; Isiaslav, a daughter of Micislas 11, King of Poland; Vseslav, a Greek princess, daughter of Constantine Monomachus; Viatcheslav and Igor, two German princesses.

Yaroslav gave an asylum to the proscribed princes, Saint Olaf, King of Norway, and his two sons; a prince of Sweden; Edwin and Edward, sons of Edmund Ironside, King of England, expelled from their country by Knut the Great.

It is very important to note that the humane and mild element not only characterizes the reign of Vladimir the Great, after his conversion, but this spirit of mildness is also the chief trait of Yaroslav the Wise's legislation. He is reputed to have published the first code of law known among the ancestors of the Ruthenians, as the Ruskaya Prava (the Russian law).

Capital punishment, death by refinements of cruelty, torture, even a public prison were unknown. These are Scandinavian principles in all their purity.

The descendants and successors of Yaroslav the Wise were often contending for power, and as there was no law in force for the succession to the throne, the principality of a deceased king was divided into several parts, according to the number of his sons.

It is only the Mongolian conquest that partly put an end to these quarrels between the princes. The Tatar armies, numbering 500,000 warriors, flooded the plains of Rus. The princes of the House of Ruric joined their ranks to have a deciding battle with the terrible foe. Such a battle was fought at the Kalka river, near the Azof sea, in 1224.

Danilo, who later on was crowned as King of Rus in 1253, had joined the other Russian princes in the battle of Kalka. In it the princes of Rus were defeated and this defeat resulted in two and a half centuries of humiliation of Ruric's descendants when they became but vassals of the Mongolian Khans.

It was only in 1480 that John III emancipated Rus from the Mongolian yoke.

King Danilo, of whom we spoke above, reigned in Galicia and his subjects were the ancestors of the Ruthenians of Galicia.

Before the Tatars evacuated Russia, Galicia and Oukraina became parts of the kingdom of Lithuania, and its prince, Olgerd, gave the Tatar invaders a heavy blow by repelling them into their plains.

In 1386 the Lithuanian Prince Yagailo married the Polish Princess

Hedvige, and was crowned King of Poland in 1386 in the city of Crakow.

In the fifteenth and sixteenth centuries the Turks and Tatars, which are akin to them, raided the settlements of Oukraina, and the population, who had to protect themselves against these incursions, banded themselves into a permanent army, the army of the Cozaks (Cossacks).

This army at last concentrated on an island situated on the river Dnieper, some hundred and fifty miles north of the Black sea. The centre of culture was in the city of Kiev, where during centuries academies flourished, and while the kingdom of the Moscow Tsars groped in darkness and ignorance, Kiev abounded with learned men who were versed in Latin, Greek and Slavonic, and who influenced even the northern Russian towns by their culture. . . .

Several centuries were spent in Oukraina in this struggle with the Tartars and also the Poles, who succeeded in holding their power for a time over Kiev and whose realm reached at a time from the Baltic to the Black Sea. After a war with the Poles, the leader of the army of Cozaks, Bogdan Chmelnitski, on conferring with his people resolved to apply to the Tsar of Moscow, Alexis, asking the protection of Moscow against the outward foes.

An alliance was then concluded between the Tsar of Russia, Alexis Michaelovitch, and the Republic of Kozaks, at Pereyaslav, and then Oukraina enters upon a new period of her history.

This event took place in 1654, when Oliver Cromwell ruled over the Commonwealth of England.

Galicia which had been meanwhile under the power of Poland during three centuries, became a province of Austria in 1772. The farming and working classes of the Ruthenian nationality were in an oppressed economical condition although for the last 50 years the poorer classes were somewhat better favored with schools than in Russia.

Another province of Austria, Boukovina, is mostly inhabited by Ruthenians known as Boukovinians. These people had been for a long time under the power of Moldavian gospodars or princes and have been less privileged with good schools than Galicia. The Boukovinians adhere to the Greek Church.

During centuries the learned classes wrote in a kind of archaic dialect which was a mixture of the church language with the vernacular Ruthenian. In Russia, after the alliance of 1654, the educated classes gradually gave up their mother tongue to use the Russian language for literature.

Some 65 years ago a patriot of Oukraina, John Kotlarevski, started a literature in the vernacular tongue. His example was followed by others and now several periodicals are being printed in that language both in Austria, Russia and America.

The national poet of the Ruthenians is Taras Shevtchenko (literally: Taras Shoemaker's-son). This son of the people, born in the province of Kiev, displayed great literary talent. He was privileged to receive his education in St. Petersburg and was developed as an eminent painter and poet. His name is a rallying-point for the national feeling of the Ruthenians and a national watch-word. His songs are filled with mournful tones, recording the wars of Oukraina and the oppression of a portion of the people in serfdom. Taras was himself born as a serf and some rich friends succeeded in purchasing his liberty.

He fell into disgrace with the Emperor owing to some temerity in the use of his pen and had to serve eight years as a common soldier on the sandy banks of the lake of Aral in Central Asia. This shattered his health and although permitted to return to his country, he died after three years in 1861.

The following verses are Shevtchenko's legacy to his people which we have endeavored to render in English rhyme, as near as possible to the original:

> Learn from other men, my brethren,
>   Love to think, love reading;
> Hear from strangers' lips the teaching
>   Yours by far exceeding!
> Hold fast to your fathers' wisdom
>   And learn from another,

For God's doom awaits the traitor,
   who forgets his mother.
Strangers will forsake him likewise,
   No good will befall him,
Both his kindred and the stranger
   An outcast will call him.

OUR GALICIANS.

The Galicians residing in Canada have proved that they can thrive as an agricultural people. They are fond of locating on bushy and slightly hilly homesteads and also near watercourses, reminding them of their old country. They understand living on very scanty provisions in the first years of their settlement and, after some years of toil, they have succeeded in obtaining here a measure of welfare which the Canadian soil and people are extending to them.

They find here ample scope for gratifying their love of liberty, and some of them have so far been identified with their new conditions, that they are proud and happy to be called Canadians.

In this respect they are faithful to the standpoint of the old Slav, who tried to identify himself with all people whose language he could understand.

Transaction No. 71, read April 19, 1906.

Charles Napier Bell, March 1871

CHARLES N. BELL

(1854-1936)

CHARLES NAPIER BELL WAS ONE OF THE FOUNDERS OF THE
Manitoba Historical and Scientific Society, serving as president in 1889
and again from 1913 to 1929. Along with Professor Chester Martin,
Provincial Librarian W.J. Healy, and others, he revived the society in
the late 1920s and early 1930s, the "Old Forts of Winnipeg" being
one of the products of that revival.

Charles Bell was born in Ontario, like so many of the other early
immigrants to Winnipeg. A native of Perth, he was the son of the
Registrar of Lanark County and the grandson of the first Presbyterian minister in the county. Bell had a taste for adventure, and in 1866,
at the age of twelve, he ran off to join the Perth Rifle Company as a
bugler, to fight the Fenians. A much greater adventure presented itself
four years later when he set out for the west with Garnet Wolseley, again
as a bugler. He travelled west with the young Sam Steele, later a famous
officer of the North West Mounted Police and the commander of Lord
Strathcona's Horse in the South African war. The two men remained
close friends and in their later years were neighbours in Winnipeg.

Like many other troops who came west with the Wolseley Expedition, Bell did not return to Ontario. He spent a year, in 1872-73, hunting and trading along the Saskatchewan River. Lieutenant-Governor
Morris asked him to write a report on his experiences when he returned to Manitoba, and, in his report, he commented on the wild
game situation, especially the state of the buffalo herds.

Bell began working in Winnipeg as a custom's officer for the Dominion. In 1886 he became secretary-treasurer of the Grain Exchange

and the next year he was hired to be secretary of the Winnipeg Board of Trade. He had various business interests, and he became the secretary of the Winnipeg Industrial Bureau, in its building at Main and Water streets, upon its completion in 1912.

He was a fellow of the Royal Geographical Society and was eventually given an honorary degree by the University of Manitoba for his work with the Manitoba Historical Society. He belonged to many other societies, among them the Minnesota Historical Society and the Geographical Society of San Francisco. As the Grand Master of the Masonic Lodge in 1895, it was Bell who laid the cornerstone of the new Masonic Temple at the corner of Ellice Avenue and Donald Street. He was the original secretary of the Winnipeg Industrial Exhibition in 1891 and he served as president of the local Canadian Club in 1912.

Charles Bell was an athlete of some note when he was young, especially in the sport of skating. He was famous for having skated from Winnipeg to Selkirk on the Red River in just two and one quarter hours in 1877, and he was also a talented figure skater. He coached speed skater Jack McCulloch, who won the 1897 World Speed Skating Championship in Montréal, and he is credited with having introduced figure skating into western Canada.

But it is Bell's passion for history that interests us here. On the second floor of his house at 121 Carlton, he created a fine library, containing many rare maps of western Canada and a remarkable collection of books, some of which he used in writing this paper. Bell's maps were bequeathed to Queen's University.

W.E. Ingersoll later remembered that "if you were a special friend he would take you home and show you the latest musty old paper he had acquired for the Manitoba Historical Society. . . . These papers were ancient and some were smelly with age; but Charlie Bell was always able to point out that there was some special reason that they should be in the possession of the MHS."[1] Ingersoll's amused tolerance was probably shared by many fellow Winnipeggers, unaware of

---

1. Winnipeg *Free Press*, May 11, 1963.

Bell's role in saving a great deal of historical documentation from destruction.

Bell was intelligently curious about the world around him; his interests included natural as well as human history. Among his friends was A.H.R. Buller, a noted botanist and professor at the University of Manitoba, who lived nearby and visited often. Bell's daughter remembered going on nature hikes at Lower Fort Garry and at their summer cottage at Minaki with her father. [2]

"The Old Forts of Winnipeg" is one of the possible research topics mentioned by Bell when he became society president in 1889; he finally wrote about them in 1927. In his introduction, Bell states he is writing the piece to provide the society with answers to the frequent questions received about these old structures. But it is also clear that he is pursuing an old interest, born the day many years before when he and his friend Sam Steele discovered the remains of Fort Gibraltar on the bank of the Assiniboine River.

In this paper we see Bell, the careful researcher, at work: he recorded all the written sources he could find on the topic and intelligently compared and evaluated them; he interviewed elderly Selkirk Settlers in the 1880s, checking the transcript of the interview with them and comparing their statements with written sources for corroboration. About the only negative thing that can be said about Bell's work is that it may contain the longest run-on sentences ever written.

Bell was described as "a genial, sunny soul, who seems to carry a summery atmosphere with him."[3] This personality, combined with his passionate interest in the subject, made him one of the Historical Society's most effective activists. [4]

---

2. Winnipeg *Free Press*, March 6, 1971.

3. *Winnipeg Tribune*, Feb. 18, 1911.

4. Information for this introduction was taken from the various clippings under "C.N. Bell" in the *Biographical Scrapbooks*, Legislative Library of Manitoba.

The Old Forts of Winnipeg

AS YOUR PRESIDENT, I AM VERY FREQUENTLY CALLED upon to afford information as to some one book which gives a concise description of all the fur traders' forts, established on the site of the present City of Winnipeg, with some particulars of the cause of their establishment. I frankly confess that I have had to reply that there is no book that I know of which gives the local history of Winnipeg in the direction referred to. Consequently, in response to many requests, I am endeavouring to give, in a condensed form, what information regarding these forts I have obtained by perusal of printed and written records available to me, combined with a personal knowledge of the ground comprised in the Winnipeg area during 57 years' residence here, and many conversations and interviews had with several of the last surviving members of the original Selkirk settlers, all of whom have long since passed away. I am fully aware of my temerity in attempting such an undertaking, but can only say in explanation that I am endeavouring to give the citizens of Winnipeg some knowledge of the history of their own city, culled from many sources not available, and, in fact, unknown, to the great majority of our people. I make no excuse, however, for placing on record the facts connected with the establishing of some of the fur trading posts, or, as they were generally termed, trading forts, which have never adequately been brought into the light so that we, living in Winnipeg, can understand and appreciate some important events in our history.

I will now review, necessarily keeping within the scope of a paper of this description, the information I have gained concerning the forts of Winnipeg. It is to be always understood that in the early days of the fur trade, in Western Canada, whether under French or British occupation, practically every trading post, especially if it was protected by palisades, was called a "fort.". . .

[Before discussing the old fur-trade forts of Winnipeg, Bell examines a "Fort Maurepas," which erroneously appears at the forks of the Red and Assiniboine rivers on some early maps.]

FORT ROUGE

It has been generally accepted, and passed on, by many writers on the subject, that Fort Rouge was built by Verendrye himself in 1738, when he made his first voyage of discovery from Fort Maurepas, at the mouth of the Winnipeg River, through Lake Winnipeg and up the Red and Assiniboine Rivers to the Mandans of the Missouri River. It is passing strange how readily this idea, erroneous as it is in fact, has prevailed. An authentic copy and translation of Verendrye's journal, or narrative, for the years 1738-39, is to be found, as in several other places, in the annual report of the Canadian Archives Department, 1889, and when hereafter I use the words "Verendrye's Journal," I refer, unless otherwise specifically stated, to this particular document, of which the opening paragraph is as follows:

> Journal in the form of a letter, from the 20th of July, 1738, date of my departure from Michilimakinak, to May, 1739, sent to the Marquis de Beauharnois, Commander of the Military Order of St. Louis, Governor and Lieutenant-General of the whole of New France, lands and country of Louisiana, by his very humble servant, Laverendrye, lieutenant of a company of the detachment of the Marine in Canada, commissioned by his orders for the discovery of the Western Sea.

There is not one word in this paragraph relating to trading in furs, but the journal reveals that at least one principal object of his expedition was the discovery and examination of the strange people called the Mandans, who, the Indians questioned had reported, were white men like the French, having a light complexion, blonde hair and blue eyes, and that they lived upon a great stream which flowed to the ocean.

Now, let us examine the journal itself to ascertain just what small part Verendrye himself announces he actually had in the establishment of Fort Rouge. After leaving the French fort or post at Kaministiquia on the 6th August, 1738, where "I had your orders published and left a copy with the French who keep the fort concerning that post, and that of Tekamamihouenne (Fort St. Pierre, Rainy Lake), to be handed to M. de Lamarque, who was to arrive there at an early date," he proceeded on his western journey. On the 22nd August, he was at Rainy Lake, and then went on to Fort St. Charles at the west end of the Lake of the Woods. There he writes:

> I deferred leaving until the 11th of September, waiting for Mr. de Lamarque, to whom I had promised not to hasten, so as to give him the opportunity of joining me, he having promised me at Michilimakinak to make haste, so that he might come with me in the autumn for the discovery of the Mandans. Seeing on the 10th of the month that he had not arrived, and everything being in good order, I left on the 11th, hoping that he would join me soon to come with me.

Verendrye arrived at Fort Maurepas, at the mouth of the Winnipeg River, on the 22nd September, where he examined the arms, published the Governor's Orders concerning the post, gave a copy of it to Mr. Lariviere (misprint in Archives copy. Should be D'Amours de Louviere), clerk to these gentlemen, (that is, to his creditors in Montreal) and selected five of his men to take with him. His next sentence is: "I went to the Fork of the Asiliboiles (Assiniboine) on the 24th. (Sept.), where I found ten Cree huts and two war chiefs, who expected me, with a quantity of meat, having been notified that I was coming."

It is somewhat strange that Verendrye gives no description of his voyage across Lake Winnipeg and up the Red River, and, as Indians were at the Forks awaiting him, it would appear that he was quite well informed on the route he had just traversed, and was in some measure at least in touch with the Assiniboine River Indians. His description of the country commences with his journey up the Assiniboine, of which river it is quite clear he previously had no personal experience after waiting at the Forks (he says in his tent) for only two days to banquet with the Indians, he sent on the canoes up the Assiniboine, and himself proceeded on foot on the north side, and so continued until he arrived on the 2nd October at the prairie portage (now Portage la Prairie), where the Indians of that region passed north to Lake Manitoba, and so on down to conduct their trade with the English (Hudson's Bay Company's traders or posts). While avowedly desirous of ascending farther, probably to the Souris, where the regular route to the Mandan country started, as proved by the accounts of all travelers and traders after his time, he found that the stage of water in the Assiniboine was unusually low, and so could not proceed further up with his canoes. He emphasized that he had no resources to repair canoes, having neither gum nor resin, and, therefore, after careful examination of the land, he built Fort la Reine, which, for many years following, was the centre of the French operations in the western country.

The journal now informs us in express terms who did build the post, always since referred to as Fort Rouge.

> On the 9th October, Mr. de Lamarque, with the Sieur Nolant, his brother, and eight men, in two canoes, arrived, which gave me much pleasure. I testified my gratitude to Mr. De Lamarque for the trouble he had taken to bring us reinforcements. I questioned him if he had left many people at Fort St. Charles, Lake of the Woods, and whom he had left at Maurepas. He answered me that he had left eight men at the first, with two traders, having brought all the canoes he had, not because he hoped to be able to load them, not having been able to bring the heavy goods, but that he had promised he would join me, and did not wish to break his word, that I

required people for my expedition, that he had brought them without injury to himself, not requiring his people during the winter. I thanked him, telling him that if he joined in our expedition, he would be saved, himself and all his people, the expense until they returned. He told me he wished to share the expense. I answered that that could not be, it was enough for me that he supplied the men and himself without the necessity of sharing the expense, which I had already provided for. I gave him room, at his request, in my fort, to build a house to lodge all his people. **Mr. de Lamarque told me he had brought Mr. de Louviere to the Forks, with two canoes, to build a fort there for the accommodation of the people of the Red River. I approved of it if the Indians were notified** *[Bell's emphasis]*.

There can be no doubt, in view of the above explicit statement by Verendrye himself, that it was de Lamarque who built Fort Rouge, and that his status was that of an independent gentleman (probably representing Verendrye's eastern creditors), but certainly a valued and trusted friend to Verendrye. The latter, in many places later on in his journal, refers to de Lamarque as being treated as an equal, consulted in all matters of importance, and sharing in all matters connected with their life and hardships as an intimate friend and companion. And this friendly relationship was extended also to de Lamarque's brother, the Sieur Nolant. Benj. Sulte affords the information that de Lamarque (Jean Nolant) was born in Quebec in 1694, and under his mother's name became the companion of La Verendrye.

Judge Prud'homme (St. Boniface Historical Society) is my authority for stating that in the spring of 1735 Verendrye himself wrote: "I had, before leaving (June 6, 1735) ceded to my tradesmen the privilege of trading and the business of the posts I had established, the previously interested parties having finished their term," and that this action was taken so that he could devote all his energy, untrammeled by commercial interests, to exploration.

It is foreign to the subject of Fort Rouge to make any extended comments on the expedition of Verendrye and de Lamarque from Fort la Reine to the Mandans on the Missouri, beyond stating that they were unquestionably the first white men to discover the upper Missouri and this Indian Nation, but the latter greatly disappointed the explorers, who had been hoping to find white people, possibly Spaniards, living on a great river that flowed into the "Western Sea." In the spring of 1739, after returning from the Mandan expedition to Fort la Reine, where they were very short of provisions, Mr. de Lamarque left for Fort Maurepas, at which place he heard his people were starving, and from the context of Verendrye's journal, it seems most probable that he visited his outpost at the Forks, although no specific statement to that effect is made. That one winter's occupation apparently comprises the history of the actual existence of Fort Rouge, except that it continued as a place on the maps—a printed name only.

It is to be noted that neither de Lamarque nor Verendrye in the journal names this post as "Fort Rouge," but, on the contrary, it is simply stated that de Lamarque had brought Louviere to the "Forks" to build a fort there for the accommodation of the people (Indians) of the Red River. Neither is it stated on which side of the river it was situated. It is reasonable to assume that the person who drew the 1740 map from the information supplied in the reports of Verendrye, instead of naming it Fort Riviere Rouge decided on the condensed form of Fort Rouge—the Red Fort. Certainly these explorers and traders did not paint their temporary rough barked log structures. It is significant in this connection that Verendrye both hitherto and afterwards named every fort established by him west of Lake Superior, after some high official person. Why did the individual who prepared this map for the Governor of Canada depart from Verendrye's previously invariable policy in selecting names for forts?

The only three writers who, so far as I have read, lay any stress on de Lamarque's connection with Fort Rouge, are Judge Prud'homme (St. Boniface Historical Society, 1916), De Land (State Dept. of History South Dakota, 1914) and Morice (Catholic Church in Western Canada, 1910).

Out of the multitude of books written on Verendrye's journeys, I refer to but two of the more ambitious to illustrate how the main feature of who was responsible for the building of Fort Rouge was completely overlooked. Dr. Bryce (*Five Forts of Winnipeg*, 1886) does not mention de Lamarque, and apparently never heard of him. Burpee (*The Search for the Western Seas*, 1908) merely refers to de Lamarque as a trader taken by Verendrye with him on the Mandan expedition. But then Burpee on two pages preceding had written that it was the two sons of Verendrye who had built both Fort Rouge and Fort La Reine, and this two years before these forts came into existence, which is just another illustration of the danger of relying on second hand authorities when the original documents are available.

The name "Fort Rouge" appears on a map, dated 1740, which, admittedly, was prepared by the Governor of New France from the information contained in Verendrye's journals, and, as thereon the Assiniboine and Red Rivers are shown as running almost parallel for a considerable distance before joining, and thus becoming the "Forks," it was quite natural for the compiler, whoever he was, to assume that the fort was placed in the immediate angle formed by the junction of the two rivers, but to anyone cognizant of the topography of the land on both sides of the Assiniboine River at the Forks, (the south side being relatively very low, subject to spring floods, heavily covered with willows and small trees, and quite open to attack by the fierce and hostile Sioux, who had already killed Verendrye's son, a priest, and nineteen of his men near Fort St. Charles, while the north bank was and still is much higher, and, in fact, the edge of a large prairie area extending both north and west, with a shallow line of heavy timber reaching back from the banks of both streams), common sense would dictate that the side to build on was the north bank, which naturally and invariably afterwards was chosen by the French and British traders for camping ground and building site purposes. Indeed, fortunately, we have evidence regarding the site of Fort Rouge.

Alexander Henry (the nephew) arrived at the Forks in 1800, and his journal, written while in camp on the north bank of the Assiniboine, under date of August 19th, contains the following entry:—"Upon this spot, in the time of the French, there was a trading establishment, traces of which are still to be seen where their chimneys and cellars stood." Henry gives a number of descriptions of his campsite, which quite conclusively prove that he was on the spot where Fort Rouge stood. (See also evidence of John McDonnell in 1793 under "Fort Bruce and Boyer", following). For fully 60 years after de Lamarque erected this fort, which, so far as is known, existed only during the winter of 1738-9, the name "Fort Rouge" appeared on many different European maps, British, French, Dutch and Italian, as if the fort was still in existence. It is curious how that name stuck in the minds of map makers, who copied it one from the other, long after the French had withdrawn from the western country, and even after the occupation of the territory by the British traders from Montreal. An impartial study of the ascertained facts must convince any student that Lamarque built the Fort Rouge post, that it was in existence for probably only one winter, and that it was on the north bank of the Assiniboine River at the Forks. That McDonnell, and afterwards, Henry, at least 50 years after Fort Rouge passed out of existence, should recognize the remains of the post, is quite within the understanding of men like Mr. J. B. Tyrrell (who edited the Champlain Society's Vol. of Thompson), who has located, and even photographed, the remains of many trading posts which had existed nearly a century before. Some forty years ago, I myself, located the ruins of old trading posts, which were erected eighty or more years previously, near the mouth of Souris River, and easily identified the sites by the cellar hollows and scattered chimney materials, and, in cases, the outline of the enclosing stockades could be traced. Also when in 1872-3, as a youth of eighteen years of age, I traveled and hunted in the North Saskatchewan country and far down south into the buffalo areas, my half-breed companions pointed out to me the easily discernable sites of traders' posts erected three-quarters of a century before. Sir Alexander Mackenzie recorded that before 1800 the marks of wheeled carriages and agricultural implements were visible about the old posts of the early French traders situated on the Saskatchewan River below the forks of that river.

LEGARDEUR DE SAINT PIERRE'S FORT

Legardeur de St. Pierre (whose journal or report is in the Canadian Archives report, 1887) in 1750 was appointed by the authorities in Quebec to succeed Verendrye, in charge of the western posts, and arrived, with his Lieutenant de Niverville at Fort Maurepas, situated at the mouth of the Winnipeg River, but the season was so far advanced that it was impossible for de Niverville to travel by canoe to Fort Bourbon on the Saskatchewan River, (his destination) and he and his men were forced to proceed overland on foot from the mouth of the river, carrying their baggage and provisions on their backs or dragging them on small sleds. Finding no provisions at Fort Bourbon, they were exposed to starvation, and passed the winter miserably in a state of famine. M. de St. Pierre reached Verendrye's Fort La Reine on the Assiniboine, which, having been abandoned since the departure of that explorer and his sons, was dilapidated and devoid of provisions. His report informs us that he started north to join de Niverville, who had become seriously ill, but turned back and did nothing further during the summer of 1751. During the winter of 1751-1752, de St. Pierre had quite an exciting adventure at Fort La Reine. On the 22nd February, he was in the fort with five Frenchmen, having sent the rest of his men out to secure provisions, which he had been without for some days, when 200 armed Assiniboines came into the fort, became very turbulent, and announced to the interpreter that they wanted to pillage the place and kill St. Pierre. The latter no sooner learned of their intention than he seized hold of a burning brand, burst open the door of the powder magazine, and smashed in the head of a barrel of powder, over which he waved the burning torch, which the Indians no sooner beheld than they, in great fear and consternation, fled out of the fort.

After spending the winter of 1751-2 at Fort La Reine, de St. Pierre in the spring left with all his men for Grand Portage, Lake Superior. The adventure of February had so frightened his employees that none of them would consent to remain during the summer to take care of the fort, so he asked the Indians to do so. However, while traveling down the Winnipeg River on his return voyage from Grand Portage, he was informed on the 29th September that four days after his departure from Fort La Reine, the Assiniboine Indians had burned it to the ground. This information, combined with the scarcity of provisions he found prevailing, obliged him to go to spend the winter at the Red River, where game was abundant. At just what point on the Red River he wintered he does not state, but most likely it was at the strategic "Forks," and, with his experience of the turbulent Assiniboines, he undoubtedly erected the customary stockaded protection for his winter houses. (See under "Fort Bruce and Boyer").

It would appear, then, that once again there was a fort, occupied but for one winter, at the Forks, and within the limits of the present City of Winnipeg.

St. Pierre was succeeded in 1753 by the Chevalier de la Corne, who caused to be built a fort below the juncture of the two branches of the Saskatchewan River, and named it Fort La Corne, which name was recognized by the first British Montreal Traders, and has continued for that place to the present day. In 1756 all the western posts were abandoned by the French, whose regime west of Lake Superior terminated.

FORT BRUCE AND BOYER

A partner of the Northwest Company, John McDonnell, while serving in the interests of his company on the Assiniboine and Qu'Appelle Rivers, in 1793-5, kept a quite complete journal, extracts from which are included in Masson's *Bourgeois de la Compagnie du Nord-Ouest*. Writing of the old French forts of the Red and Assiniboine rivers, he placed the following information on record: "At the Forks, the remains of several old posts are still to be seen, some of which were built as far back as the time of the French Government"; and again—

> three leagues above Portage la Prairie stood Le Fort des Trembles, or Poplar Fort. In the year 1780 or 1781, the Indians made an attempt to pillage the traders, Messrs. Bruce and Boyer, and, in the scuffle that ensued, two Frenchmen and seven Indians were killed upon the spot. Owing to this affair, the traders were obliged, for fear of being cut off, to re-embark their canoes

and return to winter at the Forks. The smallpox seizing the natives, and sweeping off three-fourths of them, compelled them to lay aside their intention of cutting off all the white men in the interior country.

This is a definite statement, afterwards in all essentials corroborated by Alex. Henry (nephew) in 1806 that a fort was in existence at The Forks in 1781. Sir Alexander Mackenzie in his book makes a short reference to the fight at Fort des Trembles, but says nothing of the traders' retreat to The Forks.

It is not clear from any of the accounts whether Bruce and Boyer were employees of one of the large trading concerns antedating the formation of the Northwest Company, or independent traders from Lake Superior. Boyer certainly was in the employ of the Northwest Company in 1787, when he was sent to the Peace River by Sir Alex. Mackenzie to establish a fort, and remained there for two years. Of Bruce nothing further seems to be on record.

In view of the fighting that had taken place, it may be safely assumed that Bruce and Boyer, with nearly a score of men, had their post well protected in case of an Indian attack. John McDonnell's statement, that in 1793 the remains of several old posts were still visible, which had been in existence during the French regime and before the British traders from Montreal had reached the Forks is, like the evidence of Henry in 1800, valuable as locating where Louviere in 1738, and likely St. Pierre in 1753, had each passed at least one winter on the north bank of the Assiniboine, where the latter stream merges with the Red River. It is especially valuable as a record that this post of Bruce and Boyer was the first fort we know of as built at the Forks by British traders following the close of the old French regime.

ALEXANDER HENRY'S "THE FORKS'S FORT"

Alexander Henry (the nephew), a partner of the North West Company, left us a journal, which includes a lengthy account of his life on the Red River during the years 1800-8. I was fortunate enough to discover this journal in the Library of Parliament at Ottawa in 1887,

Charles Bell's map of the old forts in Winnipeg. 1. The "mythical" Fort Maurepas, and also Fort Rouge, Fort Legardeur de St. Pierre, Fort Bruce and Boyer, Fort Alexander Henry, and original Fort Gibraltar; 2. Fort Douglas; 3. Fidler's Fort; 4. original Fort Garry; 5. second Fort Garry; and 6. traditional H.B.C. post.

and extracts from it form the substance of three papers read before the Manitoba Historical Society in 1888 (*Transactions* Nos. 31, 35 and 37), or nine years before the talented Dr. Elliot Coues published it in full with such extensive and wonderfully explanatory notes in three volumes under the title of *New Light on the Early History of the Great North West*. Henry, on September 27th, 1803, established, as an out-post of his main trading fort at Pembina, a small trading post at the Forks, under the charge of one Louis Dorion. Henry, under date of January 19th, 1804, recorded that he visited this post for inspection, and found Dorion practically starving through lack of provisions; and about two weeks later, on reaching this establishment for the second time, found his men starving, as were also his people at Portage la Prairie. As a consequence of Dorion's experience, the post was discontinued the following year, and so another "fort" at the Forks disappeared.

It is interesting to have a record of the furs that Dorion, in conjunction with another outpost, existing at the same time, at the Dead River (now Netley Creek), secured in trade for the North West Company. The list includes: 350 beavers, 24 black bears, 16 brown bears, 52 fishers, 35 otters, 200 martens, 146 wolverines and 700 muskrats, and a considerable mixed lot of other furs.

All the traders, who have left us journals describing their life and movements in the Red and Assiniboine rivers country, give more or less extensive notes regarding the Forks, which was the rendezvous where the brigades of canoes and boats, arriving from both Lake Superior and James Bay, re-sorted their trading goods to fill the assignments destined for the various posts and outposts scattered along both rivers up into the interior. Winnipeg's status as a distributing centre certainly dates from this period.

In Henry's journal we get a sidelight into the customs which prevailed at The Forks in 1806, when it is related that Henry, returning from an inspection of his post at Portage la Prairie to take to Fort William his brigade of boats laden with the winter's trade of furs at Grand Forks and Pembina and their outposts, joined his men at The Forks, and on the 4th June "played with J. McKenzie of the H. B. Co., with drum, fife, etc., and drank out a ten gallon keg of brandy." It is to be hoped that the brandy was the diluted article called "trade liquor," but in any case both parties were able to leave next day en route for Albany House on James Bay, and Fort William, Lake Superior.

FORT GIBRALTAR

The autobiographical notes of John McDonald of Garth, a partner of the North West Company, which are to be found in Masson's Volume 2, under date of 1807, contain the following passage:

"I established a fort at the junction of the Red and Assiniboine

Second Fort Gibraltar, 1821

rivers, and called it 'Gibraltar,' though there was not a rock or stone within three miles."

Thus was established Fort Gibraltar, the headquarters of not only the fur trade of the North West Company on the Red, Assiniboine and Qu'Appelle Rivers, and country adjacent to these streams, but of the operations of that company against the Hudson's Bay Company, following the establishment of the Selkirk Colony, which came into existence in 1812, with the arrival of the first contingent of Selkirk settlers.

Fort Gibraltar was erected on the north side of the Assiniboine River, where that stream joins the Red River, and extended somewhat along the bank of the latter. In the year 1871, following my service as a soldier of the Red River expedition, under General Wolseley, which reached Fort Garry in 1870 via the old fur traders' route from Lake Superior to Winnipeg, in company with my friend Corporal (afterwards General) Sam B. Steele, I took a walk down the Assiniboine from Fort Garry a few hundred yards to the traditional site of Fort Gibraltar, and there, plainly to be seen very near to the edge of the bank, were recognizable hollows representing cellars, and the mixture of semi-calcined limestone, remains of chimneys, and while at that time we were rather hazy on the subject of the history of Fort Gibraltar, it was clear to us that buildings of some kind had been on that ground, though it was also evident that almost the whole area of the enclosure that had once been there had disappeared into the river through the washing away and crumbling in of the banks. Steele drew to my attention several much decayed human bones and one skull close to the water's edge, which had apparently rolled down from near the funeral ground level of the bank through under-mining by the heavy spring flood. (Henry in 1800 refers to the extensive Indian graveyard hereabouts). I am quite satisfied that the hollows and chimney debris which we then saw were the last remains of Fort Gibraltar.

I visited, and carefully inspected this site this present month, and found that if not in the two rivers, what remains of it is now buried many feet under the cinders and general refuse of the railway yard of the Canadian National.

It is not necessary for me, in connection with Fort Gibraltar, to give any details of its history after the arrival of the first Selkirk settlers, because the history of that period has been fully covered, not only by the published statements of the North West Company, the Hudson's Bay Company, and Lord Selkirk's Colony Officials, but by a multitude of writers, who have written everything from fact to fiction regarding the aggressive acts of the two companies which took place at that time, culminating on the 17th March, 1816, in the destruction by the order of the Selkirk Colony Governor Semple of Fort Gibraltar, during the absence of the partner in charge, when even the material of the fort was pulled down, floated by the river to Fort Douglas, nearly a mile below, and used to strengthen the Colony Fort; and shortly after in the killing of Semple, the Colony Governor, and a number of his followers by employees of the Northwest Company on the site known as Seven Oaks, in the northern part of Winnipeg. As a result of this clashing of interests, Colonel Coltman was sent by the Governor-General of Canada as commissioner to inquire into the whole facts of the situation, and following this lamentable state of affairs, which almost financially ruined both companies, the rival interests came together and amalgamated under the charter name of the Hudson's Bay Company.

Whether Fort Gibraltar was re-erected by the Northwest Company in 1816 has been somewhat a matter of conjecture. Beckles Willson in *The Great Company*, states that "Fort Gibraltar had been destroyed, but the Northwester's at once set about erecting buildings to carry on their trade."

Hon. Donald Gunn, for years following the year 1813, in the service of the Hudson's Bay Company, finally settling in the Red River Colony, in his book *History of Manitoba*, wrote as follows: "The Northwest Company's fort had been razed to the ground and could not be restored; but that active and energetic body procured new materials, built new houses and stores on the old site, and commenced business anew.". . .

That the Hudson's Bay Company immediately after the amalgamation did do business in a fort at the Forks is also proved by the recorded evidence of eye witnesses like Donald Murray (see statement under "Fidler's Fort"), for the stores of the company at Fort Douglas were closed. (Also see statement of marriage entry in St. John's Church under the heading of "Fort Garry").

FORT DOUGLAS

There was in the early days of the Red River Settlement a floating tradition that the Hudson's Bay Company at one time had a post or fort on the east bank of the Red River, opposite the mouth of the Assiniboine, in what is now St. Boniface, but I have not been able to obtain much information relating to it, and it must have had a very transitory existence. It is true that Arrowsmith's map of the "Interior Parts of North America," which was inscribed by permission to the Hon. Governor and Company of Adventurers of England Trading into the Hudson's Bay, and dated January 1st, 1796, shows that a house was on that site in 1780, but gives no indication as to whether or not it was a Hudson's Bay Company's establishment. I have not come across any definite claim that such a post was established by the Northwest Company, and it is generally accepted that Fort Douglas, erected on the north side of a small coulee, emptying into the Red River, at the foot of what is now Robert and George Avenues, in the City of Winnipeg (I found the coulee outlet through the river bank to be easily discerned as late as this month) was the first Hudson's Bay Company's fort established in the Winnipeg area, and this fort was not only utilized for the stores of the company, but was the official headquarters and residence of the Governor of the Selkirk Colony after the arrival of the settlers in 1812. Fort Douglas, therefore, became the centre of the Hudson's Bay Company's and Red River settlement interests. After the Seven Oaks conflict in 1816, it was temporarily occupied by the officers and employees of the Northwest Company, their own Fort Gibraltar having been previously destroyed by the order of Semple, the Colony Governor.

The detailed history of Fort Douglas, like that of Fort Gibraltar, is so fully covered in the Government reports of the day, and books of many writers, more or less accurate or colored, according to the prejudices of their writers, and which may be obtained in any good Canadian library, that I need not further dilate on the subject.

After the conflicts, Fort Douglas continued to be the residence of the Colony Governor as apart from the Hudson's Bay Company, and one of these, Andrew Bulgar, writing under date of August 4th, 1822, gives a shocking description of the place. His words are:

> As to what is styled Fort Douglas. It is well situated, though there is a better position for a fort about 200 yards higher up, upon the land which Mr. Pritchard gave up. But as to the fort itself, it is, as Mr. Halkett can tell you, the most filthy, miserable place imaginable. It is by at least 25 feet too small, and the stockades are for the most part rotten and tumbling down. The buildings, except one, are mere log huts, very old and so full of holes as to be perfectly unsuitable. The only one that is of any value is what is called the new house, but even this is nothing more than the shell of a badly built log house, being nowhere boarded outside, and having but two rooms finished

inside, and so badly have these been done that the light may be seen through the walls in many places.

I regret that while I secured possession of a large number of letters and documents of that period, which would be very valuable in connection with a description of Fort Douglas, at his request I, many years ago, surrendered all these papers to the late Lord Strathcona, and they are no longer available as historical matter. It so chances, however, that I have in my possession the original official file of the copies of various documents relating to the Red River Settlement, which was given to Captain Robert Parker Pelly as "Governor of Ossiniboia" on his departure from London, 21st May, 1823. When either of the governors of the General Territory of the Hudson's Bay Company was present, the power of the Governor of Ossiniboia was suspended for the time being for judicial purposes.

After the repurchase from the Selkirk estate of his rights under the original deed of sale, the governors came strictly under the authority of the Hudson's Bay Company itself.

The end of Fort Douglas came with the high waters of what is locally called the great flood of 1826, when the people of the settlement were forced to flee from their homes and take refuge for a time on the high grounds of Bird's Hill or Stoney Mountain.

FIDLER'S FORT

In the year 1887 I interviewed Donald Murray, George Bannerman, John Matheson, John Polson and Mrs. Kaufman, all survivors of the original Selkirk Colony, who were old enough at the time of their arrival in 1812-15 to remember the events that transpired in connection with the disputes and local occurrences resulting from the conflict between the rival interests of the Northwest Company, the Hudson's Bay Company and the Selkirk colony government. The evidence of these survivors, bearing on a number of matters not hitherto recorded, is contained in my work *The Selkirk Settlement and the Settlers*, 1887. Evidence of the fort building activities of the two companies following the conflict of 1816 is very meagre, hence the great value of the statements obtained from persons who were residents of this locality during that period.

Mr. Donald Murray, long since deceased, was in that year a wonderfully clear minded and physically active old gentleman, and the information which he afforded me, endorsed by the other survivors, when checked where possible by the official documents of the period, agreed in almost every detail. Mr. Murray, who was born at Kildonan, Sutherlandshire, Scotland, in or about the year 1801, came to the Red River in 1815 with Lord Selkirk's fourth party of colonists, and lived there until his death, consequently he was a participant in, or eye witness of, most of the events and exciting times of what are commonly termed "the Colony Troubles."

In connection with the forts at the mouth of the Red River, Mr. Murray said, his words being taken down in writing at the time and read over to him at the close of the interview:

> The Northwest Company's fort was called "Gibraltar," and stood on the Assiniboine point, at the mouth of that river, but it has now gone into the river a good many years, I think. I do not know of any traces of any earlier fort known as Fort Rouge. The Hudson's Bay Company, however, had a fort which stood close to where Notre Dame Street, East, is now. This was the fort which Dr. Bryce was unable to locate when he wrote his book about the old forts. This fort was built by Peter Fidler about 1817-18, but he went to Brandon House in the latter year, and it was first occupied by one James Sutherland, who finished it in 1819. As nearly as I can now locate its position, it was situated between what is at present McDermot Ave. and Notre Dame St. East, but perhaps nearer Notre Dame than the other. It was near the rise in the ground, and a few hundred yards from the Red River. It was about square, the principal entrance facing exactly to the point between the two rivers. At the farther end, opposite to this gate, stood the master's house, which was larger than the others, which ranged down each side of the palisaded enclosure, about four on each

side, but I do not remember exactly how many there were. There was a walk between them and the palisades, and an open courtyard in the centre. (I still have the plan Mr. Murray drew for me of the fort. —C.N.B.) I often slept in this fort, and in 1818, when I went to Brandon House, I started from it. I do not recall that it had any particular name other than "the Company's Fort." It was quite distinct from the later Fort Garry, and stood at the same time as Forts Douglas and Gibraltar. I forget just when it disappeared, but it probably stood until the flood of 1826, and was then swept away, like the remains of Fort Douglas, then owned by Mr. Logan. If you doubt that this fort was there, just find out about a marriage ceremony I was at in it. I was the only guest from the colony invited, when the following persons were married by the Rev. John West: James Bird, the chief factor, to a daughter of Thomas Thomas; Thos. Thomas, a retired chief factor, to Miss Monture; and Jos. Bird, a son of James, to a Swamp Cree woman.

(Note: I personally examined the marriage register kept by the Rev. John West, still preserved in St. John's Cathedral, Winnipeg, and the above three entries show on the record, and are dated as at Red River Colony—C.N.B.)

It is, I think, certain that Mr. Murray's statement is in strict accord with the fact, and that there was a fort, the existence of which has been lost sight of, built by the Hudson's Bay Company as apart from their then dilapidated Fort Douglas.

Mr. Murray also made the following statement:

Fort Garry (the First) for years was only called "the Company's Fort" by the settlers, and it was not until the last fort was erected that it was regularly called Fort Garry, though, of course, that was its proper name for years before.

The Hudson's Bay Company used an old building that stood about two or three hundred yards north of Fort Gibraltar as a stable. That was after the companies joined. I do not know if they ever had a fort there before, but they used that old building as a stable when they moved out, and occupied the Northwest Company's fort about 1821. Before we came to the country, the Hudson's Bay Company had a store on the east bank of the Red River, opposite to the mouth of the Assiniboine. I think on the property where Mr. Norman Kittson (a man afterwards most prominent in the affairs of Minnesota, especially of St. Paul), later had his trading store. The company may have had a fort there, but I only know for a fact that they had some kind of a store.

THE FIRST FORT GARRY

The Hudson's Bay post, named Fort Garry, after the amalgamation, certainly was the rebuilt old Fort Gibraltar of the North-west Company, and though, after its first occupation, it was simply known as the Company's Fort, or the Forks, it was finally designated as Fort Garry, and in this connection it is interesting to note that on an occasion in the year 1887, when consulting the old register of births, marriages and deaths of St. John's Church, Winnipeg, I came across an entry under date of April 18th, 1822, of the solemnization of a marriage, with George Simpson (after-wards Sir George) attesting as witness, at "Fort Gibraltar," the next following six entries being of marriages at "Fort Garry," one of which was also witnessed by Simpson, while a star was placed opposite the first above mentioned entry, drawing attention to a footnote, which reads "Fort Gibraltar is now named Fort Garry." Without doubt on that date Simpson changed the name to remove all feeling of resentment still existing amongst the Northwestern element with the occupation of the place by the Hudson's Bay Company.

Nicholas Garry, a member of the Hudson's Bay Company's Council, after whom the fort was named, visited the settlement about this date, his name afterwards appearing, with that of Simpson, as witness to a marriage at Norway House, Lake Winnipeg, on the 12th August, 1821.

That the First Fort Garry was a good deal of a ramshackle place is described by Alexander Ross in his *Fur Hunters of the Far West* (1855). Ross, on his arrival at the Red River from British Columbia via the fur traders' overland route, in 1825, rode up on horseback from below the present Selkirk to Fort Garry, reaching the fort on the evening of the 2nd July, and described it in the following words:

> I was anxious to see the place, I had heard so much about it, but I must confess I felt disappointed. Instead of a place walled and fortified, as I had expected, I saw nothing but a few wooden houses huddled together, without palisades, or any regard to taste or even comfort. To this cluster of huts were, however, appended two long bastions in the same style as the other buildings.
>
> These buildings, according to the custom of the country, were used as dwellings and warehouses for the carrying on of the trade of the place. Nor was the Governor's residence anything more in its outward appearance than the cottage of a humble farmer, who might be able to spend fifty pounds a year. These, however, were evidences of the settled and tranquil state of the country.

This fort was occupied by the Hudson's Bay Company as their headquarters, apart from the business of the Selkirk Colony as such, and with successive Governors until the appointment of Alexander Christie in 1835, who, in that year, began the erection of the Second Fort Garry, known to the present generation, of which the rear gateway now stands in the small Fort Garry Park which extends through from Main Street to Fort Street, immediately south of Broadway, and in the rear of the Manitoba Club. The buildings of the old evacuated fort, however they were utilized, remained until 1852, when as they were in part falling into the Assiniboine, they were demolished.

THE SECOND FORT GARRY

Realizing the necessity for better and greater accommodation for the conduct of their business, which, since the coalition of the two companies, had greatly improved, in 1831 the Hudson's Bay Company built at the then head of deep water navigation, just below St. Andrew's Rapids, the large and costly establishment which became known as the Stone Fort, or lower Fort Garry. The general tradition amongst the English population was that Sir George Simpson, viewing with some alarm the increasing turbulence of a part of the Metis of French extraction, deemed it advisable in case of a clash between the Company and that section of the Red River population, to have a stronghold nearer the centre of the English speaking white and half-breed inhabitants. Indeed, it was then generally understood in the Settlement that Government of the Company would be removed to the Lower Fort.

Whatever the policy may have been in 1831, it was changed, and Governor Alexander Christie, who had been a counselor of the governors of the Company's territories, and later Governor of Assiniboia in 1833 (an office he held for two terms, 1833-39 and 1844-48), began the erection in 1835 of the large and quite imposing Fort Garry which, until 1882, was the centre of the Company's business affairs in what is now Manitoba, and as well the centre of the social life of the Red River Settlement.

The Court House and jail was originally within the fort, but a minute of a meeting of the Council of Assiniboia held 3rd July, 1843, explains that "It being found exceedingly dangerous and inconvenient to have the public jail within the walls of Fort Garry; it was resolved: That the present jail be abandoned and that a new building be erected on some suitable spot by the Hudson's Bay Company, to be in future used for that purpose." The new Court House and Jail was built immediately adjoining the fort on the northwest side, and here several important cases were tried, particularly those connected with the claim of many of the inhabitants of the Settlement, both French and English, of their right to trade in furs, and which the Company, acting under the powers of its charter, granted in 1670, resolved not to concede. This claim of the people lay at the very root of the dissatisfaction which prevailed, causing serious outbreaks, and the presentation of their claims, by some of the people, to both the heads of the Hudson's Bay Company in London and the Canadian and British Governments. I happen to have the original letter book of Fort Garry, containing much of the correspondence that took place between the Company and the leaders of the Red River people on this subject, and it affords very entertaining and instructive reading.

On several occasions detachments of Imperial troops were sent to the Red River Settlement by the British Government in response to urgent requests of the Hudson's Bay Company, and these were all in turn, during their stay, quartered within the stone walls of Fort Garry. In 1846, eighteen officers and three hundred and twenty-nine men, being a wing of the 6th Royal Regiment of Foot, with artillery and engineers, under the command of Colonel John F. Crofton, arrived, having made the long journey from England via Hudson Bay, Lake Winnipeg and the Red River. They remained quartered in the fort for two years, and then returned to Great Britain by the same route.

In the autumn of 1848, seventy pensioners arrived under command of Major Caldwell, the object of this corps being that they should form the nucleus of a local force to be recruited in the Red River Settlement, to support the enforcement of the laws of the Hudson's Bay Company. Major Caldwell remained in the Settlement until 1855, but most of the men settled down in the country.

In 1856, the Company evidently brought strong pressure to bear on the Imperial Government to send another military force to Fort Garry. In this year also, two hundred United States troops arrived at Pembina, and the first act of this body was to issue a proclamation, notifying British subjects that they must not cross the International Boundary line to hunt or trade in furs. As a result of the situation, the Imperial Government in 1857 sent a company of the Royal Canadian Rifles via the Hudson's Bay route, and these remained until 1861, when they returned to England. . . .

From 1871 a small permanent force of troops were quartered in the fort until the erection of barracks and other necessary military buildings in an enclosed space, which received the name of Fort Osborne.

The Lieutenant-Governors of Manitoba resided within the

northern enclosure of Fort Garry, to which the gateway yet remaining was the entrance, until the building known as "Government House" was erected, and which is still the official residence of that official.

Fort Garry, as built in 1835, enclosed a space of 240 feet from north to south, and 280 feet from east to west, the heavy walls being constructed of stone, with four large round bastions at the corners. The buildings, including the officers' and employees' residential quarters, warehouses and retail store were distributed within the enclosing walls. The large main gate faced the Assiniboine River, and was not far back from the bank of that stream. There were two small postern gates, one of which was in the east wall beside the retail store, and it was through this gate that Thomas Scott was taken for his execution by order of Riel and his Provisional Government in 1870. The other postern gave access, through the main wall at the northeast corner of the fort, to what was called the fur warehouse. It may be here pointed out that several years after the original fort was built an addition was made at the north end to provide quarters for the resident governor of the Company. The high walls of this added enclosure were constructed of large solid square oak logs, laid horizontally in the form of crib work, the space between the outer and inner oak walls being filled with earth, and it was at this time that the gateway still remaining in the small Fort Garry Park was erected.

In 1882, during the Winnipeg real estate boom, the Company sold the fort and the ground upon which it stood, this area having been surveyed into city lots, and the purchasers demolished the fort, except the small northern gateway, which still remains; and so passed Fort Garry, the Second, within whose walls many scenes of excitement, hospitality and commerce took place during its existence from 1835-1882. The Governor's residence was the centre of many a jollification, on the occasions when he invited visiting and resident officers and other guests to grand spreads, the table being well supplied with choice tid-bits in the form of game obtained from all parts of the Company's territory. Reindeer tongues and ptarmigan from the far north, buffalo tongues and joints from the plains, smoked bear hams, carefully prepared pemmican of deer and buffalo meat made with marrow, moose nose, beaver tail, sturgeon and whitefish, and other delicacies were provided for the guests, to be washed down by the best of teas, and generally drowned with the choicest of old liquors and wines taken from the well-stocked cellars of the fort. To be invited to dine at the Governor's table was an event to be looked forward to. The newly articled clerk on his first arrival was initiated into the mysteries of the fur trade by listening to the tremendous yarns of the officials from the interior districts, and those of us who, at a later date, had the privilege of listening to these weather worn men know what wonderful experiences they could relate. Now and then in the old days, some traveler on his way to the far west or north, in pursuit of exploration, scientific observations or hunting, passed through the Settlement, and always received a hearty welcome at the Fort; indeed the travelers who have given us books on their work and adventures in the then vast uncharted areas of the country, invariably dwell on the hospitality extended to them at Fort Garry.

This Society was largely instrumental in securing the old gateway and park for the City of Winnipeg. Representatives of the Society taking the opportunity of Lord Strathcona visiting the City, waited on him and urgently pleaded that the site be donated to Winnipeg to be used for all time as a public park. His Lordship was most sympathetic and shortly afterwards the Hudson's Bay Company made conveyance of the property to the City.

Transaction No. 3, New Series, read May 1927.

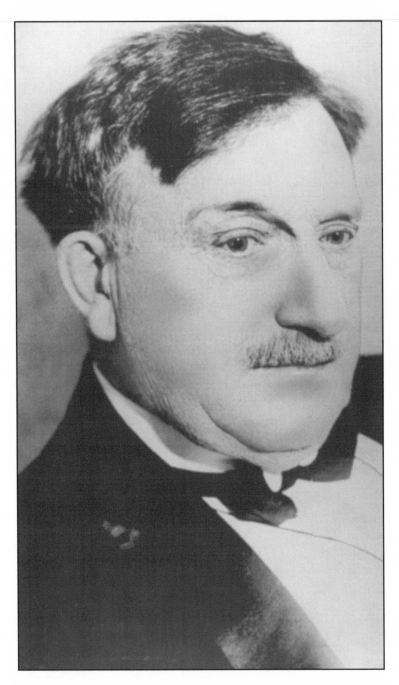

John W. Dafoe, editor of the *Free Press*, c. 1930

JOHN W. DAFOE
(1866-1944)

JOHN WESLEY DAFOE HAD BEEN, AT THE TIME OF reading this paper, a journalist since the 1880s and editor of the *Manitoba Free Press* for twenty-nine years. He had become a writer of national importance and influence in Canada and a power within the Liberal Party. His pen was mightier than any sword and his vociferous editorial campaigns had often brought defeat upon his enemies. His most famous victory was over the Conservative government of Rodmond Roblin during the Legislative Building scandal in 1915-16.

Dafoe was born in Combermere, Ontario, in 1866 and educated in Arnprior. At seventeen he went to work for the Montreal *Daily Standard* and from that time until he died he was a newspaperman. As a reporter for the Ottawa *Journal*, he sat in the press gallery and heard the speeches of the likes of John A. Macdonald and Wilfred Laurier. He was in Winnipeg, writing for the *Free Press*, from 1886 until 1892, and this paper contains some of his personal reminiscences of that time. He returned in 1901 to become editor of the *Free Press*, a post he held until he died in January 1944.

John Dafoe made the *Free Press* the leading paper in western Canada and, by the end of his career, his opinions were noted both nationally and internationally. He championed liberal causes such as lower tariffs and was a supporter of the League of Nations and greater autonomy for Canada within the British Commonwealth. He was one of a minority in the 1930s who warned of the menace posed by Hitler to the democratic world. Dafoe did not always follow the Liberal Party line, however: for example, he broke with Laurier over the conscription issue during World War I.

Dafoe was the founder of the Canadian Institute for International Affairs and he served as Chancellor of the University of Manitoba from 1934 until 1944. He was a member of the Rowell-Sirois Royal Commission on Dominion Provincial Relations.

In October 1943 a banquet was held to honour his sixtieth anniversary as a newspaperman. The huge dining room at the Royal Alexandra Hotel was full and the event was broadcast on national radio. Congratulations and tributes came in from all across the country, for, whether one agreed with him, there was no doubt that Dafoe was a national figure of great influence and importance.

During his speech on this occasion, Dafoe told a story that probably best expressed his ideals about journalism. In 1885, as a reporter for the *Montreal Star*, he witnessed his editor, Hugh Graham, defy the powerful Montreal establishment by breaking the story of the smallpox epidemic that was gripping the city. The word had gone out to ignore the existence of the disease because it would be bad for business, but Graham knew that some measures had to be taken to bring the epidemic under control. His story resulted in compulsory vaccination and a quarantine of the city. The death toll of nearly 5000 would have been much worse but for Graham's courageous act. [1] Dafoe undoubtedly saw himself as a crusading editor like Graham, using his pen in the fight for truth and justice.

Dafoe delivered the lecture reproduced here in 1932. Although he chooses to make his points by recounting amusing and very human stories about the journalists and editors of Winnipeg's early papers, if we read between the lines we can sense his deep respect for these people and their trade.

---

1. Murray Donnelly, *Dafoe of the Free Press* (Toronto: Macmillan, 1968), 199.

Early Winnipeg Newspapers

MANY STORIES ARE TOLD OF THE IDYLLIC CONDITIONS in the Red River Settlement in the middle of the last century. The settlers were supposed to live in rude comfort and in harmony. Whatever truth there may be as to this, certain it is that the serpent, in the form of a newspaper, entered into whatever Eden there was and started trouble. On November 1, 1859, seventy years and four months ago, two young newspaper men arrived with a printing plant from Toronto, and started the first paper in what was afterwards known as the Canadian Northwest. They were Englishmen, William Coldwell, 25 years of age, born in London; and William Buckingham, 27 years of age, born in Devonshire. Both were thoroughly competent reporters, with a considerable Toronto experience.

What moved these young men to come to the uttermost confines of civilization? Undoubtedly their appearance in the Red River settlement was the sequel to the newspaper campaign which had been carried on for eight years by the Toronto *Globe* in favor of the cancellation by the British Government of the Hudson's Bay Company's charter and the transfer of the territory of Rupert's Land to Canada. This campaign was inspired in the first place by A.K. Isbister, a native of this country, who had attained a position of considerable prominence in the educational and legal world of Great Britain, and whose name is perpetuated by a school in Winnipeg and by scholarship grants to the University of Manitoba. He suggested this policy to the re-doubtable George Brown, "through a mutual friend," according to a statement by Brown, and it was steadily advocated, as I have indicated, by the Toronto *Globe*.

Coldwell and Buckingham thus came here with a policy ready made for them. They were the forerunners of what came to be known as the Canadian party. The paper they founded they called the *Nor'Wester.*

An interesting description of the arrival of the first newspaper in the territory known as Rupert's Land was given by William Coldwell, one of the founders, at a dinner of the Winnipeg Press Club on April 2, 1888. Mr. Coldwell described how the paper and much of the plant had been purchased in St. Paul and transported north over the old Crow Wing Trail by Red River cart, the carts being drawn by oxen. "We made," said Mr. Coldwell, "a very wild start indeed, as one team ran away at the outset and distributed some of the type in the streets." The journey from St. Paul to the Red River Settlement took over a month, or from September 28 to November 1. "In our slow going, sleepy travel we did not exceed 15 or 20 miles a day." There were in 1859 no houses on the present site of Winnipeg, except the great log villas of Andrew McDermott and Alexander Ross along the river bank; so the *Nor' Wester* was housed in a little shack, probably near the present corner of Water and Main streets.

"Here," said Mr. Coldwell, "we commenced publication on December 28, 1859, and at the outset were greater monopolists than we had any wish to be. We were our own editors, reporters, compositors, pressmen, news boys, and general delivery agents, besides having to undertake a house-to-house canvass throughout the entire settlement. We secured a liberal subscription for our fortnightly newspaper—payment in advance. The subscription price was 12 shillings, afterwards reduced to 10 shillings per annum."

The *Nor' Wester* started right in as a paper in opposition to the existing order. They slung a pretty good pen in those days. The first number spoke of the interest of the Canadian government in the colonization of the vast country watered by the Red River, the Assiniboine and the Saskatchewan. "The country in the Northwest cannot remain unpeopled. The printing press will hasten the change," they declared. They denounced the discouragement of colonization by the authorities and asserted that the only possible future for the Red River Settlement and the territory to the west was union with Canada. The two pioneer newspaper men told the people of the Red River Settlement that they were "living in a miserable state of serfdom." What an assertion in view of the many statements, which had been made as to the idyllic conditions of rude comfort under which the inhabitants lived! They declared that the Hudson's Bay Company was utterly unsuited to the times and absurd in form, and they spoke of the "settled conviction, right or wrong, in the people's mind that the Council of Assiniboia is a puppet in the hands of the Hudson's Bay Company."

A year of this strenuous journalism was enough for Buckingham. He retired and returned to the east, where he had a considerable subsequent career as publisher of the Stratford *Beacon* and as private secretary to Alexander Mackenzie during his term as prime minister of Canada. He, jointly with Hon. G.W. Ross, became Mackenzie's biographer. He died as recently as 1915.

Buckingham's successor on the *Nor' Wester* was James Ross, a native of the settlement and a graduate of Toronto University. Coldwell and he proceeded along the lines of the policy I have indicated. It was a policy that entailed serious sacrifices for the two intrepid pioneers. Mr. Ross was postmaster at the time he associated himself with Coldwell, but he was soon fired. He was also sheriff, and he lost that job too. Subscriptions to the paper were cancelled, and socially they were pretty well ostracized, being banned from the parties held by the elite. They were regarded as a pair of obstreperous agitators, and had the word been known at that time they would undoubtedly have been called Bolsheviks!

The files of this newspaper can be seen, at the provincial library in the legislative building—its first number with the old time journalistic motto: "Naught extenuate nor aught set down in malice," and later numbers describing the course of life in the settlement. Some files have verbatim reports of lectures and addresses by such famous Red River Settlement characters as Archdeacon Cochrane. Others have accounts of mishaps at buffalo hunts, such as the death of a hunter from a seared throat got by the explosion of powder while he was blowing down his gun barrel to clear it. The unique life of the Red River Settlement is mirrored in its files. One of the most notable reporting performances of the *Nor' Wester* was a verbatim report, in the best style of the divorce reports which until recently appeared in the London papers, of the notorious Corbett case, extremely spicy details of which were set forth for the edification of a community which was greatly scandalized thereby.

Coldwell left the paper and returned to the east in 1864, and at the same time James Ross was succeeded as editor by the famous Dr. John Christian Schultz, who advocated with even greater vigour the annexation of the country to Canada. With Schultz was associated Dr. Brown, who succeeded later to the editorship.

In order that one may realize something of the difficulties with which the *Nor' Wester* had to contend, it should be stated that, in addition to other groups, there was one strong American group in the Red River Settlement. There was a constant controversy as to the future of the settlement, the American group thinking that the only destiny of the country was annexation with the United States. This was scarcely to be wondered at, as the trade tracks of the country were chiefly to the south, 1,500 carts a year going to St. Paul. Schultz and Brown had a very stormy time. They were the principals in many stirring incidents. The authorities harassed them almost unceasingly. At one time they threw Schultz into jail, but he was liberated by the populace. There are also records of mobs visiting the newspaper office to instruct the editor how to conduct his paper.

Rev. Dr. George Bryce paid the following tribute to the *Nor' Wester:* "This paper by its advocacy of union with Canada gave publicity to the cause which was chiefly instrumental in bringing that dream to pass." And Professor Chester Martin, probably nearer the mark, states: "The vigour with which those in charge of the *Nor' Wester* conducted their campaign was probably very largely responsible for the troubles of 1869-70, as it was the organ of what was known as the Canadian Party."

The *Nor' Wester* was an early casualty of the Red River uprising.

When the trouble started the paper ceased to exist, because Louis Riel commandeered it. The last issue appeared on November 24, 1869.

At this moment the indefatigable Mr. Coldwell reappeared on the scene with a new lot of type and a printing press, prepared to start a paper which he proposed to call the *Red River Pioneer*. Riel bought the plant outright for 550 pounds sterling, and to get the money he looted the Hudson's Bay treasury and carried off the cash. Riel merged the two papers and called that which he issued the *New Nation*. This he put in charge of a young American, Major H. M. Robinson, who had some connection by marriage with a family at Fort Garry. Robinson was to run the paper in the interest of Riel, who wanted it to wield an influence in support of the provisional government of which he was "President." Robinson, however, thought his chief job was to get on with the business of annexing the country to the United States. He wrote articles entitled "Consolidation," "The Future of the American Continent," and "One Flag, One Empire"—a phrase I have often heard used in another sense. Another was entitled "Annexation is Our Manifest Destiny." Riel after four months decided that was not a judicious line of stuff to put out and he put Major Robinson in an institution that was the equivalent of the modern "hoosegow." He then turned the paper over to Thomas Spence, a man who had come to the Red River four or five years earlier, an Irishman who was said to be a friend of D'Arcy McGee. Thomas Spence has a niche of fame in the history of this country, because he was the man who established the Republic at Portage la Prairie. The *New Nation* came to an end in August, 1870. In its final issue there was an editorial complimentary to Col. Garnet Wolseley who was then nearing the fort with his troops. Robert Cunningham, a representative of the Toronto *Globe*, who came in with the troops, joined forces with Coldwell and they started a new paper called the *Manitoban* in November, 1870. It was the first of a flock of weeklies. If you want to start a paper nowadays you can do it with $500,000 or $1,000,000; but those were the days when political papers could be established given a handful of type, a printer and a "slashing" writer. The *Manitoban* inaugurated the era of the small political paper. It appeared as the organ of the government party, which embraced the "old timers" or settlers and supported the Clark Administration. Then the Canadian Party published a paper called the *News Letter*, which was a very lively sheet. Still another was started, the *Manitoba Liberal*, conducted by Stewart Mulvey who, as an Irishman, was "agin the government." There was also a French paper, the *Metis*, which was edited by Joseph Royal, political figure.

In 1871 a notable journalistic event occurred in the Red River Settlement. A group of American newspaper men took a trip to the West and penetrated to the Settlement. Included in the party were Charles A. Dana, famous editor of the *New York Sun*, and Bayard Taylor, noted American poet. Telegraphic news made its first appearance in this year. Alexander Begg, the historian of the early days, began in 1872 the publication of the *Manitoba Trade Review*.

The year 1872 was an unfortunate one for the newspapers in the Red River Settlement. Dominion elections were held in that year. It appears that some one monkeyed with the voters' lists, which was a popular political pastime in those days. The elections were held on a list that was two years old. The result was that many "Canadians" could not vote. They could wreck the newspaper offices, however, and they wrecked them all so thoroughly, with the exception of the *Manitoba Liberal*, that it took them months to get going again. During this interregnum the *Free Press* decided it was an opportune time to be born; and though many other papers have come and gone since, it has refused to die. The *Free Press* was formed under a happy combination of circumstances. There was a young man who wanted to start a newspaper and another young man who had the money with which it could be started. The former was William Fisher Luxton, teacher of the only school in Winnipeg, who had gained newspaper experience in Goderich and Seaforth, Ontario. The other young man was John A. Kenny, who had just arrived in the settlement from Ontario with $4,000. The *Free Press* got off to a flying start and perhaps to that fact its long life can be attributed.

This much has to be said for the *Free Press*, that it is the only survivor of a large family of newspapers which appeared during the seventies, many of which were born only to die. One, the *Daily Herald*, edited by Mr. Fonseca, lasted two weeks. It was revived later by Walter R. Nursey, but expired after the lapse of two months. One of the papers which was born and had a brief life was the *Standard*, founded and edited by Molyneux St. John. There is a fine name for an editor! St. John was the junior member of a noble English family and had been an officer in the English army. He came to this country as a newspaper correspondent with the Wolseley expedition and remained for some years. Twenty years later he returned to the province and was for a brief period editor of the *Free Press*. At a later period he was, until his death, Usher of the Black Rod in the Federal House at Ottawa.

There was considerable excitement in conducting newspapers in the Red River Settlement in the seventies. Here is a sample: Contempt of court proceedings against Mr. Luxton were taken. Mr. Luxton had disagreed violently with the chief justice of the province as to the manner in which he conducted his court. Brought before the angry chief justice he was fined $500. Immediately sixty-four men in the court room put their hands in their pockets and produced the money. There is a signed list, in the files of the *Free Press*, of the worthies who paid the fine, and the last of the sixty-four died only a month ago in the person of W.F. Alloway.

The *Free Press* started as a weekly in 1872. In 1874 it came out as an evening daily. Later, opposition dailies began to appear. The *Nor' Wester* and the *Daily Herald* did not last long. The *Daily Tribune* was started by George H. Ham in 1878 but its career was brief and troubled. In 1880 the *Daily Times* came out in opposition to the *Free Press*, and from that time, I regret to say, there has been competition with the *Free Press*, except for one blessed period when we were monarchs over the whole scene for four or five weeks.

A complete list of the newspapers published in Winnipeg between 1859 and 1885 was given by William Coldwell in connection with his address to the Winnipeg Press Club in the latter year. Mr. Coldwell said:

> The record of newspapers from the start runs thus: 1859-70, the *Nor' Wester* published in succession by William Coldwell, Dr. John Schultz, and Dr. Brown; 1870, the *New Nation*,

published by Major H.M. Robinson; 1870, the *Manitoban*, Cunningham and Coldwell; 1870, the *News Letter*, by P.G. Laurie; 1871 the *Manitoba Liberal*, by Stewart Mulvey; 1872, *Manitoba Trade Review*, by Alexander Begg; 1872, *Manitoba Gazette*, G.F. Carruthers; 1872, *Manitoba Free Press*, Kenny and Luxton; 1873, *Nor' Wester*, E.L. Barber; 1874, the *Standard*, Molyneux St. John; 1877, *Manitoba Daily Herald*, Messrs. Begg and Walter R. Nursey; 1878, *Manitoba Telegraph*, Mr. Nursey; 1878, *Quiz*, Geo. H. Kerr; 1878, the *Gazette*, Hon. H.J. Clarke; 1879, *Winnipeg Daily Times*, C. R. Tuttle; 1879, *Tribune*, George H. Ham; 1880, *Daily Times*, Amos Rowe; 1881, the *News*; 1882, the *Daily Sun*, W. Naegle; 1883, the *New Sun*.

"All of these," said Mr. Coldwell, "excepting the last two, the *Free Press* and *Sun* (which was a year or so later absorbed by the *Free Press)* have passed into the happy land where sheriffs are unknown!" Of Mr. Coldwell, it is to be noted that illness forced his retirement from the *Free Press* staff in the early 80's. He moved to the coast and died there in 1907.

George H. Ham came to the Red River in the winter of 1874, from Port Hope. He was a member of the *Free Press* staff, first as printer and then as writer. He started the *Tribune* in 1879, which, as Mr. Ham in his characteristic way said, "he contributed to the list of busted newspapers." Mr. Ham has left a good description of journalistic activities in Winnipeg in the seventies.

"One great hardship," he wrote,

> was the frequent failure, through climatic conditions, of the telegraphic service, which came from Montreal, and from Ottawa, via St. Paul. It didn't take much of a storm to put the service out of business, but everybody sympathized with the paper's announcement that the telegraph lines were down and no dispatches had been received, and blamed the telegraph company instead of the paper for the lack of news. Three cents a word was charged for press dispatches and as the Canadian dispatches had to be repeated at Buffalo and St. Paul,

Sanskrit was easier to decipher than some of them when they finally reached Winnipeg.

In those early days no one could realize the troubles of a reporter's routine unless he experienced them. Sometimes, when the telegraph service was out of commission, no mails for three or four days, the thermometer 40 degrees below zero, and not a blessed thing doing, the situation was appalling. But the paper had to be issued, and Jack Cameron (the city editor) was a wonder, and what he didn't conjure up wasn't worth conjuring. But pleasant memories linger of those earlier days, kindly companions and congenial work and I can look back with pleasure that I was amongst those pressmen in the happy days when everybody knew everybody else in Winnipeg, or knew who they were, and the little frontier outpost had a glorious pioneer glamour which, alas, has passed away forever.

The "Jack Cameron" to whom reference has been made by Mr. Ham was the first news editor of the *Free Press*. John R. Cameron came to the settlement with the troops as a sergeant. A printer named Griffin helped him to get out the first issue of the *Free Press*. Cameron achieved considerable celebrity in the community through a column which he conducted under the heading, "Noremac's *[Cameron spelled backwards]* Nonsense." Quite a romantic story is told about him. Apparently smitten right away by the charms of a lovely young lady whom he noticed, Cameron was as suddenly overcome by religious emotion, and with enraptured voice he remarked to a companion: "I want to go to that young lady's church." He went to church faithfully and he subsequently married the fair object of his affection, though history does not record whether his church attendance record following the nuptials was as exemplary as it was previously. Cameron afterwards returned to Hamilton, the city from which he had come west, and made a reputation for himself as an editor and a humourist.

A note might perhaps be here made of the subsequent career of George Ham, whose death occurred but a few years ago. Ostensibly, during the eighties, he was a registrar under the old system of Land

Titles, but actually he was engaged in journalism, a good deal of the time, with a deputy in charge of his office. When his office disappeared owing to economies practised by the Greenway government, he joined the *Free Press* staff. He amused himself by pretending to be a green reporter; and the naive comments of the "new reporter" on things in general soon set the town rocking with laughter. He remained with the *Free Press* for two or three years until the C.P.R. saw in him the making of a useful publicity man, and his subsequent career was with that railway. He was a man of extraordinary charm and humour, with a marvellous capacity for clever, instinctive impromptu and repartee. A story is told of how he was rushed to an emergency hospital for an operation for appendicitis. He told the surgeon as he was going under the ether: "Well, doctor, you can take my appendix but please leave me my table of contents." Once he made some kind of a "bonehead" play in the handling of a newspaper article, and when taken to task for it he replied: "Well, I may not be broad-minded, but I am certainly thick-headed!" These are just samples of the sparkling, bubbling wit which made George H. Ham a most cherished companion. Many of his best stories are to be found in the book which he left behind, *Tales of a Raconteur*.

With the arrival of the railway and the coming of the eighties, Winnipeg got into the throes of the great boom. The newspapers had a brief period of glory and prosperity. The *Free Press* went from the evening field to the morning field in 1881, and that left the evening field to the *Times*, which was then under the control of Amos Rowe, who acquired his journalistic training in an auction room in Ottawa. Those were the days when the air rang with the talk about the crossing at "Grand Valley" and about "Nelsonville, the banner town of Southern Manitoba." Then in April, 1882, the newspapers announced "Edmonton, Edmonton, at last", whereupon the boom blew up.

At that time Winnipeg appeared to be the Mecca of many of the livest newspaper men of Canada. They flocked in and after a short stay a good many went out; some stayed, perhaps because they hadn't the price of a ticket. Among them were Albert Horton, afterwards editor of the Senate Hansard; A.C. Campbell, afterwards editor of the House of Commons Hansard, who is still active, in retirement, in Ottawa; John Lewis, now senator; J.P. Robertson, afterwards provincial librarian; R.K. Kerrighan, "The Khan;" and, most notable of all, Ed. Farrer, who for a short time was editor of the *Times*. In many ways Farrer was the most remarkable journalist that Canada had ever seen. He belonged to a noted Irish family and was closely connected with dignitaries of the Roman Catholic Church. He was a student at the Jesuit college in Rome, but one day he walked out of the college, left the life of seclusion, study and prayer behind him and became an adventurous journalist in Canada. He was a man of extraordinary talent as a controversialist. It was a matter of record that he had written campaign literature for both parties at the Dominion elections in 1882. It was reported that he was once seen wandering about in the early dawn and that he explained that he had been up all night trying to figure out how he could answer his own case for the other side.

Mr. Rowe had a good deal of trouble with Mr. Farrer. One amusing story is told of an encounter which Mr. Rowe had with him. Mr. Rowe, who was a dignitary of the Orange Order, went on a lecture tour in support of it, and while he was away Farrer wrote an article criticizing the order. This distressed Mr. Rowe very much. On his return he expostulated with Mr. Farrer, saying people must be wondering why it was he spoke of the order in one way and wrote of it in another.

"Don't worry, Amos," was the consoling reply of Mr. Farrer, "no one will ever accuse you of writing that article!"

There were two or three papers in succession known as the *Sun*. About 1883 the position of editor was taken by T. H. Preston, a young newspaperman of Toronto, who some years later returned east and became owner of the *Brantford Expositor*, entering upon a career as a public man, and having an opportunity, which he declined, of being leader of the Liberal party in Ontario.

The *Free Press* had a succession of notable editorial writers. One of them was W.E. MacLellan, who came from Nova Scotia to practise law but soon gave it up for newspaper work. He was a very vigorous writer of the old, slashing style type. He was induced to leave the *Free Press* and go over to a new Conservative evening paper, the *Manitoban*, which was being founded by Acton Burrows, who is still engaged in the publication of trade papers in Toronto. Mr. MacLellan, for a short time before he made his shift, wrote the editorials for both papers, which was comparatively easy since he would write an article for one paper and then write a scathing reply to it in the other. It worked very well, but he once narrowly escaped having a mishap. Having written a powerful leader for the *Free Press*, the morning paper, he wrote a telling reply to it and before going home for the night delivered it at the *Manitoban*, the office next door. It was not until noon the next day that he discovered to his horror that the first article had been thrown out of the *Free Press* by Mr. Luxton, who had rejected it upon seeing the proof. Mr. MacLellan, so the story goes, grabbed his hat and rushed over to the *Manitoban* office to have the scathing reply to the article which never appeared taken out of the evening issue of the *Manitoban*. Newspapers in those days consisted of only four pages, and they were printed on a flat press, two pages at a time. The edition had been half printed; as it contained the crushing rejoinder it was necessary to consign the whole of it to the furnace, which was a serious matter in those hard times!

The breaking out of the rebellion of 1885 provided an exciting time for the newspapers. The *Sun*, the *Times*, and the *Free Press* were put on their mettle and there was extreme rivalry between them. The *Free Press* rather objected to what it regarded as the abhorrent sensationalism of its contemporaries, and made a celebrated declaration of news policy with a view to putting its more volatile rivals to shame. The high water mark of this declaration was in these terms:

> Whether the campaign be of long or short duration, exertions will be made to give the readers of the *Free Press* exactly what the public wants and have a right to expect from any newspaper worthy of the name—reports of actual occurrences as soon as possible, as distinct from the mischievous imaginings of 'war correspondents' located in the home office. During the campaign the regular issues of the *Free Press* can be confidently relied upon for all that has transpired. When

anything happens, it will be reported. When nothing happens, nothing will be reported.

I came to Winnipeg in May, 1886, and joined the reporting staff of the *Free Press*. There were at that time four newspapers in Winnipeg: the *Free Press*, a morning paper; the *Manitoban*, already referred to; the *Sun*, and a small paper called the *News*, edited by W. T. Thompson, who is now managing editor of the Duluth *Herald*. One of the reporters on the *News*, if my recollection is right, was John J. Moncrieff, now a veteran of Manitoba journalism.

Among the other active newspapermen of that time was Fred C. Wade, who was editorial writer of the *Free Press*, and afterwards a noted lawyer and politician; he died in London some years ago as agent general for British Columbia.

The *Free Press* news staff at that time consisted of Walter Payne, who is still with us and is the dean of Manitoba newspaper men; T.E. Morden and myself. Mr. Morden, who was a reporter on the *Free Press* for well over thirty years, had an extraordinary reputation as an accurate reporter. In controversies in the legislature as to the accuracy of reports, it was always conclusive if it could be asserted that the report was by Mr. Morden. No one ever challenged either his integrity or his accuracy. He was a man absolutely without guile, except in one respect. If when late at night space became contracted and he was told to put the balance of his "copy" in four more pages, he would, in his desire to give everybody a fair show, write so fine a hand that he would get as much in these four pages as he ordinarily put into a dozen!

I was city editor of the *Free Press;* the city editor of the rival *Manitoban* was C.W. Handscomb. I was John Wesley; he was Charles Wesley. He was just one day my senior, which justified us in having a joint two day birthday celebration every year. For these and other reasons there was between us close friendship and brisk rivalry. Charlie carried his singing and acting talents to the American stage for a time, but came back to Winnipeg and to journalism and at the time of his death in 1906 was dramatic editor of the *Free Press*.

The leading reporter of the *Sun* was R.L. Richardson, who afterwards had a somewhat remarkable journalistic and political career.

The *Free Press*, in 1888, gobbled up the *Morning Call*, into which the *Evening Manitoban* had been turned. Later it absorbed the *Sun*, and for five weeks it was monarch of all it surveyed. The *Tribune*, founded by R.L. Richardson, then made its appearance and we had a competitor which was to prove permanent. For some years there was a very vigorous political duel between the *Free Press* and the Greenway government, which was supported by the *Tribune*. A gentleman who was active in politics at that time has often told me a sad story of his experience with the two newspapers. As a supporter of the Greenway government he was instructed to extirpate the *Free Press* in his constituency and get all the people to take the *Tribune*. Just as he succeeded in doing this, at a very considerable cost, there was a shift in the newspaper scene in Winnipeg. The *Free Press*, owing to a change in ownership, resumed its pristine faith in Liberalism and became an ardent supporter of the Greenway government, while the *Tribune* began to see serious faults in the administration which it formerly adored, whereupon the unfortunate politician had to do his work in his constituency all over again in reverse.

By this time Mr. Luxton had ceased to be connected with the *Free Press*. By purchasing rival newspapers he had brought new interests into the partnership which he could not control, with the unfortunate consequence that about 1893, owing to differences as to policy, he ceased to be editor of the paper. He thereafter founded a paper, reviving the old title, *Nor' Wester*, and for a short time conducted it.

This is an opportune moment to say something about Mr. Luxton. He had his defects like everybody else, but he was one of the whitest, squarest men I ever knew. He had certain journalistic principles which he strongly held and which he impressed upon the journal which he founded—traditions which are still operative and which have not had a little to do with whatever success the *Free Press* has achieved.

After his retirement from the *Free Press* and his unsuccessful venture with the *Nor' Wester*, he had a brief period of newspaper experience in St. Paul. He edited the St. Paul *Globe*, a paper now extinct, a position which it is understood he owed to his old time friendship with J.J. ("Jim") Hill. But Mr. Luxton came back to Manitoba. He took over a position in the public service, and died a good many years ago. His name will always be honorably associated with the history of journalism in Manitoba.

Associated with Mr. Luxton on the *Free Press* and afterwards on the *Nor' Wester* was an editorial writer of exceptional ability, D.J. Beaton, "Black Dan", as he was popularly called. I found myself fascinated by his extraordinary style of composing editorials. He wrote on soft copy paper with the hardest pencil he could find. His calligraphy was extraordinarily minute and no one ever saw any interlineations or changes in his copy. He would sit at his desk motionless for long periods of time until a sentence was formed letter perfect in his mind. Thereupon he would write it down. His day's work would be represented by three or four pages, but on these pages there was a complete editorial page!

Mr. Beaton gave two sons to journalism, both of whom have achieved a considerable degree of eminence. One is Welford Beaton, whose writings about the movies frequently appear in the *Saturday Evening Post*. The other is the well known columnist, "K.C.B.". Both got their original newspaper trainings as boys on the *Free Press*.

After an absence of some years I came back to Winnipeg in September, 1901 to take the editorship of the *Free Press*. At that time the newspapers in Winnipeg were: the *Free Press*, morning and evening, with E.H. Macklin in charge; the *Tribune*, with R.L. Richardson as owner and editor; and the *Telegram*, into which the *Nor' Wester*, by a series of changes, had evolved. It was an evening paper, but shortly afterwards it put out a morning edition. One of the happy consequences of the establishment of the *Telegram* was that it gave to Winnipeg one of its most valued citizens in the person of Mr. W. Sanford Evans.

Mr. Richardson divided his attention between journalism and politics. He was elected to the Dominion parliament in 1896, and thereafter, with the sole exception of the general election of 1911, he contested a constituency at every Dominion election. In addition, he fought two by-elections, all of them, after 1901, unsuccessfully until 1917 when he became Unionist member for Springfield. Mr. Richardson had a considerable gift of humour and his special contributions to his paper, embodied in the reflections and observations of "The Major", gave a good deal of amusement to his readers for a long period. He was also a very effective platform speaker.

Mr. Evans retired from the *Telegram* and newspaper life about 1905, and his place was taken by Mr. M.E. Nichols, who after some years of service entered into newspaper ventures in Montreal, but finally returned to Winnipeg to take charge of the *Tribune* under its changed ownership.

I don't propose to say much in detail about the journalism of the last twenty-five years. Members in it are still with us and it is not necessary to dwell upon them. But some general observations might be in order. I have no desire to indulge in laudation, but I think it can safely be said that Winnipeg is now and has always been well served by its newspapers, and that in many ways they have rendered a very substantial service to Canada and to Western Canada. One such service might very properly be here mentioned. It seems incredible when it is recalled that up to 1907 the newspapers of Canada bought their telegraph service from the telegraph companies, one of which, at least, was an auxiliary of a railway corporation. The impropriety of having such a service and its inadequacy were felt keenly by the Winnipeg newspapers and in the summer of 1907, finding something at last on which they could agree, they met together; Mr. Macklin and I for the *Free Press;* Mr. Nichols for the *Telegram;* and Mr. Richardson for the *Tribune.* We made a solemn vow that for better or worse, we would have our own news service, obtained from sources open to us. I remember going first to Chicago and then to New York to arrange for such an independent news service as could be obtained at that time. The result was the formation of the Western Associated Press, which began in Winnipeg and spread throughout the west. Within five years cooperative news gathering came into effect throughout Canada. As the outcome of the movement which started in Winnipeg, the Canadian Press came into existence. The Canadian Press now includes in its membership every considerable daily newspaper in Canada. It operates leased wires night and day, from Cape Breton to Victoria. It maintains correspondents in several outside capitals. Its expenditure runs into hundreds of thousands of dollars and it has rendered invaluable national service in supplying impartial, adequate news reports, and in providing for an interchange of news between all parts of Canada.

Time does not permit of the reference to papers in the province outside of Winnipeg and to the men who founded them which perhaps should be made. The first paper published in Manitoba, outside of Winnipeg, was the Portage la Prairie *Review*, by Thos. Collins, started about 1878. Other pioneer newspaper publishers of Manitoba were: C.S. Douglas, Emerson *International*; James Hooper, Morris *Herald*; Alex Dunlop, Neepawa *Press*, A. Weidman, Selkirk *Inter-Ocean*; C. Cliffe, Brandon *Mail*; F. Galbraith, Nelsonville (now Morden) *Mountaineer*; and W.I. White, Brandon *Sun*. Mr. Dunlop still publishes his paper. Mr. White, after long service in the Dominion Immigration Department is living in retirement in Saskatchewan. The others have passed on.

In addition there has grown up an extensive and varied newspaper press-trade and technical papers; farm, commercial and church papers; and a considerable number of papers published in foreign languages. A recent newspaper directory shows a total of publications of all kinds in the province of Manitoba of 149, of which seven are dailies. There are in the province 62 points at which newspapers are published. There are 22 papers published in languages other than English. Printing and publishing have become one of the most notable industries in Western Canada, and while government statistics do not separate newspapers proper from publishing, the figures show that altogether there were, in the year 1928—67 printing and publishing establishments large enough to be so regarded with a total capital of $3,699,524, with a yearly outlay for wages of $2,000,000, and total valued products of $5,383,000—a notable development in 70 years from the venture of Mr. Coldwell and Mr. Buckingham into the field of journalism!

Transaction Series III, No. 3, read April 1930.

Samuel Pritchard Matheson, c. 1908

SAMUEL MATHESON
(1852-1942)

AT THE END OF 1932, WHEN HE DELIVERED THIS lecture, Archbishop Matheson, like everyone in the province, was reeling from the sudden disclosure three months before of the loss of almost $2,000,000 sustained by both his church and the university through the mismanagement and dishonesty of J.A. Machray. For Matheson the so-called "Machray defalcations" were both a professional and personal blow because Machray was a lifelong friend, and the nephew of his predecessor, Archbishop Robert Machray. With the Machray scandal swirling around him, it may have been comforting for Samuel Matheson to remember the simpler days of the Red River colony.

Samuel Pritchard Matheson was born in 1852 in what is now East Kildonan. His family were important community leaders in the Red River colony. His grandfather, John Pritchard, had worked for the Hudson's Bay Company, survived the Seven Oaks fight, and, in 1817, began farming near the present junction of Henderson Highway and Whellams Lane. His farm there was called "The Elms" and remained in the family until the 1890s. Pritchard operated a small school in his house at The Elms for children of Hudson's Bay Company employees, the first school in the area. He was a member of the Council of Assiniboia.

Matheson was educated at St. John's College and, although his family was Presbyterian, he was ordained as an Anglican priest in 1876. He received a Bachelor of Divinity from the college in 1879. His career in the church was one of unbroken success, testifying to his natural abilities and political skills. He was also a teacher, serving as the head-master of the St. John's College School and a professor at St. John's College. He was at various times warden and chancellor of the col-lege, and he was the founder of Havergal College for girls and served as its first president.

Matheson became a Canon of the Diocese of Rupert's Land at the comparatively young age of thirty and was Dean of St. John's Cathe-dral in 1902. He succeeded Robert Machray as Archbishop of Rupert's Land in 1905. From 1909 to 1930 he was honoured by his fellow bishops with election to the position of Primate of All Canada, the senior bishop of the Anglican Church of Canada.

His service to the University of Manitoba began in 1908 when he was made chancellor of the university. He was involved in its practical administration through his work for many years on the Land Board, which was responsible for managing the federal government's land grant to the university. He was known as a shrewd judge of farmland and helped to maximize the benefit to the university of the acquisi-tion and sale of lands under the grant.

In 1934 Matheson's term as chancellor of the university came to an end and he did not let his name stand again. W.L. Morton wrote that his going "ended the last personal link with the founding of the Uni-versity and took from it a great servant who had not only graced its highest office with a venerable dignity, but had brought to his work a shrewd knowledge of men, which had failed lamentably with respect to his friend, J.A. Machray, and an administrative gift which was per-haps not adequately recognized." [1]

In his talk about floods, Matheson introduces the idea, startling now but common at the time, that there would never be another cata-strophic flood on the scale of the inundations he was describing. Many people felt that the drainage projects, which had almost eliminated the vast marshes that once surrounded Winnipeg, had made such major

---

1. W.L. Morton, *One University* (Toronto: McClelland and Stewart, 1957), 158.

floods impossible. He agreed, stating, "I am of the opinion therefore that the claim that the chances of recurring flooding are minimized by drainage is a correct one."

To illustrate that not everyone was so optimistic, he tells the story of Andrew McDermot, who always kept a York boat ready in his yard in case the waters rose again. Had he lived, he would have seen the great flood of 1950 prove Mr. McDermot right.

Floods at Red River

———•———

I HAVE THOUGHT THAT SOME NOTES ON THE THREE floods which visited this country in 1826, '52 and '61 respectively might be of interest historically to the members of our society. Various causes have been assigned for their prevalence in the early days and their comparatively rare occurrence in later years. It is contended, for example, by old timers who were here when floods did occur, that they arose from abnormally heavy snowfalls to the south, together with the fact that the swamps and low-lying land were filled almost to overflowing when the frost came in the previous autumn.

I myself recall the latter condition. The time was when in the rear of our river lots the country was composed largely of swamps, often filled with deep water and remaining so during the whole winter season. These swamps were like tumblers filled to the brim, which required very little to make them overflow. Others account for the floods by the blocking of the rivers by ice. Of course there were higher lands and elevated ridges in the rear, but between them were numerous low lying areas. In traveling weekly in the early days to Stony Mountain as chaplain of the penitentiary I encountered more than once deep swamps where, in a very wet spring or autumn, the water reached the bottom of my buggy and not infrequently came into it, with the result that I had to elevate my feet and legs on the dashboard to keep them dry. Moreover there were only certain districts by which you could make your way through these low places to reach your destination beyond them.

There was a trail going out from Old Kildonan and one also from what is now Logan Avenue that were fairly good, but not until you reached a point much farther north towards the Lower Fort was it possible in very wet seasons to get safely across the intervening swamps. I presume that may be the reason why Sir George Simpson and others, in giving evidence in 1857 before a committee of the British House of Commons on the suitability of this country for agricultural purposes, claimed that outside of a narrow strip of land along the rivers the whole hinterland was composed of deep swamps and mossy muskegs. I dare say that that was true when Sir George knew the country as it was in his day. With the system of draining which has since taken place, all this is now changed, with the result that what were deep swamps where some of us can recall shooting ducks are now cultivated fields for grain.

There were numerous creeks emptying themselves into the river containing large volumes of water. Some of these were large enough to have dams erected on them to supply motive power for several water mills which operated in those days. One of these creeks entered the river near my old home in East Kildonan, and higher up in the course was situated Long Angus Matheson's water mill, which I remember very well, and to which I had often taken wheat to be ground into flour. By means of your modern drainage system, all these creeks are now as dry as a bone, and all the water flowing down them so far from running a water mill, would not move the wings of a mosquito, unless Dr. Speechly was on hand to give it a push. *[Dr. H.M. Speechly was Winnipeg's coroner and led the city's anti-mosquito campaigns during the 1930s.]*

In motoring out to Stonewall I have often passed by what we used to call "The Bear's Swamp," a regular rendezvous not only in the spring, but during the whole summer of crowds of ducks and other water fowl, but now a high and dry farm. My father owned it and used to cut tons of hay on it. I am of the opinion, therefore, that the claim that the chances of recurring flooding are minimized by drainage is a correct one. This view, however, was not concurred in by some of the old settlers, who continued to entertain fears that we might have a recurrence of a flood at any time.

The late Andrew McDermot, for example, for so many years a leading settler in what is now the City of Winnipeg, was so confident that the menace had not passed that he kept a large York boat at the back of his house at the foot of what is now McDermot Avenue and had it carefully pitched and caulked ready for embarkation by himself and his family in the event of a recurring flood in the country. Frequently when I visited him he took me to see his boat and emphasized the fact that he kept it in prime condition for an emergency. I remember also the late Col. Ruttan, for so long our city engineer, when questioned as to his view of the possibility of floods again taking place, remarking that, while the prospects were greatly lessened by the extension of draining, and while the rivers, especially the Red River, had greatly widened and also were capable of carrying away rapidly a greater volume of water, he did not consider that the danger had entirely passed away. He gave as his reasons that, while doubtless the Red River was much broader all along its course than it once was, yet he had observed that its mouth where it entered into Lake Winnipeg, had remained the same width and he added that a funnel was only capable of carrying through itself what its small end could convey. Be that as it may, I have no desire to play the part of Noah and thus be an alarmist and picture to you the immensely increased population of Winnipeg and the Province trying to huddle together on Stony Mountain and Bird's Hill and other higher spots, where the members of our little colony in olden days camped comfortably for weeks together until the tyranny of the waters was past.

After these preliminary remarks let me now give you some particulars about those early floods, the records of which, though scanty, are still extant. The first took place in 1826, though the aboriginal inhabitants and old timers have traditions of another and a greater inundation in some former year. The following are extracts from letters of my grandfather, John Pritchard, in my possession, written in the autumn after the flood. He was an eyewitness of what had taken place and wrote this letter to a brother in England 106 years ago:

"Red River,
August 2nd, 1826.
"With feelings of gratitude to Almighty God, who, though he has afflicted, yet has spared; and in His wrath thought upon mercy, I have to relate a most calamitous event which visited us this spring.

"About the 30th of April the ice on the Red River began to give way in particular places, but did not generally break up till the first week in May, when it presented a scene of devastation dreadful to contemplate and very difficult to describe. I have before informed you, that this country is formed of one large plain of many hundred miles in extent, its western boundary the Rocky Mountains, its southern I cannot describe, but I suppose somewhere about New Mexico. It is intersected with very few rivers and the few eminences to be met with scarcely deserve the name of hills. I find it necessary to make these observations to enable you to form some idea of the terrific scene we have witnessed.

"When the ice broke up in our neighborhood, it was late in the evening. The night was dark and stormy, accompanied with rain. The flood at once rose higher than ever known by man. The crashing of immense masses of ice was loud as thunder; neither the tallest poplar nor the stoutest oak could resist its impetuosity. They were mowed down like grass before the scythe. The inhabitants fled from their dwellings, and with their cattle sought safety upon the first high lands that presented themselves.

"The water continued to rise, but not so rapidly as at first. As it rose the poor settlers daily retired and continued their sorrowful route until those on the east bank reached a hill at about eight miles, and those on the west another at about nine miles distance. From the heights they had the cheerless prospect of one general ruin. Far as the eye could discover, the earth was covered with water carrying on its surface the wreck of a whole colony. Houses, barns, stables, fences, and in fact all that could float was a prey to the destructive element.

The water continued to rise till the beginning of June. It then began to fall though by slow degrees. As it retired, we retraced our steps and from the middle of that month till the early part of July, we planted potatoes, barley and some wheat upon such lands as the water had left; and I am extremely happy to say that what we so planted looks well and through the blessings of the Almighty now promises a sufficiency for man and beast.

"You may form some idea of the extent of this flood by considering the river whose usual breadth may be compared with the Severn at Shrewsbury having expanded itself over a surface of more than seventeen miles; which is the distance between the hills on which the settlers took refuge. There, of course, it was contracted and its width above must have been considerably greater. The depth was thirty five feet above its common level, being more than twenty feet higher than the former flood which was considered a very high one. It is worthy of remark that the three churches, the residence of the clergy and the house of our social prayer meeting, with the exception of the windmill, should be the only buildings which have not been carried away or so much injured as not to deserve notice. It is no less remarkable that the sites of these buildings were not chosen on account of their central position.

"I have now given you the outlines of this disastrous event, and turn in grateful remembrance to Him who directs all things; who in exhibiting the greatness of His power and the justness of His wisdom did not withold his merciful kindness. Incredible as it may appear, not one human life has been lost, and so few cattle perished that they are not worth mentioning.

"I am writing this on the site of my usual residence, 'The Elms', opposite Kildonan Church where Mrs. Whellams now lives. I returned the day before yesterday after an absence of twelve weeks. I am living under a shed of boards, but before the winter sets in I hope to have a comfortable house. A considerable number of the settlers have left the country and gone to the United States, a few others will return to Europe. The old residents still remain and are very actively employed in re-establishing things as heretofore; so that I expect next summer the remembrance of the flood alone will be retained. To view the country now and compare it with what it was a few weeks ago—a sea of devastation or desolation—it is impossible not to exclaim, O Lord how wonderful are Thy works! Truly the wilderness has become a 'fruitful field' and 'the desert rejoices and blossoms as the rose.'"

Extract from letter August 21, 1826.

"Since my last we have received further accounts of the recent flood and I very much fear for the safety of the American Settlements on the lower parts of the Missouri and St. Peter's Rivers. Report says that some of their military posts have been overwhelmed and many soldiers drowned. We are also informed that several Indian Villages have fallen victims to these destructive waters. It is now clearly ascertained that they flowed from the Rocky Mountains and passing over the banks of the Missouri (their usual channel to the Gulf of Mexico) overflowed the adjacent country; and were conducted here by the Riviere a La Souris which falls into the Assiniboine River about one hundred miles from this place.

"Our crops continue to look well; both wheat and barley are in full ear and the potatoes sufficiently large for the table. When you consider that seven or eight weeks ago we were only sowing after the flood you will join in praise to Him in Whom we live and move and have our being, for His providential care towards His creatures."

This will give you an idea of the extent of the flood if we picture to ourselves the conditions when the Red River arose thirty-five feet above its usual level. It is no wonder that only our two high spots at Stony Mountain and Bird's Hill escaped being submerged. It seems extraordinary that under the providence of God there were no human fatalities and so few even among animals and livestock generally.

We come now to speak of the flood of 1852, twenty-six years afterwards. Here again I cannot speak as an eye-witness, for, though I was born in that year, 80-odd years ago, either my parents or myself with Scottish caution saw to it that I did not appear on the scene until the waters had completely subsided. So, I shall have to depend upon the particulars given by Bishop Anderson in his *Notes of the Flood*, which were published shortly after the event.

Bishop Anderson begins his notes as follows:

"This little sketch does not profess to be a narrative of the late flood as a whole but of its effect in that part of which I am in the centre. Its effects were very different in different places; they varied almost with every reach of the river and according to the level of the bank at each spot. It was perhaps the most disastrous among the Canadians around and above the Upper Fort; it was very severe in the Upper and Middlechurch districts, Middlechurch and St. Andrews near Lockport. It affected a good deal the lower part of the Assiniboine; while the upper part of the district of St. James and Rat River and the Indian settlements were almost untouched. My own suffering was greater for my having so much on my hands and so many around me. Some have even called our buildings a village. The schools and households numbering sixty to provide for daily might almost be so termed. There was my own house with the Collegiate school, where all were boarders, chiefly from a distance; a little below us the large house of St. Cross, a similar establishment for young ladies. Across the creek, over which I had lately thrown a long bridge, was the farmyard, stables, etc., and the parochial day school attached to the Upper Church, at the far end of which some of my servants lived." (There used to be a deep creek between what is now Church Avenue and what is now the St. John's Park and it was there that those buildings stood.)

It would take too long and possibly might be tedious to follow consecutively the whole narrative, so that I shall content myself with giving you excerpts illustrative of how events progressed. On Sunday, April 25th, we find the following note:

"The ice having partially broken up rendered it unsafe to cross the river. A few, however, came over in the morning and more to the afternoon service. Large masses of ice passed during the evening and the following day. The water had risen much, even before the ice gave way, and continued doing so during the week, there being no outlet for it as yet towards the lake. The rise was sometimes a foot or a foot and a half in twenty four hours.

"Sunday, May 2nd: By this time the prospect became alarming. I determined in consequence to give notice of a day of prayer and humiliation."

At the service on that day the Bishop preached in the morning from a text in the Prophet Amos:

"It is He that buildeth His stories in the heavens and hath founded His truth in the earth; He that calleth the waters of the sea and poureth them out upon the face of the earth. The Lord is His Name." In the evening he spoke on St. Paul's experience when shipwrecked, on the text: "The rest, some on boards and some on broken pieces of the ship, and so it came to pass that they escaped all safe to land." The narrative goes on with the encouraging words: "The evening was placid and calm" and every breast was filled with hope. But on May third a different story is told: "These expectations were encouraged by the slight rise during the night, but from 10 a.m. to 2 p.m. the waters came so fast as to lead to very painful forebodings. Some houses opposite to us were already abandoned, their inmates tenting on little knolls behind. We hear of one settler taking a bateau right through his house; another with a boat at his door to carry off his goods. From the fort we hear that more than fifty deserted houses may be seen. The owners of some, wholly reckless of the future and regarding their return to them as uncertain, have in some cases offered them for sale and some houses changed hands in this way for thirty shillings and two pounds." Circumstances became worse and worse, until we find that people were notified during the church service on May fifth that anyone who chose might lodge wheat in the gallery of the church for safety, thirty bushels were brought immediately after. Many besides deposited the articles they most valued to themselves, as clocks, saws, seed, etc. One individual brought as much as 100 bushels of grain of different kinds for storage. On May seventh the note is as follows: "A morning of more wintry aspect. Six hundred weight of flour lodged in the gallery of the Church. Horses of the Hudson's Bay Company I passed down, sent for security to the stone Fort. They were seen fording and swimming the creeks, now swollen to rivers. In every direction there are processions of cattle, horses and carts going to Little Stony Mountain; the creaking sound of the wheels is melancholy to hear. One stable is seen drifting down the river. The most melancholy sight of the day had been when those tented on the ground moved off and passed over the swollen water to the north of the church. All walked right through the stream, men and women up to their waists. The cattle were swum over and the carts with difficulty got through. Others were housed by us for the night."

Later on the Church at St. John's which had been a house of refuge as well as a storehouse for valuables, was flooded, for the Bishop writes: "I went over to the Church and found the water had entered it. It was a melancholy sight to look down from the gallery and as I viewed the Church yard lying under water (the present cemetery at St. John's) I thought, what could be done in case of death? There had been two funerals the day before at St. Andrews; what could I do if death occurred in the upper settlement?"

Apparently for a time part of the district of St. James was immune from trouble, and a great many went there in canoes or boats and took refuge in the parsonage, which was not yet finished. We are told that as many as thirty-five camped in one room. Later on, however, practically the whole population had to repair to Stony Mountain, Bird's Hill, etc., and camped for many weeks on these higher spots. Such is the account of an eyewitness of the flood of 1852, which proved a serious setback to the settlement and, like a good many other misfortunes, tested the courage and constancy of those early pioneers who laid the foundations of the old Red River Colony with wonderful pluck and perseverance and of what subsequently became our Province of Manitoba. In these days of depression and difficulty may we, imitating their faith, continue steadfast and keep on our feet. Some of us ought to feel proud that we are descended from those intrepid pioneers who in the midst of disasters never said die. . . .

I need not weary you with any further details of the disaster of 1852. I have said enough to indicate that it was sufficient to put a serious damper on the progress and development of the little colony at that date. For the records of the two floods which I have described I have had to depend upon the notes which I have gathered from those who were here when they occurred. In 1861, however, there was an inundation of which I was an eye-witness, though I was only a small boy. It was only of a partial extent and did not cover nearly as large an area as the two previous ones. The fact is, these succeeding floods seem to have grown less, both in extent and in their destruction, as time went on, which is an encouraging feature, bearing upon the possibility of any recurrent ones. That of 1861 appears to have made so small an impression on the public that I have searched in vain for any reference to it in the histories covering that period. Only the low lying lands were affected and as far as I can recollect not many houses were flooded. In portions of Kildonan and Middlechurch considerable inconvenience to the inhabitants was caused, with the result that homes were abandoned and a good many people migrated as they did in '26 and '52 to the higher lands.

The farm where I lived at the time was on the east side of the Red River opposite Old Kildonan church. It was located on the river bank and near it quite a deep creek (on which there was a dam and a water grist mill higher up) to which I have already referred, emptied itself into the river near our house. For that reason possibly our farm was seriously affected, in fact, it was covered with water reaching back for about a mile from the river. Just about the time that the floors of the houses were flooded the men removed our goods, chattels and livestock to a higher spot not far from where Transcona now stands. Those of us who were left behind, an aunt, a sister and myself, remained upstairs, which in those days was termed "the loft", and where quantities of wheat and other cereals were piled up. It was arranged that within a day or two the men were to come back for us and take us out to where tents and board shacks were being built in the meantime to receive us. A heavy storm, however, ensued and we were left there for several days in great anxiety.

In the meantime the water continued to rise rapidly and I remember bringing a canoe, which was tied to a tree outside, into the downstairs rooms of the house, and for a time paddling about throughout the building, which was a commodious one, for it had been used for a boarding school by my grandfather in the early days. I recall that as time went on, the canoe came nearer and nearer to the ceiling of the house, until I had to duck my head when paddling about. One day I espied sitting on the roof of the stable (we called it the byre in those days) a very favorite white hen, but when I essayed to go out in the canoe to fetch her I was strictly forbidden on account of the possible risk.

One morning, however, when the surface of the water seemed smooth, we saw a hay rick and a portion of a stable with hens on it floating by. I slipped out quietly from downstairs in the canoe, paddled to the byre and rescued my hen. Holding her tightly between my knees, I used my hands for paddles, made my way back to the house and went aloft with the hen, which I remember made straight for a pile of grain and feasted on it, for apparently she had been starving for several days. The next day the hen rewarded us for my escapade by laying an egg, which we relished very much, for our supply of tasty food was becoming decidedly low.

Some days afterwards my uncles arrived in a York boat which they had borrowed from Donald Murray, I think it was, and took us out through an upstairs window and conveyed us out to the place where they had established our camp and temporary quarters. On the way out when we had reached land and discarded the boat we came across some livestock which had been left behind on the way out. Carts met us there and among the livestock was a pig and a fine litter of young ones. The mother and family were placed in a cart with a low rail round it and I was commissioned to drive it to our destination. When we came to what was called Bunn's Creek and had to wade through it with the oxen cart, and when the water came into the cart, Mrs. Pig and her progeny became restless and, resisting my endeavours to keep them in, jumped into the stream and swam to the other side. When we collected them together I recall how some of the little pigs were bleeding around the throat and I was told that, while pigs could swim when they were compelled, they always incurred the danger of cutting their own throats with the sharp points on their hoofs, and if they swam far they were liable to cut themselves so seriously that they bled to death. Be that as it may, our little piggies arrived safely in camp and grew into fine porkers.

Life in our temporary encampment was quite pleasant. We had plenty of food and not too bad shelter and, as there were several families near each other, we had not a little social diversion. I remember how plentiful game was. Prairie chickens, partridges, plovers, etc., abounded on the ridges near us and a deep swamp hard by, encircled by reeds and rushes, seemed to be full of ducks. An uncle who was a good shot kept us supplied with all the game we needed. Every boy in those days had a bow and arrows and one morning, not to be beaten by my uncle, I crept into the reeds and, concealing myself, waited for the near approach of some ducks, which were swimming in the pond. When a large mallard swam close to me I let him have an arrow in the head. He tumbled into the water and, lest he should revive, I hurriedly waded after him, despatched him and carried him proudly to the camp. My foster mother said that I was becoming a Nimrod, but as I did not know the difference between a Nimrod and a ramrod I failed to appreciate the compliment.

On Sundays we used to ride on horseback—for the swamps were too deep to go through in carts—to Bird's Hill some miles away, where the settlers from Middlechurch were camped. They attended church services there conducted by the Rev. John Chapman, who rowed out in a boat from his parish on the river about three miles away, and who had been living in the gallery of the church, in which he had also taken refuge in the flood of '52. Twenty-six years before, Bishop Anderson speaks of Mr. Chapman holding services on the same spot and also in the large tent of Mr. Pritchard, who, as he states, had been debarred by infirmity for many years from regular attendance at public worship. . . . I recall very vividly an incident which occurred at one of those services at the end of which Mr. Chapman made a painful announcement to us to the effect that Dr. Bunn had passed away that morning. The Doctor was very popular from end to end of the settlement, and was not only an able practitioner but a most devoted family physician. He was the much loved "Dr. McClure" of Ian McLaren's book *Beside the Bonnie Briar Bush*. I was only a boy of eight at the time, but I shall never forget the profound impression made. I had seen women break down into convulsive tears but I had never seen full grown men collapse and try to hide their emotions by disappearing one by one into the grove hard by to weep there. A good family physician is a possession of great price.

I am afraid that I have kept you too long already, but let me add, that, as in the case of the other two floods, though we planted nothing much before July, in the good providence of God, nature seemed to adjust itself to our needs and mishaps, with the result that both grain and vegetables matured in time to supply adequately our wants.

Transaction Series III, No. 3, read December, 1932.

Appendix

MANITOBA HISTORICAL SOCIETY TRANSACTIONS:

FIRST SERIES 1882 - 1906

McArthur, Alex. *The Causes of the Rising in the Red River Settlement, 1869-70.* Winnipeg: s.n., 1882. Transaction no. 1.

Rae, John. *The Arctic Regions and Hudson's Bay Route.* Winnipeg: s.n., 1882. Transaction no. 2.

Panton, J. Hoyes. *Gleanings from the Geology of the Red River Valley.* Winnipeg: Manitoba Free Press, 1883. Transaction no. 3.

Bryce, George. *Winnipeg Country: Its Discovery and the Great Consequences resulting.* Winnipeg: s.n., 1883. Transaction no. 4.

Burman, W.A. *The Sioux Language.* Winnipeg: s.n., 1883. Transaction no. 5.

Dennis, William. *The Sources of North-Western History.* Winnipeg: Manitoba Free Press, 1883. Transaction no. 6.

Bell, Charles N. *Navigation of Hudson Bay and Straits.* Winnipeg: Manitoba Daily Free Press, 1883. Transaction no. 7.

Bryce, George. *In Memoriam: Late A.K. Isbister, M.A., LL.B., honorary member.* Winnipeg: Manitoba Daily Free Press, 1883. Transaction no. 8.

Bryce, George. *Notes and Comments on Harmon's Journal 1800-1820.* Winnipeg: Manitoba Daily Free Press, 1883. Transaction no. 9.

Panton, J. Hoyes. *Fragmentary Leaves from the Geological Records of the Great Northwest.* Winnipeg: Manitoba Daily Free Press, 1884. Transaction no. 10.

Agnew, Niven. *Our Water Supply: Suggestions as to the Water we Drink and where to Get it from.* Winnipeg: Manitoba Daily Free Press, 1884. Transaction no. 11.

Murdoch, William. *The Red River.* Winnipeg: Manitoba Daily Free Press, 1884. Transaction no. 12.

Rowan, J.H. *The Red River.* Winnipeg: Manitoba Daily Free Press, 1884. Transaction no. 13.

Seton, Ernest Thompson. *The Prairie Chicken. Scientific Description of the Bird and its Habits. Hints on Rearing and Domestication.* Winnipeg: s.n., 1884. Transaction no. 14.

Panton, J. Hoyes. *Gleanings from Outcrops of Silurian Strata in the Red River Valley.* Winnipeg: Walker & May, 1884. Transaction no. 15a.

Scoble, Thomas C. *Our Crop Markets.* Winnipeg: Manitoba Daily Free Press, 1885. Transaction no. 15b.

Seton, Ernest Thompson. *Prairie fires.* Winnipeg: Manitoba Daily Free Press, 1885. Transaction no. 16.

Bell, Charles N. *Some Historical Names and Places of the Canadian North-West.* Winnipeg: Manitoba Free Press, 1885. Transaction no. 17.

Bryce, George. *The Mound Builders.* Winnipeg: Manitoba Free Press, 1885. Transaction no. 18.

Bryce, George. *The Old Settlers of Red River.* Winnipeg: Manitoba Daily Free Press, 1885. Transaction no. 19.

Panton, J. Hoyes. *Notes on the Geology of Some Islands in Lake Winnipeg.* Winnipeg: Manitoba Free Press, 1886. Transaction no. 20.

Goodridge, R.E.W. *On the Proposed Change of Time Marking to a Decimal System. A plea that the duodecimal system be retained.* Winnipeg: Manitoba Daily Free Press, 1886. Transaction no. 21.

Bowerman, A. *The Chinook Winds and other Climatic Conditions of the North-West.* Winnipeg: Manitoba Free Press, 1886. Transaction no. 22.

Seton, Ernest Thompson. *A List of the Mammals of Manitoba.* Winnipeg: s.n., 1886. Transaction no. 23.

Bryce, George. *The Souris Country: Its Monuments, Mounds, Forts and Rivers.* Winnipeg: Manitoba Free Press, 1887. Transaction no. 24.

Drummond, Lewis. *The French Element in the Canadian Northwest.* Winnipeg: Northwest Review, 1887. Transaction no. 25.

McCharles, A. *The Foot-Steps of Time in the Red River Valley, with special reference to the salt springs and flowing wells to be found in it.* Winnipeg: Manitoba Free Press, 1887. Transaction no. 26.

McArthur, Alex. *A Prairie Tragedy: The Fate of Thomas Simpson, The Arctic Explorer.* Winnipeg: G.C. Mortimore, 1887. Transaction no. 27.

McArthur, Alex. *Our Winter Birds.* Winnipeg: The Manitoban Printing Company, 1887. Transaction no. 28.

Bell, Charles N. *Some Red River Settlement History*. Winnipeg: Call Printing, 1887. Transaction no. 29.

Bryce, George. *Sketch of the Life of John Tanner, a Famous Manitoba Scout: A Border Type*. Winnipeg: Manitoba Free Press, 1888. Transaction no. 30.

Bell, Charles N. *Henry's Journal, Covering Adventures and Experiences in the Fur Trade on the Red River 1799-1801*. Winnipeg: Manitoba Free Press, 1888. Transaction no. 31.

McMicken, Gilbert. *The Abortive Fenian Raid on Manitoba: Account by One Who Knew its Secret History*. Winnipeg: Manitoba Free Press, 1888. Transaction no. 32.

Bryce, George, and Bell, Charles N. *Original Letters and Other Documents Relating to the Selkirk Settlement*. Winnipeg: Manitoba Free Press, 1889. Transaction no. 33.

Annual Report for the Year 1888 and President's Inaugural Address. Winnipeg: Manitoba Free Press, 1889. Transaction no. 34.

Bell, Charles N. *Continuation of Henry's Journal, Covering Adventures and Experiences in the Fur Trade on the Red River, 1799-1801*. Winnipeg: Manitoba Free Press, 1889. Transaction no. 35.

Taylor, James. *Lord Selkirk's Deed from the Hudson's Bay Co.* Winnipeg: Manitoba Free Press, 1889. Transaction no. 36.

Bell, Charles N. *Henry's Journal*. Winnipeg: Manitoba Free Press, 1889. Transaction no. 37.

Bryce, George. *Two Provisional Governments in Manitoba Containing an Interesting Discussion of the Riel Rebellion, with an Appendix Embodying the Four Bills of Rights Verbatim*. Winnipeg: Manitoba Free Press, 1890. Transaction no. 38.

MacFarlane, R. *Land and Sea Birds Nesting within the Arctic Circle in the Lower Mackenzie River District*. Winnipeg: Manitoba Free Press, 1890. Transaction no. 39.

Bryce, George. *The First Recorder of Rupert's Land*. Winnipeg: Manitoba Free Press, 1890. Transaction no. 40.

Bryce, George. *Surface Geology of the Red River and Assiniboine Valleys*. Winnipeg: Manitoba Free Press, 1891. Transaction no. 41.

Bryce, George. *Older Geology of the Red River and Assiniboine Valleys*. Winnipeg: Manitoba Free Press, 1891. Transaction no. 42.

Bryce, George. *"Seven Oaks": an account of the affair of Seven Oaks; the Circumstances which led up to it; a description of the Contestants; the Events of the Conflict, including the Death of Governor Semple and his followers; and a Report of Proceedings of the gathering for the Unveiling of the "Seven Oaks*

Monument," *June 19th, 1891.* Winnipeg: Manitoba Free Press, 1891. Transaction no. 43.

MacBeth [sic], John. *Social Customs and Amusements of the Early Days in Red River Settlement and Rupert's Land.* Winnipeg: Manitoba Free Press, 1893. Transaction no. 44.

Schultz, J.C. *The Old Crow Wing Trail.* Winnipeg: Manitoba Free Press, 1894. Transaction no. 45.

Bryce, George. *Early Days in Winnipeg.* Winnipeg: Manitoba Free Press, 1894. Transaction no. 46.

Schultz, J.C. *A Forgotten Northern Fortress.* Winnipeg: Manitoba Free Press, 1894. Transaction no. 47.

Bryce, George. *Worthies of Old Red River.* Winnipeg: Manitoba Free Press, 1896. Transaction no. 48.

Bryce, George. *The Lake of the Woods: Its History, Geology, Mining and Manufacturing.* Winnipeg: Manitoba Free Press, 1897. Transaction no. 49.

MacBeth [sic], R.G. *Farm Life in the Selkirk Colony.* Winnipeg: Manitoba Free Press Co., 1897. Transaction no. 50.

Atkinson, George E. *The Game Birds of Manitoba.* Winnipeg: The Manitoba Free Press Co., 1898. Transaction no. 51.

Bryce, George. *Sketch of the Life and Discoveries of Robert Campbell, Chief Factor of the Hon. Hudson's Bay Company.* Winnipeg: Manitoba Free Press Co., 1898. Transaction no. 52.

Atkinson, A.E. *Manitoba Birds of Prey, And the Small Mammals Destroyed by Them.* Winnipeg: Stovel Co., 1899. Transaction no. 53.

Bryce, Marion. *Historical Sketch of The Charitable Institutions of Winnipeg.* Winnipeg: Manitoba Free Press, 1899. Transaction no. 54.

Burman, W.A. *The Present Status of Natural Science in Manitoba and the Northwest.* Winnipeg: Manitoba Free Press Co., 1900. Transaction no. 55.

Fonseca, W.G. *On the St. Paul Trail in the Sixties.* Winnipeg: Manitoba Free Press Co., 1900. Transaction no. 56.

Bryce, Marion. *Early Red River Culture.* Winnipeg: Manitoba Free Press Co., 1901. Transaction no. 57.

McLean, W.J. *Notes and Observations of Travels On the Athabasca and Slave Lake Regions in 1899.* Winnipeg: Manitoba Free Press Co., 1901. Transaction no. 58.

Jónasson, Sigtryggur. *The Early Icelandic Settlements in Canada.* Winnipeg: Manitoba Free Press Co., 1901. Transaction no. 59.

Atkinson, George E. *Insectivorous Birds of Manitoba.* Winnipeg: Stovel Co., 1903. Transaction no. 60.

Hunt, Frank L. *Britain's One Utopia*. Winnipeg: Manitoba Free Press Co., 1902. Transaction no. 61.

Dugast [sic], Georges. *The First Canadian Woman in the Northwest; Or the Story of Marie Anne Gaboury, Wife of John Baptiste Lajimonière, Who Arrived in the Northwest in 1807, and Died at St. Boniface at the Age of 96 Years*. Winnipeg: The Manitoba Free Press Co., 1902. Transaction no. 62.

Ross, Alexander. *Letters of a Pioneer*. Edited by George Bryce. Winnipeg: Manitoba Free Press, 1903. Transaction no. 63.

Bryce, George. *Treasures of Our Library*. Winnipeg: Manitoba Free Press Co., 1904. Transaction no. 64.

Atkinson, George E. *Rare Bird Records of Manitoba*. Winnipeg: Manitoba Free Press Co., 1904. Transaction no. 65.

Bryce, George. *Among the Mound Builders' Remains*. Winnipeg: s.n., 1904. Transaction no. 66.

Laird, David. *Our Indian Treaties*. Winnipeg: Manitoba Free Press Co., 1905. Transaction no. 67.

Atkinson, George E. *A Review-History of the Passenger Pigeon of Manitoba*. Winnipeg: Manitoba Free Press Co., 1905. Transaction no. 68.

Turner, John Percival. *The Moose and Wapiti of Manitoba: A Plea for Their Preservation*. Winnipeg: Manitoba Free Press Co., 1906. Transaction no. 69.

Bryce, George. *A Great City Library*. Winnipeg: Manitoba Free Press Co., 1906. Transaction no. 70.

Sherbinin, Michael A. *The Galicians Dwelling in Canada and their Origin*. Winnipeg: Manitoba Free Press Co., 1906. Transaction no. 71.

Bryce, George. *A Sketch of the British Association for the Advancement of Science*. Winnipeg: Manitoba Free Press Co., 1906. Transaction no. 72.

Illustration Acknowledgements

All illustrations reproduced in this book are provided courtesy of the Provincial Archives of Manitoba, except for the following:

Cover: *Upper Fort Garry* (1907) by Frederick Challener, reproduced courtesy of the Government of Manitoba Art Collection. Photograph provided courtesy of the Winnipeg Art Gallery. Photograph by Ernest Mayer.

page 8: Cartoon of George Bryce from Newspaper Cartoonists' Association of Manitoba, *Manitobans as We See 'Em* (1910)

page 130: The Winnipeg Lodging and Coffee House, from the original publication of "The Charitable Institutions of Winnipeg"

page 176: Michael Sherbinin (1907) from George Knysh, *Michael Sherbinin in Winnipeg* (1994)

page 152: Catching pigeons, from Samuel G. Goodrich, *Recollections of a Life* (1857)

page 203: Charles Bell's map of the old forts of Winnipeg from the original publication of "The Old Forts of Winnipeg"

page 205: Fort Gibraltar from the original publication of "The Old Forts of Winnipeg"